Your Official America Online® Guide to Digital Imaging Activities

Your Official America Online® Guide to Digital Imaging Activities

by David Peal

AOL Press

Dulles, VA

Your Official America Online® Guide to Digital Imaging Activities

Published by

AOL Press

An imprint of Hungry Minds, Inc.

909 Third Avenue

New York, NY 10022

www.hungryminds.com

www.aol.com (America Online Web site)

Library of Congress Control Number: 2001090676

ISBN: 0-7645-3613-3

Printed in the United States of America

10 9 8 7 6 5 4 3 2 1

1B/SZ/QW/QR/IN

Distributed in the United States by Hungry Minds, Inc. and America Online, Inc.

For general information on Hungry Minds' books in the U.S., please call our Consumer Customer Service department at 800-762-2974. For reseller information, including discounts and premium sales, please call our Reseller Customer Service department at 800-434-3422.

is a trademark
of America Online, Inc.

is a trademark of Hungry Minds, Inc.

Welcome to AOL Press™

A OL Press books provide timely guides to getting the most out of your online life. AOL Press was formed as part of the AOL family to create a complete series of official references for using America Online as well as the entire Internet — all designed to help you enjoy a fun, easy, and rewarding online experience.

AOL Press is an exciting partnership between two companies at the forefront of the knowledge and communications revolution — AOL and Hungry Minds, Inc. AOL is committed to quality, ease of use, and value, and Hungry Minds excels at helping people understand technology.

To meet these high standards, all our books are authored by experts with the full participation of and exhaustive review by AOL's own development, technical, managerial, and marketing staff. Together, AOL and Hungry Minds have implemented an ambitious publishing program to develop new publications that serve every aspect of your online life.

We hope you enjoy reading this AOL Press title and find it useful. We welcome your feedback at AOL Keyword: **Contact Shop Direct** so we can keep providing information the way you want it.

AOL Press

About the Author

David Peal teaches in the Educational Technology Leadership MA program at George Washington University in Washington, D.C. As the former editorial manager of AOL's Internet Connection, he developed forums about the Internet and helped create AOL's first comprehensive online source of Internet help. In addition to this book, David has written four other books for AOL: *Your Official America Online Guide to Pictures Online, Your Official America Online Internet Guide, Student's Guide to the Internet,* and *Picture This! An Easy to Use Digital Imaging Guide.* He also wrote *Access the Internet* and developed one of the first newsletters devoted to commercial use of the Internet. He was a finalists judge for the education category in the 2000 Global Information Infrastructure (GII) awards.

Credits

America Online

Technical Editors
Keith Fleming
Jennifer Consalvo
Dan Pacheo
Sam Ro
Dan Shilling
Stephanie Diamond

Cover Design
DKG Design, Inc.

Hungry Minds

Project Editor
Paul Levesque

Acquisitions Editor
Carol Sheehan

Copy Editor
Rebecca Huehls

Technical Editor
Keith Underdahl

Permissions Editor
Carmen Krikorian

Publishing Director
Andy Cummings

Editorial Manager
Leah Cameron

Media Development Manager
Heather Dismore

Editorial Assistant
Amanda Foxworth

Project Coordinators
Bill Ramsey
Ryan Steffen

Layout and Graphics
LeAndra Johnson
Kathie Schutte
Brian Torwelle

Proofreaders
Vickie Broyles
John Greenough
Jennifer Mahern
Marianne Santy
Charles Spencer

Indexer
Liz Cunningham

Acknowledgments

I am grateful to AOL's Kathy Harper for giving the green light that got this project started and providing the guidance that kept it on track. For answering many questions about AOL's "You've Got Pictures," thanks to Jennifer Consalvo, Senior Program Manager ("You've Got Pictures"), and Keith Fleming, Director of Marketing and Programming ("You've Got Pictures"). Thanks also to Dan Pacheco for again answering questions about Groups@AOL.

At Hungry Minds, Inc. (formerly IDG Books Worldwide), thanks go to Walter Bruce and Andy Cummings for their continued support. Thanks to Carol Sheehan, who worked with AOL and me for many weeks to refine the outline into the blueprint for the book you have in your hand. This activity book itself is the result of highly complex activity, and primary thanks thus go to Paul Levesque, Project Editor, for closely reading the manuscript and adeptly coordinating the editorial team: Rebecca Huehls, Copy Editor; Keith Underdahl, Technical Editor; and Amanda Foxworth, Editorial Assistant.

Thank you Amy Fuchs for quickly, ably, and professionally writing many of the activities, especially in Chapter 6.

At MGI Software, thanks to Shelly Shofer, Kristen Boucher, and Chris Taylor. Mr. Taylor answered numerous technical questions and helped me discover the breadth of PhotoSuite's possibilities. Special thanks to Wayne Ing, Technical Support Analyst, who tried valiantly to prevent my computer from eating PhotoSuite alive.

Closer to home, inadequate words of thanks go once again to Carol, Ella, and Gabriel for inspiring so many of the book's ideas and images.

I would like, lastly, to be able to acknowledge you, as reader. Please send suggestions for improvements and ideas for new activities to AOL screen name `dpeal`. Thank you!

Contents at a Glance

Table of Contents

Introduction

This book is about the things you can make with AOL, a PC, a camera, graphics software, and an inkjet printer. Here are ten things you can make with this equipment right now:

▲ A custom mousepad for your kids or your company

▲ Certificates for work or home

▲ Digital pictures to help you sell, well, anything online — whether it's on eBay or in AOL's classifieds

▲ A congratulations banner or poster

▲ Professional business cards, brochures, and flyers

▲ Your own business cards and an online résumé

▲ Cartoon versions of family snapshots for young children to color

▲ Picture postcards featuring you, your car, your kid, or anything else

▲ Greeting cards that say and show exactly what *you* want

▲ A visual property inventory to protect yourself from theft and damage

The book walks you through more than 50 activities like these. Most of the activities have two things in common. First, they are made or designed on the computer but become useful only when printed onto regular paper, card paper, magnets, labels, and all the materials onto which you can directly or indirectly print these days. The fact is, business cards, bookmarks, and paper airplanes are useless until printed and applied to some daily purpose or another. Second, the activities involve *digital pictures,* which are photographs and other images that you can view and use on a computer. The activities in this book show you how to acquire such pictures, use them in projects, and share them both online and as tangible things, from greeting cards to business brochures.

What You Need

What you really need in order to benefit from these activities is the feeling that, when you sit down in front of a computer, you are in charge of the computer and not the other way around. With that much courage, you can be free to use your hardware and software as mere tools and on your terms. The following things are also helpful:

▲ **An AOL account,** which you probably already have. Why do you need one? You can use your AOL membership to:

Definition

Digital pictures are photographs and other images that you can display, change, and store on a computer and then share *between* computers (*online*, in other words). *Digital imaging* encompasses all the tools that enable you to make and manipulate digital pictures, or to turn photographic prints into digital pictures. These tools include cameras, video recorders, scanners, graphics software, and printers.

Note

This book assumes you have a Windows computer, which for better or worse, is the platform for which the latest graphics software is written.

- Take advantage of the free "You've Got Pictures," AOL Hometown, and Groups@AOL services
- Explore the digital-imaging resources available on or through AOL
- Join an AOL community or create a new one
- Share your pictures online with friends and others
- Shop for the next version of your graphics software when it comes out or order labels for your printer

▲ **A PC.** Of course you need a computer. In the world of digital imaging, you need a computer with, if possible, a little more of everything. The good news is that prices of just about everything continue to drop. Even today's less-expensive new PCs are fully equipped for a wide range of digital-imaging activities.

▲ **Lots of RAM.** You need 64MB of RAM (random-access memory) or more to run graphics programs — and to run several programs at once, which is very helpful in many digital-imaging activities. Lots of hard-disk space is good too, so you can install those big programs and store your future collection of digital pictures. You can go pretty far with 10GB (gigabytes), but another 10 or 20GB affords you ample elbow room as your collection of pictures and software grows. Also, consider a CD-R or Zip drive to copy and store your digital pictures and other multimedia files, so you never feel pinched.

▲ **Graphics software.** Most of the activities in this book use MGIsoft's PhotoSuite 4.0 or higher. This software offers a full range of features for editing, organizing, and sharing digital pictures, and for using those pictures in projects. If you have an AOL DigiCam or PhotoCam, a version of PhotoSuite probably came with your camera.

PhotoSuite has competition, of course, and for several activities I used a long-time favorite, Learning Company Print Shop. Other popular graphics programs include Adobe PhotoDeluxe and Jasc Paint Shop Pro. I leave the more sophisticated graphics products such as Adobe Photoshop out of the picture, because of their steep learning curves and limited support for projects.

A few activities are based on Microsoft Office products: Publisher, Word, and PowerPoint. Microsoft also makes well-regarded graphics software called Picture It.

▲ **A color inkjet printer.** For under $150, you can buy a very capable inkjet printer that can produce sharp, glossy color photographic prints and accept the specialty papers used to make cards, stickers, labels, T-shirts, and even magnets.

▲ **A camera.** You need a camera, too. Any kind will do, whether a point-and-shoot film camera, a 35mm camera, or a digital camera of any kind. In Chapter 2, you can find out about "You've Got Pictures," an AOL service that allows you to digitize pictures from your regular negatives so you don't have to give up the pleasures of prints.

How This Book Is Organized

Part I (Chapters 1-4) is designed as a reference guide to AOL's services for storing digital pictures, creating visual Web pages, and finding information about all aspects of digital imaging.

▲ Start with Chapter 1 if, well, you don't know where to start and are perplexed by the many products and unfamiliar concepts.

▲ Chapter 2 is a compact guide to AOL's "You've Got Pictures" service, which allows you to store and share your digital pictures online.

▲ Chapter 3 provides a mini-reference to AOL Hometown, the integrated set of free services where you can view, create, and share Web pages.

▲ Chapter 4 introduces more than a dozen essential online and Web resources where you can find more information about the latest in digital-imaging products, technologies, ideas, and projects.

Part II steps you through more than 50 activities for children, the family, and the home business. You can follow these activities in any order. Different activities may suit different roles you play throughout the day.

▲ Chapter 5 has activities that kids can do themselves or that kids younger than eight or so can do with assistance. You can adapt many of these kid-related activities for adult uses as well.

▲ You can find twenty-some activities for the entire family in Chapter 6. These activities aim to be useful as well as fun.

▲ Chapter 7 surveys the essential needs of people who work at home or have a home-based business, with detailed instructions for making brochures, signs, business cards, résumés, and more.

Throughout Part II activities are meant to stand on their own, but you'll quickly notice that you can adapt many activities for purposes other than the ones suggested here, and that activities are related to each other in many ways. Lastly, use the book's Glossary whenever you stumble across an unfamiliar term.

Book Elements and Conventions

The subject matter may be novel as several technologies come together and, at the same time, become easier to use. The book itself, however, aims to be as familiar and easy-to-use as possible. That's the beauty of books. For now, at least, they're the most familiar way of learning *anything,* all without a single click.

Web Addresses

I've indicated the address of Web sites in a special font, as follows: `www.avery.com`. I've left out the `http://` part (standard in Web addresses), because with the AOL browser you don't have to type it. To visit Avery.com (the label vendor), type `www.avery.com` into the AOL toolbar's address box and click Go.

Definition

A CD-R drive (short for CD recordable) lets you save pictures, music, and other files to recordable CDs, which are available at any computer store. These CDs can hold more than 600MB, an enormous amount of storage space for most purposes, and are great for digital pictures. For a huge amount of information about CD-Rs, check out `www.cdrfaq.org`.

Note

You don't need a digital camera in this book, though you will have more fun if you do! Digital cameras are catching up with 35mm's in resolution but are more slowly coming down in price.

Note

If you like your film camera, you may want to invest in a scanner. Chapter 1 has some more information on scanners, as does AOL Keyword: **Scanners**.

Tip

You should always feel free to alter the activities in this book to suit your needs, moods, taste, equipment, abilities, sense of whimsy, and amount of time.

AOL Keywords

Sometimes you will see (in parentheses, usually) the words *AOL Keyword* followed by a word in boldface. This means that you can find related services and information on America Online. In the address box on the AOL toolbar, type the keyword (the word in bold) and click Go. That's right: AOL Keywords and Web addresses can both be entered into the address box.

Boldface

Sometimes, when you need to type something specific into a text box, the characters you need to type appear in boldface. For example, to show you the best words to do a search on AOL, I might say something like this: To find pages for your kids to color, type **kids coloring pages** into the AOL Search box.

Commands

Sometimes, I provide instructions for doing something. The ⇨ symbol means to do one thing and then do another. Usually, you do something like opening a menu and choosing an option from that menu (as in the common Windows command, choose File⇨Open).

When you click a sequence of options in the activities that use MGI PhotoSuite, you see text similar to the following:

Click Collages⇨Blank Canvas

In this case, you click Collages in the left pane and a new pane appears where you select Blank Canvas from the Collages options.

Numbered Steps

A unique feature of this computer book is the arrangement of the step-by-step procedures. Each activity in Part II takes two pages; a few are spread over 4 or 8 pages as well. On the left side are the step-by-step procedures. On the right you will find icons and figures. The figures have "callouts," numbered icons that correspond to the numbered steps of the procedure. The figures are thus an integral part of the book, meant to be used for reference when following a procedure.

Icons

You will find the following helpful icons sprinkled throughout the margins of this book.

These suggestions provide shortcuts or hints.

Cautions keep you on your toes. Don't worry, though; you won't find too much teacherly scolding in this book.

Notes emphasize certain points in the text, containing the information you really, really want to know.

This icon defines terms that may be new to you. Sometimes the definitions can help you better understand what is said in the text.

This icon indicates references to the sections or chapters in this book, or other books, that explore a specific topic in more detail or include helpful, related procedures.

This icon alerts you to an AOL area or Web site with insights into a topic in the text. For every Find It Online icon, you can find many other resources, so here's a tip: Read the introduction to Chapter 4 to find out how to do a search and uncover what you need if you don't find it in this book or in the Find It Online icons.

PART

I

AT HOME: DIGITAL IMAGING WITH AOL

1

STARTING OUT WITH DIGITAL PICTURES

IN THIS CHAPTER

▲ Understanding the many uses of pictures

▲ Making the transition from pictures to digital pictures

▲ Getting digital pictures with "You've Got Pictures," digital cameras, and scanners

▲ Buying the right gear

▲ Bringing digital pictures into your life

Chapter 1

Starting Out with Digital Pictures

Feeling overwhelmed by your computer, printer, software, and other high-tech gear is common. This book aims to help you manage this gadgetry so it doesn't manage you. The way to do that, you'll see, is to avoid becoming obsessed with technology. Instead, you'll put your tools to work for you by making simple things from masks to business cards. The focus is on digital pictures — electronic versions of familiar snapshots. After your pictures get into your computer, there's no end to what you can do with them.

That's where this book comes in. It's a guide to what you can do with digital pictures. You can navigate this book at your own pace, according to your own interests, but please read at least this chapter. It puts digital imaging in perspective. After beginning with pictures, it introduces *digital* pictures and concludes with guidelines for using them in your daily life.

Understanding Pictures and Their Purposes

Pictures — whether they're photos or drawings, tangible or digital — serve all kinds of uses in print, on the Web, on bulletin boards, in wallets, and everywhere else in daily life.

▲ In books and on the Web, pictures can provide examples of what's in the text.

▲ For young readers, pictures can repeat what's in the text, to support the complex process of figuring out what words mean.

▲ For adults, pictures can amplify or clarify what's in the text.

▲ In a coffee-table book or book of photographs, pictures often have intrinsic interest.

Of course, pictures can simply illustrate something, for example the buffalo nickel shown in Figure 1-1, which someone is auctioning online at eBay (AOL Keyword: **Ebay**).

Pictures can carry a great deal of information themselves. Pictures illustrate home-improvement ideas, for example, better than words. Figure 1-2 shows an illustration from AOL's home-improvement area, which is part of AOL's House & Home channel. Generally, pictures can present a visually complex situation or a complex procedure more efficiently than words. Take, for example, a map that provides directions to a bowling alley or piano recital. You can type out instructions, but if people are coming from several directions, you must type out a different set of instructions for each person. Moreover, most of us can't remember more than a handful of facts or steps at a time, let alone complicated turn-by-turn driving directions. A map or two can satisfy more people, more easily, with less chance of confusion.

Figure 1-1. Someone is selling this buffalo nickel on eBay (AOL Keyword: **Ebay**), and provides this picture to give potential buyers a good sense of the item for sale. Words, in this case, can mislead, but pictures cannot. That's the assumption at least.

Finally, whether photos or freehand images, pictures can be purely expressive. Scribbles created in kids' software or pencil sketches of a bowl of fruit do not just represent the image formed by light hitting the retina. They're doodles. Perhaps they bring out some feature that is significant, or just interesting, to the person doodling. That's what counts. After all, wizards and woozles, gryphons and heffalumps all come straight from the imagination. Graphics software provides the tools to coax these beasts into your screen, onto paper, and out to the World Wide Web.

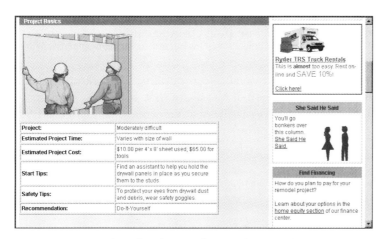

Figure 1-2. Hanging dry wall made easier, thanks to this digitized drawing and the accompanying text.

Find out how to prepare pictures for eBay in Chapter 7.

An AOL *channel* is one of about 20 major content areas available on AOL. In AOL 6.0, the Show Channels button is available on the lefthand side of the toolbar. (When the menu is displayed, the button reads Hide Channels.) Click it to see a listing of channels. In AOL 5.0, channels were part of the AOL Welcome Screen.

Scanning is a technique for turning a print (or anything on paper) into a digital form, which means it can be used on a computer. A scanner is a device that is attached to a computer for scanning. I discuss scanners later in this chapter.

Introducing Digital Pictures

Before digital pictures, the tiresome chores of getting reprints, mailing images, and gathering the clan for slideshows were a hassle at best. Large pictures and old photographs perhaps couldn't be shared at all, or only at great expense. That's where *digital pictures* come in. A digital picture is just a picture changed into a form that a computer can store and display. Figure 1-3 shows a digital picture that had been scanned from a print photo thumbtacked on a wall. When a picture is digital, it can be used in many ways.

Digital pictures offer a number of advantages over traditional, print pictures. You can edit digital pictures to correct exposure, create effects, and enhance images. A lot is covered under the word *enhance,* as you'll see in this book: removing specks, creating special effects, cropping the image to improve the composition, and so forth. And you can share digital pictures, primarily by sending them from one person to another using AOL and the Internet.

Figure 1-3 shows the digital version of a paper print. The difference in how the digital and paper versions look is insignificant, but the difference in what you can do with them is huge. For one thing, I was able to quickly improve the colors and crop unwanted parts of the digital picture.

Any new picture you take with a film camera is just a few short steps away from becoming a fully fledged digital picture, as is any snapshot or family photo that you already have. The next section looks at two important devices that can turn pictures into digital images: digital cameras and scanners. Then I'll also introduce "You've Got Pictures," a way to get digital pictures from a film camera.

Getting Digital Pictures with Digital Cameras and Scanners

Today's digital cameras *create* digital pictures. Instead of using film, whose negatives are printed onto paper, digital cameras record images as files. These files can be viewed on the camera itself using a small screen that is usually built into the back of the camera. They can also be transferred to your computer for storage, editing, and sharing. The most common way of getting these pictures into your computer is with the help of a cable that you plug into the camera and computer. Figure 1-4 shows AOL's popular PhotoCam Plus digital camera.

What about those old photographs and other pictures you want to use online? You can convert your prints into digital pictures by using a *scanner,* a piece of hardware that works like a photocopier. Instead of making a paper copy of a picture, however, the scanner creates a file, which you can view, edit, and share online. Figure 1-5 shows a popular scanner that's available at AOL Keyword: **AOL Shop Direct**.

Figure 1-3. This digital picture began life as a standard snapshot — a print developed by a local drugstore.

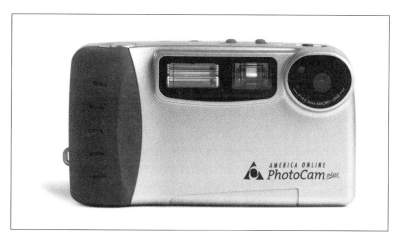

Figure 1-4. AOL PhotoCam Plus, an affordable digital camera for taking pictures for online use.

The term *digital pictures* usually refers to digitized photographs, or the pictures that a digital camera creates. Sometimes, however, the term *digital pictures* can refer to cartoons, drawings, and clip art.

When you crop an image, you cut out nonessential parts to improve it or remove a part that you don't want. Generally, cropping removes only the edges of an image.

The AOL Digital Imaging Made Easy CD-ROM is a good place to learn about scanners and digital cameras. *Your Official America Online Guide to Pictures Online* (Hungry Minds, Inc.) covers this equipment in more detail. The CD and book are both available at AOL Keyword: **AOL Shop Direct**.

Figure 1-5. You can purchase this simple scanner online through AOL.

Scanning has become easier and less expensive over the past few years. At $100 or less, good scanners are quite affordable, and many come with rebates or even come free with a new PC. With a scanner, you can convert just about anything on paper into a file that your computer can store and display, and that you can edit and share.

To use a standard scanner like the one shown in Figure 1-5, you simply place your photo face-down on the scanner's glass surface and press a button. Usually, you can operate a scanner entirely from your PC by using the scanner software. From AOL version 5.0 and above, you can operate a scanner with Picture Finder, AOL's handy digital image viewing and editing feature. When the scan is completed, the scanner's graphics software usually opens automatically, allowing you to view your new digital picture, edit it, save it, or open it within another program.

Collecting Your Pictures Online: "You've Got Pictures"

AOL's "You've Got Pictures" service gives you a single online place where you can keep all your digital pictures. With your pictures online, you can very easily share them with other people. "You've Got Pictures" now offers unlimited online storage space for free, where you can keep your digital pictures as long as you are an AOL member.

How do you get your digital pictures into your online storage space at "You've Got Pictures"? Here's what you do, depending on the type of camera you have:

▲ **Digital camera (or scanner):** You can simply copy your pictures (a quick and easy process called *uploading*) from your PC to "You've Got Pictures." Chapter 3 shows the exact steps for doing this.

▲ **Film camera:** The same photo retailer who develops your paper prints can scan and post them to "You've Got Pictures."

After your digital pictures are online at "You've Got Pictures," you can share them one at a time or several at a time (as *albums*). You can also order products made from your pictures, such as T-shirts, sweatshirts, coffee mugs, and mousepads. Whatever their source, you can *download* these digital pictures (copy them to your PC) for activities like the ones you can find in Part II.

Putting digital pictures online takes little effort. Using your film camera, you can have your prints turned into digital pictures and posted to you, courtesy of "You've Got Pictures." For old prints and *anything* on paper, such as kids' drawings, you need a scanner. If you're gungho about digital pictures, treat yourself to a digital camera, which you can learn all about at AOL Keyword: **Digital Photo** or on the AOL Digital Imaging Made Easy CD.

Going from Pictures to Projects

What next? To use your digital pictures to make bookmarks, CD labels, mousepads, and a myriad of other things, you usually need to have graphics software and a printer, though sometimes a word processor alone will suffice.

The major consumer graphics programs in this category are not only inexpensive (under $50), but are also becoming dramatically easier to use, even fun for adults and kids alike. The competition among vendors really helps you; you'll find an increasing number of creative features in big-but-affordable graphics software products, such as MGI's PhotoSuite program, shown in Figure 1-6. To boot, chances are good that if you do have a digital camera or scanner, it came with a free edition of a major piece of graphics software. (Scanners and printers as well often come with new PCs or can be purchased along with a new PC at a discount.) The only downside to all this great software is that it's always improving. Your free software may need to be upgraded within a year; upgrading at least once is usually worthwhile, because you can get new features, a full version (if you started with a "lite" edition), and vendor support. Later in this section, you'll find a brief overview of specific programs.

Cross-Reference

For more about Picture Finder, the digital image viewing and editing feature available on AOL version 5.0 and above, see Chapter 4.

Cross-Reference

"You've Got Pictures" is the subject of Chapter 2.

Cross-Reference

Chapter 4 introduces online resources such as CNET, AOL's Decision Guides, and Shop@AOL, where you can learn about and purchase digital-imaging products. Chapter 4 introduces online resources such as CNET, AOL's Decision Guides, and Shop@AOL, where you can learn about and purchase digital-imaging products.

Figure 1-6. PhotoSuite 4.0 allows you to add creative touches to digital pictures, such as this neat bubble caption.

Most graphics software products have four major purposes, outlined below. These days you'll see more and more programs offering the ability to publish projects for the Web. Keep an eye out for Web features in the future.

▲ **Retrieving pictures:** Graphics software can use a digital picture from many sources, including your computer's hard drive, a scanner, or a digital camera. When you use PhotoSuite or almost any graphics software, you need to tell the program where a digital picture is located before you can retrieve it.

▲ **Editing pictures:** Editing includes all the tweaking you can perform on each digital picture. Some types of edits affect the entire picture — like cropping (removing extraneous details) or increasing the contrast. Other types of edits let you control parts of a picture, even the individual picture elements, or *pixels*, the very small blocks of color that make up a digital picture. Pixel-level editing lets you do things like remove dust marks.

▲ **Making things out of your pictures, such as the cards, certificates, and other projects in this book:** Graphics software varies greatly in how you actually make things. Higher-end products give you the tools for doing anything, but they provide little guidance for making specific projects. Products designed for the average consumer are not only easier to use, but also help you make exactly what you want.

▲ **Organizing pictures:** After you get into digital pictures, you quickly build up large collections of them, just as many people have years and years of snapsnots squirreled away in shoeboxes and albums. Many graphics programs give you the tools to name, search, and arrange your pictures for easy retrieval.

A number of excellent (and inexpensive) graphics software products are on the market today. The following list covers some of the more popular programs, but the list is necessarily highly selective. The list doesn't include special-purpose programs like KidPix (for kids) or Adobe Photoshop (for graphics professionals).

▲ **MGI PhotoSuite:** AOL's PhotoCam Plus and many other digital cameras are sold with a special version of MGI's PhotoSuite program, shown in Figure 1-6. PhotoSuite offers a good mix of editing control and step-by-step projects. It stands out for its broad support for retrieving, editing, organizing, and project-making.

▲ **Adobe PhotoDeluxe:** PhotoDeluxe is a well-established and popular graphics program that comes with many hardware devices. It offers easy-to-use photo-editing tools for adjusting contrast and color, among other things. PhotoDeluxe comes in a home version as well as a business version; both have numerous templates for making projects.

▲ **Jasc Paint Shop Pro:** This sophisticated software offers great control over image editing but very little project support. You would use Paint Shop to create some amazing special effects or do refined edits, and then use the resulting images in a project-builder like PhotoSuite.

▲ **Print Shop:** An old-timer in the market, Print Shop has recently been souped up and includes 175,000 pieces of clip art! Print Shop probably supports activities better than editing and organizing.

You need software to do many of this book's activities, which are mostly based on PhotoSuite. It's hard to go wrong with any of the major graphics programs, however. In fact, a simple word processor (if you consider Microsoft Word *simple*) can suffice for many activities, as you'll see in Part II. For some guidance and ideas, compare product reviews and prices at AOL Keyword: **CNET**.

Printing Digital Pictures

In the world of consumer and small-business pictures and projects, inkjet printers rule. An *inkjet,* true to its name, is a type of printer that uses small cartridges of colored inks that move back and forth across the page spraying tiny drops of ink, a few trillionths of a liter per drop in some cases, onto a page. The colored inks combine in correct amounts to re-create an image as close as possible to your digital picture.

Inkjets, like the one shown in Figure 1-7, are everywhere, but they sometimes go under different names. *Bubble jet* is what Canon calls its inkjet, and some of the seemingly fancier "photo printers" are high-quality inkjets. For under $150, you can buy a good-quality inkjet printer. Inkjet printers differ in details such as the size and types of paper they support, the number of sheets they hold, and their color and black-and-white printing speeds (measured in printouts per second). Overall, the general-purpose color inkjet produces excellent printouts of photos as well as text.

Note

You'll see the term TWAIN when bringing digital pictures into a program. TWAIN refers to the ability of a piece of software, like PhotoSuite, to retrieve a digital image directly from hardware attached to your computer, such as a scanner or a digital camera.

Note

This book is not about a specific software package. Although I use PhotoSuite as the source of many activities for the sake of consistency, you can use products like PhotoSuite, PhotoDeluxe, Print Shop, Photo Impression, and so on, interchangeably for most activities.

Tip

Many excellent graphics programs and utilities can be downloaded for free, or for a nominal charge, over the World Wide Web. (A *utility* is a program that does one thing well, such as archive your files or create moving images for the Web.) At AOL Keyword: **Shareware**, you can find some good graphics software. You can purchase many of the programs in this section at AOL Keyword: **Shop Direct**.

Preserving Digital Pictures

Almost by instinct, people know how to care for old photos: Keep them dry and avoid touching the surface. Old photographic prints in particular, at least if they have family significance or historical value, require an album with waterproof binding, stiff pages, and a protective plastic overlay. Printouts of digital pictures don't have quite the aura of photographic prints, perhaps because of their lower resolution and low-quality paper. All that is changing quickly as paper and resolution improves, which is reason to treat digital photos as if they will last for decades. Here are some things you can do to preserve your printouts of digital pictures:

- **Consider a photo-quality inkjet printer.** If you're in the market for a printer, this type can create quality prints.

- **Consider ink quality.** Epson claims that a new line of its printers uses inks that last for 200 years. (This claim has not tested in practice, of course.) Because ink can be the greatest cost in an inkjet, investigate both the quality of the ink and the lifespan of ink cartridges before you buy a new printer.

- **Treat a digital printout like a fine photograph.** Use quality, acid-free, glossy, white inkjet paper. Hold pictures by their edges.

- **Store digital printouts carefully.** Put them in a sealed box or album, away from light. Within an album, keep printouts in plastic sleeves made of Mylar, not PVC (a type of plastic). Don't tape or glue the pictures to a surface. Keep them away from moisture and extremes of heat. Better yet, just visit a reliable photo store and discuss your storage needs.

You may be thinking, "So what? I can always print the file again if anything happens to the printed copy." Yes, but files can become corrupted or erased accidentally. To be safe, keep printouts of your favorite digital images as backups. If you're like me, you wouldn't want to lose even one favorite image.

Most inkjet printers require two ink cartridges (a color cartridge and a black-and-white one), each of which typically costs $20 to $40. A big part of the price is the precision-made ink nozzles and electrical contacts needed to connect the cartridge to the rest of the printer. These nozzles can be damaged if mishandled and can become clogged if your printer is used heavily or is hardly used at all. Be sure to follow all the manufacturer's instructions for handling, installing, aligning, and cleaning your printer to get the longest life and best performance. If you will be making heavy use of your inkjet, ask your dealer about refillable ink cartridges for any printer you are considering.

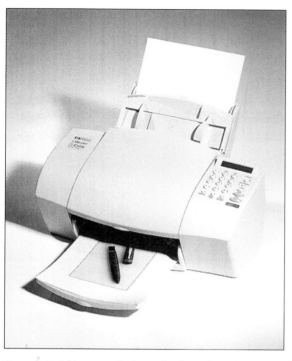

Figure 1-7. Inkjet printer. In the market for such a printer? Learn about them at AOL Keyword: **CNET**, make a choice at AOL Keyword: **Decision Guides**, and purchase one at CNET or AOL Shop Direct.

Variations of the inkjet serve specific purposes:

▲ If you travel a lot, consider a *mobile printer,* a lightweight inkjet. Often somewhat lower in resolution (sharpness), these printers are used for on-the-spot printing while you are traveling or on vacation.

▲ If you need a scanner and a printer for occasional use, consider a *multifunction device,* a printer-scanner-copier. Bear in mind that most scanners these days double as copy machines. The important benefit to the multifunction machines is that they take up less space than two or three separate machines and offer separate scanning and printing functions.

Inexpensive inkjets can produce outstanding photographic prints from your digital pictures, if you keep several points in mind:

▲ **Use inkjet photo paper.** Such paper comes in many styles, such as high-gloss, low-gloss, matte, and premium. Papers can be found online (AOL Keyword: **Printer Supplies**) and in most office-supply stores. Some paper is coated on both sides, so you need not throw away a sheet if the picture was not centered or was printed at too small a size or too low a resolution. Epson, Kodak, Avery, and Invent-It are just some of the excellent vendors in this market.

Tip

If your needs are specialized, consider a printer optimized for your needs. If you work primarily with words, a laser printer may be cost efficient. If you are a graphics or photo pro, look into *dye sublimation* printers, which make sharp, richly colored photographic prints.

Note

The resolutions of digital cameras vary, which is why you can find a broad range of prices. Before you buy a digital camera, consider whether you want to print your pictures and how big you want those prints to be. For prints that are 8 x 10 inches or larger, you need a megapixel camera.

Cross-Reference

Use CNET's online reviews and articles to learn more about specialized printers (AOL Keyword: **CNET**). See Chapter 4.

Using Your Inkjet to Make . . . T-shirts?

In making projects, the key ingredient is often an inkjet printer. Inkjets offer affordable color printing, and they accept all kinds of papers and other printable materials. For instance, they take transfers (for making T-shirts), card stock (for making business cards), glossy paper (for those photos), greeting card paper (for those birthday and holiday cards), and countless sizes and styles of labels. Other printable materials let you use your inkjet to make jigsaw puzzles, illustrated refrigerator magnets, and other fun items. You *will* impress people, or at least young children, with these things.

AOL's Printing Supplies Web site, part of the Print Central site profiled in Chapter 4, simplifies the reordering of printing supplies. For the major printer brands, Print Central can automatically detect your printer model (if you have one installed) and can show you the papers, inks, and other materials available for that model. Part II of this book is full of ideas for using all those materials.

▲ **Check the resolution and picture size.** The resolution (sharpness) of the print is a result of two factors: the resolution of the picture and the size of the picture on the paper. If your original image was shot at your camera's lowest resolution (in pixels per picture), printing it at a large size such as 8 x 10 inches will probably give you a low-quality print. If you use a higher resolution on your camera (such as a megapixel or above) and you print the image at 4 x 6 or 5 x 7 inches, then the results could approximate the quality you can achieve from photo retailers.

Graphics software products all let you control the size of your printout, but many of these programs have a default size that fills up a third or half of a page. This default size is usually too big for good printouts, especially if you don't have a megapixel camera (a camera with a resolution greater than 1280 x 980). For a quality print, all you have to do is use your graphics program to reduce the picture's size. In PhotoSuite, for example, choosing File⇨New⇨Photo lets you create a canvas of any size (such as 2 x 3 inches or 5 x 7 inches), and in either orientation (tall or wide). When you add your photo to the canvas, you can then size it to the canvas. Also, when you go to print any picture in PhotoSuite, the Print Preview window includes a ruler that lets you adjust the dimensions of your picture. In Print Multiples mode, you can create several pictures on a single page, usually in a small enough size to ensure a good-quality (sharp) print.

▲ **Take advantage of your printer's properties.** Many inkjets, for example, have a best-quality mode, which you can use for special pictures. Inkjets often have Paper Type lists, which allow you to choose from a variety of specialty papers, including transfers and photo papers. To set your printer's properties, choose Start⇨Settings⇨Printers; then double-click your printer's icon and choose Printer⇨Properties. Or, just look at your printer's manual to find out about these options and how to set them.

Tips for Making Great Projects

You probably have most of what you need already: any kind of camera, AOL, and a computer. You will have more fun, too, if you have graphics software and a printer. Here are some general tips to bear in mind as you begin applying all these tools, together, in support of specific projects.

1. Start with a Purpose

Because graphics software comes packed with so many goodies, becoming sidetracked on even the simplest project is incredibly easy. The greater the challenges with your task, the more easily fun features like filters and paintbrushes can distract. Actually, playing with this software is *good* because that helps you learn how to use it, but working on a focused project is often the best way to learn a tool well, because you *have* to get the tool to do what you want it to do. That's why the activities in Part II are designed as simple, step-by-step activities; you can always see where you are and where you are going.

2. Mix Media but Avoid Multimedia Goulash

Combining words and pictures often makes for a strong project. Both carry a lot of information, directly and indirectly, and anyone who reads the comics knows that text and words can be highly complementary. Pictures, in particular, maintain attention better and are remembered longer than words.

Using media together, especially a seemingly simple combination of text and pictures, is more complex than creating a pure-text word-processing document or a pictures-only photo album. Here are a few considerations to help you make judicious use of these media:

▲ Avoid overusing text or writing complex descriptions when a simple image, like a map, will do. Organize your words on the page in a way that clarifies the information you want to convey, as in a birthday invitation providing the time, place, event, and driving instructions. Or, use bullet lists to present a list of items with a similar structure (like a list of household chores) but without a necessary sequence. For sequences, use numbered lists.

▲ Use only the pictures you need, despite the appealing idea of using as many images as you can possibly cram into every project. Graphics don't help when they distract readers from your message.

A good time to ignore these rules is when kids are working on their at-home projects; letting kids explore sometimes makes sense. For school projects, however, they may need gentle guidance away from showy presentation and toward content. Fancy reports (with pictures, borders, and the like) rarely impress a teacher as much as well-thought-out work that uses graphics software to serve some larger purpose.

Judicious use of media applies even more to what you do on the Web. In making a Web page, you want to snag and keep people's

Don't overlook the specialized printers. For people who work primarily with photographs, the so-called dye sublimation printers create sharp, richly colored photographic prints. These photo printers are not recommended for text because of the expense. Similarly, a color laser printer can be prohibitively expensive for doing routine printouts of digital pictures. However, laser printers can be more cost-effective than ink jets for people who print a lot of text.

AOL has all you need to make and share Web pages. Chapter 3 introduces this big subject.

Kids, like adults, like some degree of control. For many reasons, including undeveloped fine-motor control, some kids can't effectively undertake computer activities. Printing out pictures and making things for them to do offline can offer the experience of control and the feeling of effectiveness. Of course, they should have as much control as feasible in designing on the computer itself. Even a small role can make many kids proud of the result.

attention; it's too easy to lose attention online because people can so easily slip away in search of other sites. Decide on your purpose, choose the best possible text and pictures to achieve your purpose, and then arrange your elements to make your point. Remember that pictures are more often perceived as a nuisance when they slow down the time it takes for a page to appear in someone's browser.

3. For Kids, Use Computers to Make Real Things

Computers work primarily with a limited part of two human senses: seeing and hearing. They display words and pictures for your eyes, and play music and all sorts of auditory cues for your ears (like "You've Got Mail," when you sign onto AOL).

To thrive, children, and younger children in particular, need a much more stimulating environment than anything the PC can provide. They need to learn how different things feel to the *touch:* sponges, towels, carpets, smooth glass, dirt, grass. The stimulation helps them build and refine concepts. They need to work in messy media like finger paint as well as the neat ones available on the screen. Another important sense relates to awareness of one's body in space. This sense is developed and tuned through activities such as maintaining balance and assessing the movement of kids, dogs, and anything else that moves; in this way kids understand how gravity affects their bodies and other objects. At a computer, kids just don't have the opportunity to duck or fall down!

The projects in Chapter 5 mix computer and offline activity. Much of the work, in fact, *must* be completed away from the computer. This book shows you some places on the Internet where you can find pictures to print and then color on paper. Offline activities using computer-generated parts can exercise *all* the senses. Nothing beats flying a real paper airplane, after all.

4. Find Ideas Everywhere

The idea for digital projects comes from many places — experience, software, and your imagination.

Many of the ideas for activities in this book grew right out of kids' experiences. The elementary-school-aged children in my neighborhood, for example, have gone through the same trademarked obsessions as kids elsewhere in the U.S. in recent years, from Beanie Babies to wizards (see Figure 1-8). A few obsessions have had greater staying power, such as building toys. Along the way, these kids have created collections (calling for labels), formed clubs (calling for ID cards, certificates, and signs), and started a Lego page for the Web. For every such obsession, there's at least one digital activity. Again, this book is just a place to start.

Some ideas are suggested directly by the fill-in-the-blank *wizards* and templates of newer software products like PhotoSuite and oldtimers like Print Shop. Microsoft's Publisher (part of the MS Office suite) includes a large set of business-grade project templates, which can be recommended for many business projects (cards, brochures, Web sites, and more). Publisher, for example, offers some templates for making sophisticated Web sites, which would otherwise call for fancy programming. All these products simply make things possible that you probably didn't know you could do with a computer and your pictures. If you suspected you needed a fancy business page before, you have no excuse not to make one now.

Projects also come from the imagination. Avid photographers are always imagining pictures, even when they don't have a camera with them. A cameraless photographer, for example, might see finished pictures while looking at a dried-up rose the week after Valentine's Day. The same mindfulness applies when you get the hang of making things with digital pictures, graphics software, and a printer. For example:

▲ If you make CDs for people using your PC's spiffy new CD-writer, you could create personalized CD covers and labels, with the recipient's name, creation date, track listing, art, and a personal message.

▲ If your child forgets routines, make a visual chart so she always knows what to do next.

▲ If you are the gift-giving sort, a digital project doesn't cost much and makes an impression.

Project opportunities are everywhere.

Tip

An upshot of these considerations is that you should seriously consider getting an inkjet printer if you don't already have one. Inkjets take your on-screen projects and give you something tangible to work with such as making a bookmark or a paper doll.

Cross-Reference

See Chapter 4 for online destinations that offer ideas.

Definition

In software, a *wizard* has nothing to do with Harry Potter and magic potions. A wizard is simply a tool that steps you through a project, giving you a limited number of choices at each point to get you started as quickly as possible.

Figure 1-8. This Wizard certificate was made in KidPix. The cat picture (look closely) contains a face; this creepy cat was quickly put together in PhotoSuite.

5. Learn a Little More about Your Tools

Knowing a little more about your software and hardware can open new activities to you. For example, suppose your graphics software supports stitching. *Stitching* joins a series of photographs to make a panorama (a picture showing a very wide scene that could not be directly photographed in a single shot). See Figure 1-9 for an example. For large software products, you won't regret the time spent trying new features.

Figure 1-9. This panorama was made with a free utility called PhotoVista, which is included with PhotoSuite 4.0 (Platinum version).

The same goes for cameras. If you buy a digital camera with unfamiliar features, flip through the manual. AOL's PhotoCam Plus, for example, lets you correct "white balance" and compensate for tricky lighting situations. If you know your tools, you can easily take better pictures and, as a result, make better projects. Why better? Because you will be happier with them.

6. Experiment!

Feel free to adapt what you find in this book or elsewhere to your needs, equipment, time, and creativity. Your purposes are what count, after all.

Wrapping Up

All this information can seem like a lot to take in, with all that shiny new equipment and cool software, bursting with features and promises. The way to take control is to start with what you want to do. If you're not sure what to do, use the Table of Contents to skim the list of activities in Part II in the Table of Contents for some possible places to start. Know your tools and materials so you can create the results you want. Most of all, relax and have fun with all the new tools at your disposal. This is one computer task that can actually become a part of your life.

2

"YOU'VE GOT PICTURES":
THE EASIEST PATH TO GETTING
DIGITAL PICTURES ONLINE

IN THIS CHAPTER

▲ Getting pictures online through "You've Got Pictures"

▲ Sharing pictures through e-mail and the Web

▲ Creating photo gifts and getting prints

▲ Managing your rolls and albums in My Pictures

▲ Uploading pictures to "You've Got Pictures"

▲ Downloading pictures for use in projects

Chapter 2

"You've Got Pictures": The Easiest Path to Getting Digital Pictures Online

Digital pictures differ from ordinary photographic prints in one simple way: They are electronic. Because digital pictures are electronic, you can do special things with them, including the following:

▲ Transfer digital pictures from one computer to another using AOL, so that they can be shared with others.

▲ Manipulate digital pictures with software. Manipulating digital pictures means you can use graphics software (such as PhotoSuite, PhotoDeluxe, Print Shop, and many other excellent programs) to brighten them up; remove dust marks, scratches, and other blemishes; and play around with special effects like warping and filters.

▲ Print digital pictures onto different kinds of materials, including greeting-card (heavy) paper, precut business-card paper, banner paper, transparencies, sticker paper, and so on.

You might be asking yourself whether you need a digital camera to get digital pictures, and fretting that such a camera is not only expensive but also requires technical savvy. The answer to both of these concerns is no. Instead of a digital camera, you can use a regular film camera to get digital pictures, thanks to AOL's "You've Got Pictures," an exclusive AOL service that makes getting, storing, sharing, and using digital pictures *online* as easy as possible. If you have a scanner or digital camera, you can also use "You've Got Pictures" as an online home for your self-made digital pictures, and as an easy way to share pictures or order photo-quality prints.

"You've Got Pictures" can be reached at AOL Keyword: **Pictures** or **YGP**. Or, when using AOL 6.0, simply choose File⇨You've Got Pictures from the main menu. If you are not on AOL, you can reach "You've Got Pictures" on the World Wide Web at `aolsvc.pictures.aol.com`. Just as when you sign onto AOL, you need to type in your screen name and password to use "You've Got Pictures" on the Web. Figure 2-1 shows the opening view of "You've Got Pictures," an AOL screen that takes you to My Pictures, your area for viewing and using your digital pictures, as well as to "You've Got Pictures"-related features that are profiled in Chapter 4.

Getting Digital Pictures into "You've Got Pictures"

"You've Got Pictures" gives AOL members the opportunity to store an unlimited number of digital pictures online. How do you get your digital pictures online in the first place? The method you use depends on where your pictures are when you start. Here's what you do with the following kinds of images:

Figure 2-1. You start at this AOL screen name when you use AOL Keyword: **YGP** or **Pictures**. From here, you can participate in photo communities and find photo resources. By clicking one of the buttons on the left, you can start working with your digital pictures.

▲ **Negatives or pictures on a roll of film:** You can have your pictures developed at a photo dealer who offers "You've Got Pictures." Go to AOL Keyword: **Photo Developer** to find a photo developer near you.

▲ **Pictures that you've taken with a digital camera:** You must first transfer the files from the camera to your PC (following your camera's instructions) and then upload them to "You've Got Pictures."

▲ **Photographic prints or other images on paper:** If you have a scanner, you can create scanned images of your prints and upload the image files from your computer to "You've Got Pictures."

Before you choose a photo developer, weigh factors such as price, convenience, whether you want one-hour or several-day service, and whether the photo dealer has other services you want to use. Does the dealer frame pictures? Create prints of various sizes and qualities? Carry photo supplies and do repairs? Although most retailers offer the service at a standard price, you may find some variation.

Receiving Your Pictures Online

Developing film used to mean dashing down to your favorite photo processor, dropping off your film, and then dashing back after a few days to pick up your prints. "You've Got Pictures" can save you some of this dashing about because picking up your digital pictures is as easy as getting your e-mail. Just sign on to America Online, go to "You've Got Pictures" (AOL Keyword: **Pictures**) and with a couple of clicks, you're looking at your pictures. Just to make sure, AOL also sends you e-mail notification that your pictures have been posted to your online account.

Cross-Reference

For a complete reference book on "You've Got Pictures," with detailed guides to buying digital cameras, scanners, and printers, see *Your Official America Online Guide to Pictures Online* (Hungry Minds, Inc).

Find It Online

If you are an AOL member, you do not have to be on AOL to view pictures stored in "You've Got Pictures." You can access the "You've Got Pictures" Web site (aolsvc.pictures.aol. com) on any Internet-connected PC.

Tip

To find out the names and addresses of local retailers who offer "You've Got Pictures," visit AOL Keyword: **Photo Developer** and provide the required zip code (or city or state). Participating photo developers include one-hour developers, the large drug stores, and many large supermarkets that develop film, as well as mail-order developers.

Note

Screen names with Parental Controls set to Kids Only or Young Teens cannot access "You've Got Pictures."

One-hour services will have your prints ready in an hour or so and post your digital pictures on-line the same day. Overnight developing usually takes two days, including the time it takes to post your pictures to "You've Got Pictures." If you use a mail-order lab, you have to wait for the U.S. Postal Service to get your photos from the photo lab.

In addition to an e-mail announcement, AOL lets you know right when you sign on if your pictures have been posted. If your digital pictures have arrived, the handy "You've Got Pictures" icon on the Welcome screen gives you a visual hint. As shown in Figure 2-2, you see a colorful picture emerging from the yellow film cannister, which is otherwise closed. If that isn't enough, you also hear, "Welcome! You've Got Pictures," when you sign on. Just click the "You've Got Pictures" icon to go directly to My Pictures, where you can view your new roll of film.

Your pictures should be posted in a few days or hours. If your pictures don't appear in a reasonable amount of time, you need to follow up. The developer may have incorrectly entered the information you provided, or you may have provided the incorrect name and address (most likely because the information you supplied didn't match your official AOL account information).

Here's how to proceed. Every roll of film that "You've Got Pictures" scans has a unique Roll ID and an Owner's Key, both of which are printed on a card that comes inside the envelope containing your prints. At AOL Keyword: **Pictures**, click the Find Your Roll button in the left-center part of the main screen (refer to Figure 2-1). Type the Roll ID and Owner's Key into the appropriate boxes on the screen that appears and click OK. Your new roll will appear in the New Pictures tab, ready to view. Repeat these steps for each roll you are expecting. If you need additional help, click the Help button in the upper-right corner of the screen.

Getting Around My Pictures

The My Pictures area, from which you can access the "You've Got Pictures" main screen (AOL Keyword: **Pictures**), is the area in "You've Got Pictures" for viewing and using your digital pictures.

As shown in Figure 2-3, My Pictures consists of the following three tabs:

▲ **New Pictures.** When you receive a new roll, it first appears on your New Pictures tab. After you view even a single picture on that roll, the whole roll is stored on the My Rolls & Albums tab. Buddy Albums that you haven't viewed yet, which are discussed later in this chapter, also first appear on the New Pictures tab.

▲ **My Rolls & Albums.** Viewed rolls of film, your own albums, and Buddy Albums that you have used to create your own albums appear on this tab. Later in this chapter, you find out how to use Buddy Albums as the basis of your own albums — a good way of maintaining a joint collection of digital pictures. (After you've made a Buddy Album your own album, it's no longer considered a Buddy Album.)

Figure 2-2. "You've Got Mail" (the mailbox flag is up) and "You've Got Pictures" (the film roll shows a protruding picture).

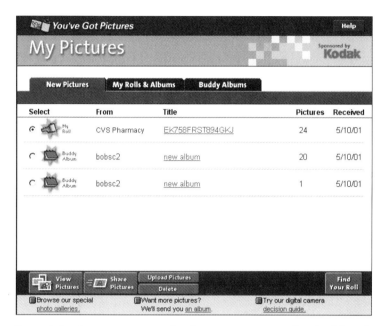

Figure 2-3. When you receive new digital pictures, you can view them by clicking the New Pictures tab — if it is not already displayed. After you view your pictures or the ones that others have shared with you, the pictures are automatically transferred to one of the other two tabs.

Tip

If you don't hear the "You've Got Pictures" message even when the "You've Got Pictures" icon lets you know that your pictures have arrived, make sure your sounds are turned on. If your audio system has a Mute button, make sure that sound is enabled. If the sound is enabled and you still don't hear the message, then change your AOL 6.0 preferences, as follows: Choose Settings➪ Preferences and, in the Preferences window that appears, click Toolbars & Sound. Make sure a check mark is next to the Enable AOL Sounds check box.

2

"You've Got Pictures": The Easiest Path to Getting Digital Pictures Online

▲ **Buddy Albums.** After you view a new Buddy Album, the album appears on this tab.

In a nutshell, the first two tabs consist of the pictures you take, plus the pictures you have gathered into *albums*. The final tab is the place for photo albums that others have sent to you using "You've Got Pictures."

The pictures you upload, the rolls and Buddy Albums you receive from others, as well as the albums you create yourself are all saved online for free. You thus have more pictures to share with others, to use in projects, and to add to your Web pages.

What's New in "You've Got Pictures"?

If you used "You've Got Pictures" before June 2001, you will now notice several improvements to the service including the following:

- Most important, the original version of "You've Got Pictures" had a limit of 50 pictures. In the new version of "You've Got Pictures" you have unlimited storage space for your digital pictures. This means that *all* pictures are saved in the new version of "You've Got Pictures"; you don't have to manage individual pictures or maintain fewer than 50 pictures, as you used to. The only requirement to maintain your free storage space is that you visit the "You've Got Pictures" area at least once every 6 months.

- AOL's first version of the "You've Got Pictures" service had four tabs instead of three. In the new version of "You've Got Pictures," the My Rolls & Albums tab takes the place of the old Saved Pictures and Albums tabs.

- You can now upload several pictures at the same time. Procedures are provided later in this chapter.

- The gift store has been streamlined and made easier to use.

- Rolls no longer expire.

- Sharing is easier — no need to create an album to share multiple pictures, and sharing pictures (one or multiple) automatically creates a Buddy Album.

All these changes work together. The multiple-picture upload tool takes advantage of the unlimited storage capability. With all those online pictures, you will have more to share by e-mail and albums, as well as in the form of photo gifts.

Viewing Your Pictures

In the main My Pictures window, you can view any of the individual pictures in any of your rolls and Buddy Albums. Here's how:

 At AOL Keyword: **Pictures**, click the Go to My Pictures button to access the main My Pictures window. Click any of the three tabs where you have digital pictures.

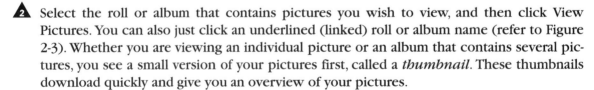 Select the roll or album that contains pictures you wish to view, and then click View Pictures. You can also just click an underlined (linked) roll or album name (refer to Figure 2-3). Whether you are viewing an individual picture or an album that contains several pictures, you see a small version of your pictures first, called a *thumbnail*. These thumbnails download quickly and give you an overview of your pictures.

To see a larger version of any thumbnail, just click it or click in the picture's check box and then click the View Larger button at the bottom of the window. Your image is now enlarged, and to its right and left, you will see Next and Previous buttons respectively, so you can see enlarged versions of other pictures, in the same order they appear in the thumbnails screen (Step 2). See Figure 2-4.

Figure 2-4. Thumbnails give you an overview of your digital pictures. Select a picture and click View Larger to see a larger version.

Sharing Digital Photos

Whether you're a proud gardener showing off your first homegrown pumpkin or a shutterbug eager to pass around those vacation snapshots, "You've Got Pictures" adds a whole new dimension to the act of sharing. Here's a brief overview of how you can share your digital pictures using "You've Got Pictures":

▲ **E-mail.** This is the easiest way to pass around your digital pictures. You can find detailed procedures for using e-mail to share pictures in the next section.

▲ **Albums.** An album provides a way to gather individual pictures to share with someone else, or with dozens of others, on AOL or the Internet. See the section "Sharing Collections of Pictures (Albums)," later in this chapter.

▲ **Gifts.** At the "You've Got Pictures" store, you can have products made out of your digital pictures: T-shirts, sweatshirts, coffee mugs, puzzles, and mousepads, not to mention prints. See the section "Sharing Your Digital Pictures as Prints and Gifts," later in this chapter.

An *album* is a collection of digital pictures. An album that someone else on AOL shares with you is called a *Buddy Album.*

All pictures that you share via AOL are subject to AOL's Terms of Service (TOS). It's a good idea to look over the rules regarding shared pictures at AOL Keyword: **TOS**. Also, read the "You've Got Pictures" Guidelines in the "You've Got Pictures" Help area.

If you want to share your photos with an even bigger audience, you may prefer to put them on a Web page or create a photo collection in Groups@AOL. Chapter 3 is about the Web, and Chapter 4 includes a profile of Groups@AOL.

2

"You've Got Pictures": The Easiest Path to Getting Digital Pictures Online

Sharing a Picture by E-Mail

Amazingly quickly, a new form of human communication has become commonplace: *electronic mail,* or *e-mail,* or just plain *mail.* Did you know that an e-mail message can carry more than a simple text message? It can include your digital pictures, too. AOL gives you several convenient ways to access your e-mail: It's built into "You've Got Pictures," it's integral to the AOL service (using the AOL toolbar's Read and Write buttons), and it's even available through AOL Mail on the Web (www.aol.com/aolmail) when you're away from your computer. Depending on where you access your e-mail on the service, you can use different e-mail features to send your digital pictures to others.

Sharing by E-Mail (1): "You've Got Pictures"

"You've Got Pictures" lets you send a single digital picture, several digital pictures, or an album to someone else or to several others. Unlike AOL's regular e-mail, described in the next section, "You've Got Pictures" is optimized for sending pictures, not written messages.

To share selected pictures from a roll or album, take the following steps:

1 Go to My Pictures, which you can access from the "You've Got Pictures" main screen (AOL Keyword: **Pictures**).

2 Click the tab with the pictures you want to share. You can share one picture, many pictures, or a whole album.

- **To share an entire roll or album:** Click the radio button by a roll's or album's name to indicate that you want to share it. Note that you can share both your own rolls and albums and Buddy Albums (albums shared with you).

- **To share one or more individual pictures from a roll or album:** Click View Pictures to display all the thumbnails for a roll or album. Then select a picture by clicking the check box to its left. (If you change your mind, click again to deselect the picture.) For the selected album or roll, you can choose as many or as few pictures as you want to send.

3 Click the Share Pictures button to bring up the window shown in Figure 2-5.

4 In the Send To box, type the recipients' AOL screen names or Internet e-mail addresses. As in regular AOL e-mail, you can enter many names by simply separating the e-mail addresses with commas.

If you have sent albums or pictures before, the names of previous recipients (up to 20) are stored in your Share List. You can see the list by clicking the Add Names from Share List button in the Share Pictures window. Check the addresses you want to use, and then click the Add Names button to place the names in the Send To box and return to the Share Pictures window.

5 Type a greeting or picture description (or anything else for that matter) in the E-Mail Message box. Whatever you type, it will have to be under 500 words.

6 When you are done, click Send.

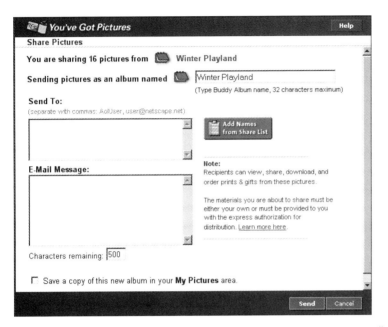

Caution

If you know your Internet recipient from AOL Instant Messenger, you cannot use the AIM screen name as the Internet e-mail address. E-mail addresses start with a user name (like the AOL screen name), include an at symbol (@), and end with what is called the domain name, which comes after the @ symbol. For example: *cgattgacagtc@helix.nih.gov.*

Note

Although non-AOL members can receive Buddy Albums and view them on the Web, they cannot create their own albums.

Tip

Because inserted pictures can be slow to download, you might consider notifying people in the Subject line that a picture is attached.

Figure 2-5. The Share Pictures window lets you specify who receives your pictures or album. Type e-mail addresses or select them from the Share List. The list will include names (e-mail addresses) only if you have already used this feature to send people pictures.

Your recipients will get automatic e-mail from screen name AOL BuddyPics, containing your message, the first photo in the picture set or album, and instructions on how to view the additional pictures. AOL members can also retrieve their pictures directly by going to their My Pictures area and looking in the New Rolls tab. Non-AOL members receive a message from AOL BuddyPics@aol.com. The message will contain a link to the picture or album, which will be available on the Web from any computer.

Legal Concerns

Exercise care when you share albums. Anyone who receives an album from you can view the photos, order gifts or prints from the photos, create new albums, and forward the photos to others.

If you used an earlier version of "You've Got Pictures," it is important to realize that albums work somewhat differently in the new version of "You've Got Pictures." You used to be able to revoke buddies' access to an album that you shared by simply removing their names from the Share List, the list of e-mail addresses that is automatically created when you use "You've Got Pictures" to send someone a picture or album. Now, sending a Buddy Album is like sending an e-mail message: After you send the album, it's out of your control. That's where the copyright concerns come in.

If any of the pictures you share in an album include pictures of strangers, you should never use such pictures in any commercial or legally dubious way. You should assume that pictures you find online or scan from a publication are copyrighted and should, of course, use such pictures only for noncommercial purposes. You can find out more by clicking the Learn More Here link in the Share Pictures window, shown in Figure 2-5; you can access this link and read the information it provides right before you send pictures.

Sharing by E-Mail (2): AOL Mail

AOL members can use AOL's regular e-mail features to compose a message with digital pictures embedded right in the body of the message. With your regular AOL e-mail, you can easily

▲ Combine your image and text message together in a pleasing design, as shown in Figure 2-6.

▲ Conclude with a signature that is automatically appended to your message and that can contain your contact information or whatever you'd like to add.

▲ Include customized colors and fonts.

▲ Have a record of (and reuse) your message after you have sent it.

To insert a picture into an AOL e-mail message, you must, of course, have the picture on your hard drive or on another drive. If the picture is on "You've Got Pictures," you can download it by following the procedures in the "Downloading Pictures to Your Computer" section later in this chapter. After the picutre is on your hard drive, follow these steps:

❶ Click the Write icon on the AOL toolbar to open a Write Mail window, as shown in Figure 2-6.

❷ In the Send To box, type the AOL screen name of the recipient. For your message to reach more than one person, just separate the addresses with commas.

❸ In the Subject box, type some words indicating what the message is about.

4 Type your e-mail message in the big box in the bottom half of the window. Writing your e-mail message before you insert the picture is a good idea, because positioning your picture(s) is easier when you already have some text in the message box.

5 Click the Insert a Picture button on the Write Mail toolbar (see Figure 2-6 — the button looks like a camera). From the drop-down list, choose Insert a Picture.

6 In the Open dialog box, navigate to the folder containing your digital picture, select it, and click the Open button. If you want, repeat Steps 5 and 6 to insert additional pictures in different places in the message.

Cross-Reference

For a complete review of AOL's e-mail features, see another book that I wrote, *Your Official America Online Internet Guide,* 4th edition (Hungry Minds, Inc.).

Tip

AOL's File⇨Open command has a Preview Picture option. Click any picture file listed in the dialog box to take a peek at that image and make sure it's the one you wish to use.

Note

Only AOL members can view the formatting effects you add to the text in your e-mail messages. Internet recipients see just the text.

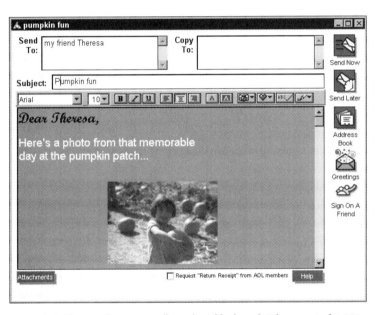

Figure 2-6. This pumpkin picture will travel quickly through Cyberspace in this AOL e-mail message.

If you like, you can immediately click the Send Now button after inserting your picture(s) and send your message on its merry way, but that would be a bare-bones approach to sending pictures via e-mail. I recommend that you take advantage of AOL's many possibilities for enhancing your message. The following list gives you an idea of what's available:

▲ You can use all the usual text-editing techniques, including copy, paste, cut, and delete.

▲ You can select the image with your mouse and center the image on the page or align the image against the left or right margin. On the Mail toolbar (just above the message window), use the second group of three buttons to change the alignment of either text or pictures.

▲ Often you will need to resize your image, because the higher the resolution (quality, or sharpness), the more room the picture needs. You are prompted to resize large images when inserting them, but you can resize a picture after you insert it as well by selecting a picture, right-clicking, and choosing Resize from the pop-up menu. Then select a percentage of your choice, with 100% being the size of the original figure.

▲ Go ahead and select a background color to set the mood for your e-mail. On the Mail toolbar, the Font Color and Background Color buttons are just to the right of the alignment buttons and to the left of the little picture of a camera.

One final word about sending and receiving digital pictures inserted into messages. If you have set up other screen names for your account (for example, children's screen names), you already know that you can customize the secondary accounts associated with the screen names to prevent them from receiving any mail from the Internet or certain domains on the Internet. In addition, you can allow secondary accounts to receive some forms of e-mail but explicitly block them from sending and receiving mail with pictures and files. Start at AOL Keyword: **Parental Controls** and follow the on-screen instructions to customize any secondary accounts as you see fit.

Sharing by E-Mail (3): AOL Mail on the Web

Did you know that you can read your AOL e-mail and send messages on the Web — without using the AOL software? The advantages of being an AOL member are thus available even when you are using a computer that doesn't have the AOL software installed. As long as the computer has an Internet connection, you are just a few clicks away from reading and sending e-mail. All you have to do to get started is visit the AOL Mail site at `aolmail.aol.com`.

Web e-mail messages sent through AOL Mail can include *attached* digital pictures. Why would you want to do this? Suppose you're using someone else's computer or you're on the road and don't have access to your AOL software. If you want to send a digital picture via that site, you have to have the picture's file with you — on a floppy or Zip disk — and then attach the digital picture to your e-mail message.

Follow these steps to e-mail a picture from the Web:

 Go to `aolmail.aol.com`.

 In the Sign On page, type your AOL screen name and password and then click Enter AOL Mail. After correctly entering this information, a page appears, asking you to confirm your desire to use AOL Mail. Click the button.

A page displaying the messages in your AOL mailbox appears. If you want to read a message, click the link for that message.

 To send a message, click the Write icon at the top right-hand corner of the AOL Anywhere (mail) window. To reply to a message from someone else and include a digital picture as an attachment, open the message and click Reply.

A new, smaller window appears, which looks like the Write Mail window shown in Figure 2-6. As you do in the AOL Write Mail window, fill in the standard information — addresses of your recipients (use commas to separate the addresses of multiple recipients), the subject of your message, and the message.

 Now add your digital picture. At the bottom of the Write Mail window, notice the Attach File box. Click the Browse button next to the box and hunt for the digital picture you want to include. It can be on your A: drive (likely, if you're using someone else's computer), a Zip drive, the C: drive, or elsewhere. Select the digital picture file and click Open. The picture appears in the Attach File box.

 When you're ready to send your message, click Send. For both AOL and non-AOL members, the picture is available as an attachment to the e-mail message.

Unlike regular AOL Mail, AOL Mail on the Web lets you attach only one image, and for now, you can't insert an image directly into the message.

You can also visit "You've Got Pictures" at (aolsvc.pictures.aol.com), but you will need to provide your screen name and password, just as when you sign onto AOL each day using your own computer. There, you can download any digital picture to the PC you are using and then attach it to any of your Web-based e-mails. Don't forget to delete the downloaded image from the other person's PC after you have sent the file.

Many home graphics programs make creating attractively formatted collections of albums easy, but they don't always provide direct ways of sharing them online. Some programs, like PhotoSuite, create Web pages based on albums. Using AOL Hometown, which I discuss in Chapter 3, you can easily make those pages available for anyone by posting them to the Web.

Sharing Collections of Pictures (Albums)

Picture this: Your child is just learning to walk. Naturally, you want to share your photos with friends and family members, so you've been taking roll after roll of snapshots. You could send your pictures off one, two, or three at a time, but "You've Got Pictures" offers a better way to share a collection of photos instantaneously with others located anywhere: Put your photos in online albums and then send the whole album to anyone who's online.

Albums are a fun, easy way to organize your favorite photos and share them with others. Where do you get the digital pictures for albums? An album's digital pictures can come from any or all of the following sources:

▲ Individual pictures in your own rolls and albums, which are found on the New Pictures and My Rolls & Albums tabs of the My Pictures screen

▲ Your Buddy Albums (that is, albums that others have shared with you), which are found on the Buddy Albums tab of the My Pictures screen

▲ Pictures uploaded from your own computer directly into an album

After you choose the photos for your album, you can personalize it by adding a background color, album descriptions, and captions for individual pictures. When your album is ready, you can share it with individuals in the same way you share a digital picture. See "Sharing by E-Mail (1): 'You've Got Pictures,'" earlier in this chapter.

Creating an Album

To create an album, follow these steps:

1 At AOL Keyword: **Pictures**, go to My Pictures (with the three tabs visible, as in Figure 2-3).

2 Click the New Pictures tab to view a new roll, the My Rolls & Albums tab for previously viewed rolls and existing albums, or the Buddy Albums tab for albums others have shared with you.

3 Select the pictures you want to include in your *new* album by clicking in the check boxes to the upper left of each individual picture. If you want to select all the pictures, click Select All Pictures. Handpicking the best shots is a good way of sharing the best pictures from a roll of film.

4 Click Create New Album. The Edit My Album screen appears (see Figure 2-7) showing all the pictures you chose. Use the Edit buttons at the bottom to choose a new layout (including background color), add a title to the album, write captions, or add more photos from other places. (For more on the Edit buttons, see "Customizing an Album," later in this chapter.)

5 When you are satisfied with the way your album looks, click Save.

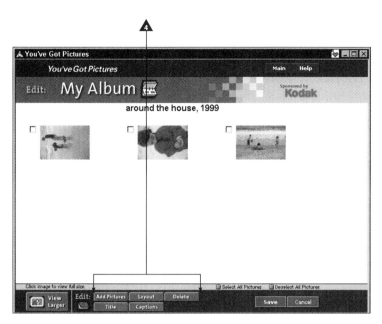

Figure 2-7. This album was created from three pictures in another album, whose name (*around the house, 1999*) can still be seen. Read "Customizing an Album" to learn how to remove a picture from an album.

Adding Pictures to an Album

Just as kids get older and families get larger, you can expect your regular photo albums to grow in size and heft. A digital album often grows a lot faster than the physical variety, because it's easier to add to and many people can add pictures by modifying Buddy Albums. You won't regret learning how to add pictures to your online albums. Here's how:

1 At AOL Keyword: **Pictures**, click the tab containing the album to which you want to add pictures. (It will be either the My Rolls & Albums tab or the Buddy Albums tab). Click the underlined (linked) album name, whether it's your own or a Buddy Album.

2 Click Edit Album. The Edit My Album window appears (see Figure 2-7).

3 In the Edit My Album window, click Add Pictures. You're taken back to My Pictures, where you have access to all your online pictures.

See the information about photo goofs and how to fix them in Chapter 6, which gives hints for making the most of shots that didn't come out.

Deleting pictures is even easier than adding them. From the Edit My Album screen, select pictures to delete only from this album, click the Delete button, and then confirm your choice by clicking Delete again. The pictures won't be deleted from other albums of which they are a part.

See the Photo Collage and Scrapbook activities in Chapter 6 for creative ways to store and present collections of pictures.

With "You've Got Pictures," you can edit an album in the ways described in this section, but you cannot yet edit individual digital pictures. For that, you need to download your pictures and open them in your graphics software (PhotoSuite, Print Shop, PhotoDeluxe, or another program).

4 Click the appropriate tab to locate the roll, album, or Buddy Album that contains pictures you want to use. Select the roll or album you want and then click Next.

5 Select the digital pictures that you want to add to your the album you're editing by clicking the check boxes to the left of each picture you want to use. Click a check box again to de-select a picture if you change your mind. If you want to select or deselect all the pictures, use the Select All Pictures or Deselect All Pictures button.

6 When you are finished selecting pictures for your album, click OK. The selected pictures appear in your album. From the Edit My Album screen, repeat this process starting with Step 1 to add more pictures from a different source. When you are done, click Save. Clicking Cancel ends the editing process without changing the album.

Here's another way of adding pictures to an album: You can upload pictures from your hard drive to one or many albums. From My Pictures, on the correct tab, first click the circle for the album to which you want to add pictures. Then click Upload Pictures and follow the steps in "Uploading Photos to 'You've Got Pictures'" later in this chapter.

Customizing an Album

Customizing an album means spiffing it up for the circle of people with whom you will be sharing it. (Also called *editing,* customizing is carried out in the same Edit My Album window used in the previous section.) Or, for your own sake, you can customize your albums with titles that will help you find and use your pictures in the future. This kind of editing gives you a set of useful choices. In addition to adding and deleting pictures, which I explain in the previous section, you can specify how many pictures appear in a row, provide captions for individual pictures, and give a name to the entire album. You can also give the entire album a distinctive colored background.

▲ To get started customizing one of your own albums, open it from the My Rolls & Albums tab and then simply click Edit Album at the bottom of the window to access the editing features of the Edit My Album window.

▲ To customize a Buddy Album, start by opening the album from the Buddy Albums tab. Select all the pictures, or any combination of individual pictures, to indicate which ones you want in your own album. Click Create Album.

Whether you are editing an album or a roll, or creating a new album based on a Buddy Album, you'll be working in the Edit My Album window (refer to Figure 2-7). The following buttons give you all your editing options:

▲ **Add Pictures.** This button returns you to the main "You've Got Pictures" page, where you can access your new and old rolls as well as your own albums and Buddy Albums. After you've selected pictures to add to the album, as explained in "Adding Pictures to an Album," your album appears again with your new pictures included.

▲ **Layout.** Clicking this button lets you choose how many photos are displayed per line: one, two, or four (default). Choose "one" for the largest possible picture displays, "two" for medium-sized pictures, and "four" for the smallest pictures. Click OK to save your changes.

The Layout feature now includes a set of colors that you can use as the background for your album. Make a choice, if you wish, and proceed.

▲ **Delete.** Select the pictures in your album that you want to remove, click the Delete button, and confirm the removal. Your album reappears without the selected pictures.

▲ **Title.** Click this button to type a new album name of up to 32 characters, plus a description of up to 500 characters. Click OK when you're done. If you're creating an album for organizational purposes (to archive pictures, for example), you might want to include the date, place, occasion, season, and so on. If you're planning to share your album with others, be sure to give it a concise name that describes the pictures in the album.

▲ **Captions.** If you want to add a descriptive or humorous caption to any photo, click the Add Caption button. The first photo in your album appears, along with space where you can type a caption of up to 32 characters. You can then click the Previous Pictures and Next Pictures buttons on the caption page to add captions to other pictures. If you prefer to add a caption to a specific picture, select it in the album before clicking Add Caption.

Be sure to save your album when you're finished customizing it. After saving it, you can preview your album so that you know how it will look to others (see Figure 2-8).

Figure 2-8. A customized album, based on Figure 2-7, with a picture deleted, an accurate title, a caption suggesting a story, and a colorful background, which you cannot see here.

Unlike the previous version of "You've Got Pictures," if you make changes to an album that you've already shared with others, you need to send the album again so that people can see your changes.

If you want the pictures in your album to display in a particular order, add each picture individually in the order you prefer. Pictures are displayed left to right, top to bottom. The most recently added picture is in the bottom-most row, on the right.

If you sign off before you're able to save any changes to your album, your modifications will be lost. To prevent this from happening, save your changes from time to time by clicking Save.

You can edit any album you create at any time. Just open the album and click the Edit Album button to see the list of customization options.

Receiving Buddy Albums

When someone sends *you* an album, the "You've Got Pictures" icon on the Welcome screen shows a small bit of film sticking out of its film canister. (You'll also receive an e-mail message from AOL BuddyPics with the news.)

To access an album that someone has shared with you, go to AOL Keyword: **Pictures**, click the New Pictures tab, select the new album, and click the View button. After you view the Buddy Album, it is stored on the Buddy Albums tab. Buddy Albums offer many familiar options: You can view full pictures, e-mail a picture, create a new album, download one or more pictures, and order prints and gifts based on a picture.

Managing Albums

If you like albums, spend a moment and find out how to manage them and expand their potential. Here are some tips for making the most of your albums:

▲ **Develop a naming system:** Names (called *titles* in "You've Got Pictures") can include an initial (to indicate who took the pictures), the date or season, the subject, or any other way of referring to the collected pictures. If you use abbreviations consistently, you can identify your various albums at a glance.

▲ **Delete unwanted albums:** Albums, like anything else, can become outdated. Rather than keep unwanted albums that are merely cluttering up your My Pictures space, you can simply delete them. If you need to delete an album, click the My Rolls & Albums or Buddy Album tab, select the album you want to delete, and click the Delete button. After you confirm the deletion, your album is removed. If you want to keep any digital pictures in an album to be deleted, make sure to add those pictures to another album as described above.

▲ **Download pictures you are no longer using actively online:** If you are pretty sure that you are not going to be using a digital picture for any online purposes, remove it from your My Pictures space by downloading it to your hard drive. (See "Downloading Pictures to Your Computer," later in this chapter, for more on downloading digital pictures.) You can always upload the picture back to your My Pictures space at a later date if you change your mind.

Sharing Your Digital Pictures as Prints and Gifts

Another valuable way of sharing your pictures — after e-mail and albums — is by using them to create prints and gifts. At the "You've Got Pictures" store, you can order prints or add your photos to popular gift items such as coffee mugs and T-shirts. In the new version of "You've Got Pictures," the store has received a facelift and now offers more choices.

To use your pictures in a print or gift:

1 Go to My Pictures, which you can access on the YGP main screen (AOL Keyword: **Pictures**); find the roll or album containing the picture you want to use; and click the roll or album to view the thumbnails (small pictures).

2 Select the picture that you would like to use with your prints or gifts by clicking in the check box next to the picture. You can select more than one picture if you like.

3 Click the Photo Store button. An introductory page tells you about Kodak's picture services. Click Print@Kodak button to proceed to the store. Another page tells you that the selected picture is being retrieved.

4 The Select Your Products page appears. Here, you choose how you want to use the selected picture(s) — on a print or on a gift.

Make sure each picture you chose in Step 2 is sharp enough for use on the objects you want to purchase. At the bottom of the Select Your Products page, you can see the picture(s) you selected in Step 2, along with its dimensions in pixels (for example, 768 x 512). Make a note of these numbers, because they define your picture's resolution, and most prints and products have guidelines regarding the minimal resolution required for good-quality reproductions. Figure 2-9 shows the resolution guidelines that are available throughout the "You've Got Pictures" store.

Product	Mimumum Resolution	# of "MegaPixels"
4x6	508 x 762	1
5x7	635 x 889	1
8x10	1016 x 1270	1.3
11x14	1024 x 1300	1.5
16x20	1168 x 1460	2.0
20x30	1200 x 1792	2.1
11 oz Mug	333 x 458	.5
15 oz Mug	333 x 458	.5
MousePad	762 x 1143	1
Puzzle	762 x 1143	1
Tshirt	1016 x 1270	1.3
Sweatshirt	1016 x 1270	1.3

Figure 2-9. The larger the product, the larger the digital picture required. This online table tells you exactly how big your digital pictures should be, in pixels, for any product.

Find It Online

The table of recommended minimum resolutions shown in Figure 2-9, plus clear information about preparing photos for use as gifts, is available from a link at the bottom of all three gift-selection pages: Prints and Enlargements, Large-Format Prints, and Gifts & Novelties. Click the Make Your Pictures Look Their Best link. Wherever you see the blue Resolutions link, click it to see the table.

Definition

A *pixel* is the smallest unit of a picture — a tiny dot of color. *Megapixel* is camera makers' term for a million pixels per picture (not per square inch). A picture that is 768 pixels tall and 512 pixels wide is about 400,000 pixels square (less than half a megapixel). A resolution of 1152 x 872 pixels, however, would just exceed a megapixel. For prints, you usually want higher-resolution than for comparably sized on-screen images, because paper is simply capable of displaying more pixels in a given area than a monitor is.

If you selected more than one picture in Step 2, you decide on the Select Your Products page whether to use all the pictures in the same way (for example, on a T-shirt) or each in different ways (for example, one picture on a T-shirt, another on a 5 x 7 print, and so on).

- If you selected one or more pictures in Step 2 and want each picture made into the same gift or print (for example, a 5 x 7 print), proceed to Step 6.

- If you selected more than one picture in Step 2 and want them made into different prints or gifts (for example, a 5 x 7 print and a T-shirt), proceed to Step 7.

 If you selected one picture or several and you want each picture made into the same print or gift:

    i. On the Select Your Products page, select the print size or gift item you want to use from the drop-down list to the right of the Print All button. Prints and gifts are listed together.

    ii. Select a quantity for each gift or print. For example, if you selected two pictures in Step 2, you might order three 4 x 6 prints of each picture. See Figure 2-10.

    iii. Click Print All. You are taken directly to your Shopping Cart; go to Step 8.

For more information about any print size and any gift, click one of the three buttons on the left of the Select Your Products page (Prints & Enlargements, Large Format Prints, Gifts and Novelties). Figure 2-11 shows the Gifts and Novelties area. For every gift and print, you can find prices and minimum recommended resolutions. Prints come in a total of six sizes, from 4 x 6 inches to 20 x 30 inches. For the former, images must be at least 508 x 762 pixels; for the latter, 2.1 megapixels — more than 2 million pixels per inch!

 If you selected several pictures and want them made into more than one print or gift:

    i. On the Select Your Products page, click Customize.

    ii. On the next page, use the drop-down list adjacent to the thumbnail of each selected picture to indicate the print or gift you want to make out of the picture. For each, select a quantity.

    iii. Click Add to Order when you have chosen a quantity and print or gift for each image. (Note for people using Step 6: you won't see this button; clicking Print All takes you directly to your Shopping Cart.)

 Regardless of how and what you choose, the next window shows your Shopping Cart, with the gift item or print size, quantity, and prices, together with a subtotal (see Figure 2-12). Sales tax and shipping are added when you check out. In the Shopping Cart you can:

- Remove a gift or print by clicking Remove.

- Change the quantity by using the drop-down list to the right of each image.

- Cancel the order by clicking the button at the bottom of the page.

- Continue shopping by clicking the button at the bottom of the page.

Click Check Out when you are ready to go.

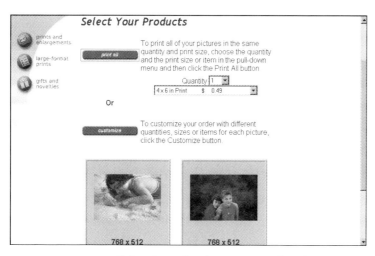

Figure 2-10. Use Print All if you have selected one picture, or if you have selected several pictures and you want the same print or gift to be made of each picture. Use Customize if, after choosing several pictures, you want each picture made into a different print or gift.

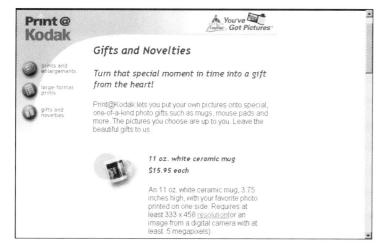

Figure 2-11. Ordering a gift. This coffee mug displays your digital picture and can be sent to anyone as a gift. Notice that the description includes the recommended minimum resolution for this picture (333 x 458). Your selected picture or pictures' resolution is provided at the bottom of the Select Your Products page.

Tip

Compare your picture's resolution with the recommended resolutions provided for the prints and gifts. For example, in Figure 2-11, the coffee cup requires a picture of at least 333 x 458 pixels (a fairly low resolution). When you select a print or gift in Steps 5 thorough 7, a small yellow triangular warning sign (with exclamation point) appears by the thumbnail of your picture when the picture's resolution is less than the recommended resolution.

Note

You can't have a single picture made in two different print sizes or a print and a gift. In all cases, each selected print can be made into only one picture or gift.

Clicking Check Out takes you to the Delivery and Billing page. At the top of the page, your subtotal for the ordered items appears in bold.

- On this page you must choose a delivery option, type credit-card information, and type the address to which you want the items sent.
- Make sure to put a check in the box indicating your agreement with Kodak's Terms and Conditions. You can't proceed with your order if you don't check this box.
- Click Continue to proceed to Step 10. Continue Quick Checkout if you're using that service. (Cancel returns you to My Pictures; Return to Shopping whisks you back to the store.)

 The next page — Checkout — displays your total charge which includes the subtotal, shipping, and tax. Confirm the order (a thumbnail of the image(s) is also provided), and click either Complete or Cancel. Clicking Complete concludes the transaction.

The Thank You page summarizes what you ordered and how much you paid, and provides a Customer Reference Number for later use. You also receive an e-mail message that confirms your transaction.

Because your "You've Got Pictures" purchases are customized, your return privileges are limited. Obviously, you are covered if your order is damaged or if there's a discrepancy in your order (check your order carefully against your confirmation notice when you receive it). Be sure to save the original packing materials and file your claim within 30 days of receipt. In the "You've Got Pictures" store, you can find the following handy links at the bottom of each page: Help, Order Tracking, and Privacy & Policies.

AOL Quick Checkout

To speed up your online purchasing, you may want to sign up for AOL Quick Checkout, which securely stores information for up to ten of your credit cards, your address, and the addresses of those to whom you frequently send gifts. Then when you make a purchase at "You've Got Pictures" or at any other online merchant participating in Quick Checkout, you'll finish in record time. Visit AOL Keyword: **Quick Checkout** to find out more.

Uploading Photos to "You've Got Pictures"

Getting digital pictures from your photo developer means you don't *have* to buy a digital camera to get digital pictures. Through a participating photo developer, you can have the digital pictures created and posted directly to your AOL account when your film is developed.

Figure 2-12. The Shopping Cart shows you what you are buying, how many of each item, and the subtotal. Here you can remove items and change quantities.

On the other hand, a scanner and digital camera give you greater control of the creative process. As your collection of scanned and digitized images on your hard drive grows, you may want to upload these pictures to "You've Got Pictures" in order to store them and share them with others.

Uploading means copying a file from your computer to one of AOL's computers, so that others can view the file. Uploaded images are stored on "You've Got Pictures" along with your other saved rolls and albums. Anything you can do with pictures processed by a "You've Got Pictures" photo developer can be done with any pictures you upload from your computer. You can, for example, share them with others using the "You've Got Pictures" Share feature described earlier in the chapter. And you can turn your own digital creations into photo gifts. Because of the resolution guidelines mentioned earlier, you may want to do exactly that: scan prints, upload the resulting high-resolution images to "You've Got Pictures," and use them to make large prints and high-resolution products such as T-shirts and sweatshirts.

Here's how to upload multiple digital pictures to "You've Got Pictures":

1 At AOL Keyword: **Pictures**, click the Upload Pictures button.

At the bottom of the Shopping Cart page, you'll see a link to information about Quick Checkout, plus a Quick Checkout button if you have already joined. Because this service stores both your billing address and credit card data, using Quick Checkout can expedite the transaction — you must provide this information in any case for every purchase. When you use the Quick Checkout link in this or any store, all you have to provide is your Quick Checkout password and confirm your information. Information in the Delivery and Billing page is automatically filled out for you. See the "AOL Quick Checkout" sidebar.

Print the Thank You page for a record of your transaction, should you need to follow up for any reason. Read the helpful Order Tracking and Privacy & Policies links if you want to know more.

2 To upload several pictures into an existing album, click the One of My Albums radio button and select the album from the drop-down list of your existing albums. To upload several pictures into a *new* album, click the New Album radio button and then type a name for the new album in the text box.

3 After you make your selection, click the Next button. The second step of the Upload Multiple Pictures window appears, as shown in Figure 2-13.

4 In the left-hand pane of the window, navigate to the folder on your hard drive containing the images you want to upload. The contents of the folder are displayed in the right-hand pane.

5 Select two or more pictures in the pane, or click Select All Pictures (or Deselect All Pictures).

6 Choose a transfer speed for uploading your images. Original Size Upload takes longer but is of a higher quality. The Faster Upload option is quicker, but there is some loss of quality.

7 After choosing your transfer speed, click Upload Pictures.

8 The bars shown in Figure 2-14 show the progress of your upload in number of files uploaded (top) and progress of currently uploaded file (bottom).

9 When your files have been successfully uploaded, a new page shows thumbnails of the uploaded pictures, indicates the album into which they have been uploaded, and gives you the choice of viewing that album or uploading more pictures (into any album).

Uploading a single picture is similar to uploading several pictures.

1 At AOL Keyword: **Pictures**, click Upload Pictures. The Upload Multiple Pictures window appears.

2 From the first step of the Upload Mulitple Pictures window, click the link labeled Single-Picture Upload Tool.

3 On the Upload Pictures page (Figure 2-15), follow the instructions for finding and selecting a file to upload.

4 Click Preview Picture to make sure you've got the right picture, and click Upload Picture when you're ready to go. You'll see the uploaded image when it's uploaded and available online.

5 You can now either view the album into which the picture was uploaded, or upload another picture.

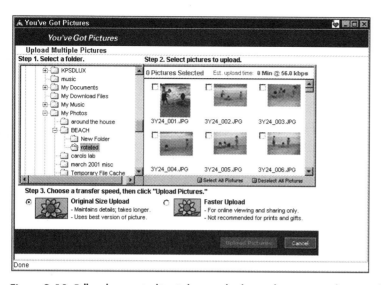

Note

The first time you try to upload more than one picture, you will be asked to first download the Multiple Picture Upload tool from AOL. Follow the on-screen instructions before proceeding with the steps in this chapter.

Figure 2-13. Follow the steps in this window to upload several pictures into the same album.

Figure 2-14. When you upload several files, these bars track their progress.

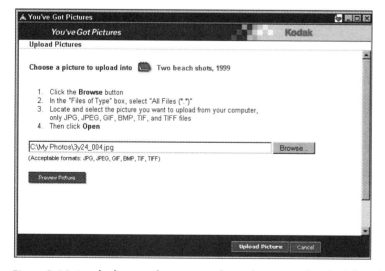

Figure 2-15. In uploading a single picture, use this window (you get here by clicking the Single-Picture Upload Tool link in the first step of the Upload Multiple Pictures window).

Downloading Pictures to Your Computer

If "You've Got Pictures" is such a useful way to collect your digital pictures, and if the new version offers unlimited online storage, why would you want to download pictures to your own computer? Here are a few reasons:

▲ To use your digital pictures in photo activities for work or home, including greeting cards, family trees, newsletters, and invitations. That's what this book is all about. In other words, "You've Got Pictures" may be the source of your pictures, but editing them and creating projects with them are usually done on your PC.

▲ To edit individual digital pictures with AOL's Picture Finder. To do pixel-by-pixel editing, you need image-editing software such as PhotoSuite. The range of editing effects is endless and offers considerable control over your pictures.

▲ To use your digital pictures in Web pages. In order to upload pictures to AOL Hometown, where you make and publish your pages, you must first download them to your PC, whether from a digital camera or from "You've Got Pictures."

▲ To use your digital pictures with AOL e-mail, as described earlier in this chapter, or with AOL Mail on the Web.

The process of downloading pictures involves more steps than the process of uploading pictures. To make the process easier to follow, each of the four major steps—downloading, extracting, viewing, and managing—has been broken down into more detailed steps in the next few pages.

Step One: Downloading Your Digital Pictures

When you download files of any type, you are merely copying them to your computer. In doing this, you are *not* removing them from the source from which they are downloaded. "You've Got Pictures" gives you the opportunity to download one or several pictures at a time. You can even download an entire roll, album, or Buddy Album. To download digital pictures from "You've Got Pictures," use the following steps:

1 At My Pictures (AOL Keyword: **Pictures**), click the tab with the roll, album, or Buddy Album that contains the pictures you want to download.

2 Select the pictures you want to download by clicking in the check box next to each picture. If you want to download all the pictures in the roll or album, click Select All Pictures in the lower-right corner of the window.

3 Click Download Pictures.

4 The service asks you to select the quality (resolution) of your downloaded pictures. The quality you choose affects download time and the image's size. Different resolutions are suited for different functions, so you may want to think about how you'll be using your photos before you choose a resolution. Your options include the following:

- **Web Sharing Quality:** This option saves your images at a resolution of 384 x 256 pixels, and the download time is only about 15 seconds at 28.8 Kbps. On-screen, your images will be approximately one fourth the size of most monitors. Choose this option if you want to share your pictures anywhere online — in e-mail, AOL Hometown Web pages, Groups@AOL, AOL's classifieds, Personals, eBay, and so on.

- **Enhanced Quality:** This option saves your images at a resolution of 768 x 512 pixels. At 28.8 Kbps, your pictures will take about 1 minute 30 seconds to download, and when you display them, they'll take up the full screen of most monitors. Choose this option if you want to use a picture as a screensaver or to make projects (such as T-shirts and mousepads) requiring medium resolution pictures.

5 Click Next.

6 The File Download dialog box appears with the Save This Program to Disk radio button selected, as shown in Figure 2-16. Click OK.

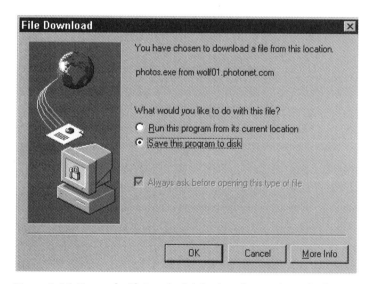

To simplify downloading, you need to change a setting for the AOL browser so that it automatically notifies you when files (your pictures, in this case) are downloaded, making it easy to find and view them. On your Windows desktop, right-click the Internet Explorer icon and choose Properties. Open the Advanced tab. In the Browsing category, make sure the Notify When Downloads Complete option is selected. Click OK.

For a profile of Picture Finder, see Chapter 4 and for an activity using Picture Finder, try the fixing photo goofs activity in Chapter 6.

You can find a thorough introduction to AOL Hometown in Chapter 3.

Figure 2-16. You see the File Download dialog box when you begin the downloading process.

7 The Save As dialog box now appears, as shown in Figure 2-17. Whether one picture or many, your picture(s) are included in a single file, which by default is called `photos.exe`. The default location for saving the file is America Online's Download folder.

Note: See the sidebar, "Renaming Files to Protect Your Downloaded Pictures" if you're not sure whether you want to change the file's name and location. If you do want to make changes, use the Save In drop-down list to choose where the file with your pictures will be saved. In the File Name text box, give the file a name that can help you identify it. Write down the file and folder names so you can easily retrieve the pictures later.

8 After you've noted the location and filename, click Save. Your pictures are then downloaded.

9 When the download is complete, you either see a Download Complete dialog box or you return to the page that was open when you began your download, depending on how you have set up your browser.

Step Two: Extracting Pictures

Before you can view your pictures, you need to extract the pictures from the file you just downloaded by following these steps:

1 If your browser shows a Download Complete dialog box, click the Open Folder button to get to your downloaded file. Otherwise, navigate to the folder containing the file you downloaded.

2 Double-click the downloaded file.

You can now view your digital pictures.

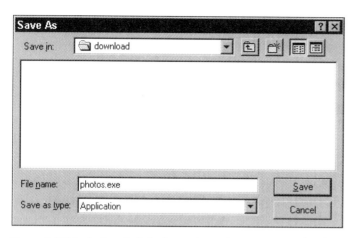

Figure 2-17. In the Save As dialog box, indicate where you want to download your picture(s).

Step Three: Viewing Your Downloaded Photos

AOL's integrated Picture Finder, which I also discuss in Chapter 4, helps you find, view, and do simple editing on all digital pictures stored on My Pictures. Just follow these steps:

1 With AOL open, choose File⇨Open Picture Finder.

2 Find the directory with your downloaded pictures and then click Open Gallery.

3 Your pictures appear in the Gallery's picture viewer. Use the arrows at the bottom to browse through them if you have multiple pictures.

4 Click any picture to view it. Then you can enlarge it and apply simple editing effects, such as cropping.

Step Four: Managing Your Downloaded Pictures

"You've Got Pictures" assigns arbitrary filenames to pictures to make sure the filenames are unique. The unique names ensure that your picture files aren't replaced each time you download new pictures. Unless you rename the picture files that you want to keep, you have no way of retrieving them later. To rename your picture files, follow these steps:

1 Still using Picture Finder, select any picture that you want to re-name. From the AOL menu bar, choose File⇨Save As. The Save Graphic As dialog box appears.

Note

If you can't remember where you saved your file, choose Start⇨Run and then click the Browse button. A dialog box appears that allows you to browse folders for the file, which is called `photos.exe` if you did not rename it. When you find the file, click OK. A plain black window appears, where you can watch the progress as your photos are extracted. Each photo is assigned a numeric filename, such as `21792.jpg`. When the window is done listing the photos, close the window by clicking the X in the upper-right corner.

Tip

You may want to rename your files with AOL Picture Gallery open, so you can quickly match the filename to what's in the actual picture.

Tip

Choose Cut instead of Copy if you want to remove the file from the folder into which it was downloaded and avoid cluttering your hard drive.

2   In the File Name box, type a new filename for the picture but don't change the file type (the three letters after the period in the filename). If you wish, you can select a new location for your file from the Save In drop-down list. You may, for instance, want to save your pictures in the folder where you'll be using them, such as `C:\My Photos\Vacation`.

3   Click Save when you're done.

Renaming Files to Protect Your Downloaded Pictures

Whether you're downloading one picture or several, "You've Got Pictures" saves them by default in America Online's Download folder as a file called `photos.exe` (on the Mac, the file is called `photos.sit`).

As I explain in "Step One: Downloading Your Digital Pictures," you can change both the name and the location of the downloaded file. You may want to give the picture(s) a more descriptive name such as *Florida vacation* to help you find your pictures more easily. Likewise, if you prefer to download your pictures to another location, navigate to that folder on your hard drive. Note the download location and filename so that you can find the file later.

If you retain the default name (`photos.exe`) and location (America Online's Download folder), you will see a message saying, `There is already a file named photos.exe. Would you like to replace it?` the next time you download from "You've Got Pictures."

- If you replace the file, make sure you have already extracted pictures from the original file and saved your pictures somewhere on your hard drive (see the section "Extracting Pictures" in this chapter).

- If you don't want to replace the file, click No. Make sure to give the file a more descriptive name, give it a new location (folder), or both.

After you've extracted pictures from `photos.exe` (or whatever you want to call it), the individual picture files have their own names and can be stored in any folder, so you don't have to worry about accidentally replacing them with new pictures.

Wrapping Up

Digital pictures have few of the limits of paper prints: They're easier to share, they're usable in all sorts of new activities (what this book is about), and they give you much more control over your pictures. In "You've Got Pictures," AOL has made the entire process of getting, storing, sharing, and using digital pictures broadly and affordably available. Chapter 3 and all of Part II of this book provide ideas for what to do with the digital pictures you retrieve from "You've Got Pictures," as well as from other sources such as a digital camera, scanner, or a clip-art collection.

3

AOL Hometown: Putting Your Images on the Web

In This Chapter

▲ Creating a Web page *fast*, with 1-2-3 Publish

▲ Making a more complex page and site with Easy Designer

▲ Editing your 1-2-3 and Easy Designer pages

▲ Publishing other pages on AOL Hometown

▲ Uploading files to AOL Hometown

▲ Adding pages to a Hometown community of similar pages

Chapter 3

AOL Hometown: Putting Your Images on the Web

Even if you have never seen a page on the World Wide Web, you have probably seen the (now common) TV ads mentioning a company's Web address or know someone who finds information on the Web. A Web page is simply an electronic document consisting mostly of words and pictures, like a page of a book. Unlike a book, however, a Web page can be viewed by anyone in the world who has a computer, an Internet connection, and browsing software. AOL has a built-in browser and connects you to the millions of computers where pages are kept. The secret of the Web is its simplicity: You can effortlessly see pages located in many countries around the world. The Web is so simple, in fact, that you can even create pages that Web users everywhere can see.

People make Web pages for every imaginable reason, and so can you. Here are some possibilities:

▲ The World Wide Web can provide gallery space for your digital photography. Linking your page to others' collections, small or large, can turn a gallery into a small museum.

▲ You can use a Web page to display a digital version of your résumé and enhance it with a digital picture. Then, your résumé is available to potential employers at any moment.

▲ You can share photographs of your paintings, paper airplanes, antique cars, coin collection, or anything else.

▲ A Web page can help promote a home business and provide information about your services to existing and potential customers, and you can add a few pictures of your products to make your message more compelling.

▲ A Web page can also be a great way for everyone in the extended family to see the latest pictures of the kids and to catch up on the family news. A Web family tree can be jointly maintained.

Whatever your purposes, AOL Hometown provides all the tools you need to build and share your own Web pages. Over the years, Hometown has gathered a nearly comprehensive and nicely integrated set of services, including:

▲ Easy-to-use software to make pages, with many templates to simplify the process further

▲ My FTP Space, an online place to store your Web pages and image files

▲ A place to host all your pages (`hometown.aol.com`) for everyone to see

▲ Communities of shared interest and friendship, containing small groups of pages on related themes

▲ Complete online help

This chapter gives a complete tour of AOL Hometown, where you can find everything you need to share your projects and digital pictures with everyone (or, more likely, a handful of friends). The best way to learn about AOL Hometown's Web page tools is to try them out. Don't worry about mistakes: Editing your pages (or starting over from scratch) is as easy as creating them in the first place.

How to Visit a Web Site on AOL

AOL has content only for AOL members and gives you complete access to the Web, the Internet's multimedia smorgasbord. The online world — AOL and the Web together — is the place to learn about digital-imaging products and techniques. Chapter 4 reviews a handful of outstanding Web sites devoted to digital imaging.

The Web consists of *pages*, each of which has an *address* (www.aol.com is AOL.com's address). An address allows you to fish any page out of the sea of more than a billion pages. A collection of pages is called a *Web site*.

To visit any Web page, simply type its address in the address box on the AOL 5.0 or 6.0 toolbar and then press Enter. The figure shows a Web address in the toolbar and a page of Newseum's Web site, which appears when you press Enter (www.newseum.org/pulitzer). By clicking a link, you can jump to another page. To find out if something on a page contains a link, watch your mouse arrow. The arrow turns into a pointing finger if it's hovering over a link, as shown in the figure.

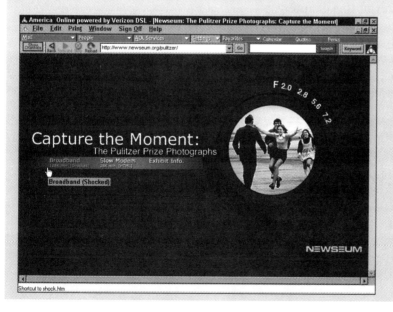

Most people with Web pages learn from each other's work. On AOL, the place to start seeing others' work is the Member Spotlight section at AOL Hometown (AOL Keyword: **Hometown**). See "Adding Your Pages to a Hometown Community," later in this chapter.

Think of a template as a fill-in-the-blank form that you use to create a Web page. Hometown provides a layout consisting of placeholders, which you replace with your own words and pictures. Throughout Part II you'll encounter templates when you use graphics software to make projects.

For more about using "You've Got Pictures," see Chapter 2. To find out about Groups@AOL, go to Chapter 4.

Welcome to AOL Hometown

AOL Hometown (AOL Keyword: **Hometown**), shown in Figure 3-1, provides a destination on the World Wide Web for AOL members and non-members alike. It's the place to go to create your own Web pages as well as view pages made by others. Non-AOL members with Web access can use Hometown by going to the Web site at `hometown.aol.com`.

Members and non-members alike can use up to 12MB of online storage space for their digital pictures, Web pages, and anything else they wish to make available to others. For AOL members, that's 12MB *in addition to* your unlimited storage space for digital pictures on "You've Got Pictures" *and* in addition to the 12MB of space allocated to every Group@AOL you create or join.

Choosing the Right Tool

Hometown provides two tools for making Web pages: 1-2-3 Publish and Easy Designer. These tools take a different approach. It's important to recognize the differences between them before you start. If you have particular needs or prior experience, you may want to use third-party Web tools, including the tools built into Microsoft's Office suite. Pages built with these products, too, can be uploaded to Hometown, stored there, and shared with others.

▲ **1-2-3 Publish.** Use this tool if you want to create a page and publish it quickly in AOL Hometown. Choose a template, add your digital pictures and other content, put in some links, and you're done. See "1-2-3 Publish: Fastest Path to the Web," later in this chapter, for more information.

▲ **Easy Designer.** This tool lets you do more than 1-2-3 Publish and gives you more control of your page's content and visual design. Because you can link multiple pages with Easy Designer, you can expand the amount and organization of your content. Easy Designer also allows you to add pictures wherever you want. For more on Easy Designer, see the section, "Step Up to Easy Designer," later in this chapter.

▲ **Other Web page editors.** If you use another Web tool — such as Macromedia Dreamweaver or Microsoft FrontPage — to create pages, you can upload them to your Hometown storage space at AOL Keyword: **My FTP Space.** Also, you can save files you create with any Microsoft Office application as HTML or as Web pages and then upload them to My FTP Space. After you upload your files, adding them to AOL Hometown is a snap, and you can even include them in a Hometown community.

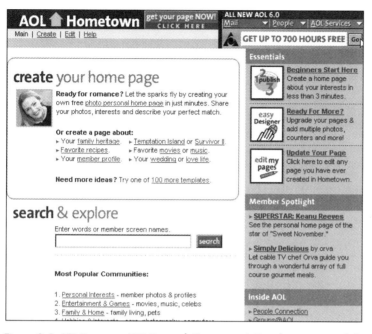

Figure 3-1. AOL Hometown (AOL Keyword: **Hometown**). From here, access tools for making pages, searching other people's pages, and editing your own.

Getting Your Digital Pictures Ready

Before starting on your Web page, it's a good idea to gather any digital pictures (along with any text that's already written) that you want to use in your page. To help you keep track of your files, consider keeping them in one folder on your hard drive or at least in a manageable number of folders. Into this folder, you can also download pictures from other sources, such as a Photo CD, a digital camera, or scanner.

If you have digital pictures on "You've Got Pictures" and want to use these pictures on the Web, you first have to download them to your hard drive (see Chapter 2 to find out how to do this). From your hard drive, you can then upload your pictures to AOL Hometown.

You can upload digital pictures to AOL Hometown in two different ways:

▲ AOL Hometown's Web tools—1-2-3 and Easy Designer—can upload digital pictures for you, one at a time, while you are making a page. The how-to is provided later in this chapter.

▲ Also on AOL, you can use the built-in uploading software known as FTP to upload any file you want to your online storage space (start at AOL Keyword: **FTP**). For more on FTP, see "Uploading Pages Created with an HTML Editor to AOL Hometown," later in this chapter.

If you start a page with 1-2-3 Publish, you can continue editing the same page with Easy Designer. If you start a page with Easy Designer, however, you cannot edit it in 1-2-3 Publish. If you're comfortable with Easy Designer, however, you probably wouldn't want to use 1-2-3!

FTP stands for File Transfer Protocol. You can use FTP software to move your own files around the Internet, and when you download programs, FTP is often at work in the background moving files to your computer. Most important, it's the way your files — Web pages and digital pictures — move from your computer to AOL's computers, which you learn how to do in "Uploading Pages Created with an HTML Editor to AOL Hometown," later in this chapter.

Digital cameras and scanners are introduced in Chapter 1; "You've Got Pictures," in Chapter 2.

3

AOL Hometown: Putting Your Images on the Web

1-2-3 Publish: Fastest Path to the Web

With 1-2-3 Publish (AOL Keyword: **123 Publish**), you start with a *template,* which walks you through the initial layout process for setting up your page. Templates offer you a series of choices by providing the blanks that you fill in.

Figure 3-2 shows the My Family Tree Page Template. Some steps on the template ask you to choose from several predefined options (as in Steps 1 and 2); others ask you to type your own text (as in Step 3). In either case, just make your choices and fill in the blanks or make your selection, an approach you'll appreciate if you are in a hurry. Currently, you can choose from about 100 different templates in 1-2-3. If you are a photographer, you may want to show off a sample image by using the My Photography Page. All the templates are available on 1-2-3's opening page. Just click the one you want, and you are ready to go. Scroll down a bit to see any templates that don't appear in the opening window.

The following steps list walks you through the My Family Tree Page template. Exact steps vary by template, so this procedure is provided only as an example. None of your choices is permanent, by the way, so don't worry about the details. You can see how to modify your work later in the chapter.

After you select the template you want from the 1-2-3 Publish page, do the following:

1. Choose a background color for your page by selecting one of the four radio buttons. A background color is like a gigantic rug for your page and can give it a distinctive feel.

2. Select a banner from one of the available options. A *banner* is a picture that goes at the top of the page, defining the purpose and content of your page.

3. Type a descriptive or attention-grabbing title in the Title field. The words in your title function as a headline and appear below the banner, in large bold type. Titles are usually one or two lines long.

4. If you want to add a digital picture, click the Browse button next to the 1-2-3 Step where you can (optionally) upload a picture. Then, find a picture on your computer's hard drive and double-click to include it on your page.

5. From the available options, choose a horizontal divider to separate the short sections of your page-to-be. In Web lingo, this divider is called a *rule.*

6. Personalize your page by adding your own text in the text fields. 1-2-3 Publish gives you three sections to work with. For each section, you can use the headings provided or create your own.

7. If you want to steer your viewers from your page to other Web sites, you can add hyperlinks to a maximum of three Web addresses. When viewers click a hyperlinked Web address, their browsing software displays (more or less quickly) the related site you want them to visit. Simply type a Web address (also known as a URL, or *Uniform Resource Locator*) into an online links text field. Pay close attention to the spelling, dashes, and other such details when typing in your URL. A misspelled URL could send your viewer to the wrong Web site — or not send them anywhere at all.

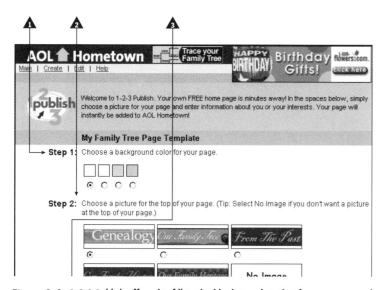

Figure 3-2. 1-2-3 Publish offers this fill-in-the blank template that focuses on genealogy.

8 Click Save My Page to see your home page and save it in AOL Hometown. Or, Click the Preview My Page button to see what your page looks like, whether the links work, how your pictures look, and so on.

9 If you clicked the Preview My Page button in Step 8, click the Modify button at the top of the Preview page if you want to make more changes to your page. After making any changes, click the Preview My Page button again. When you're happy with the look of your Web page, click the Save button on the Preview page to upload your page to AOL Hometown.

Sharing Your Page with the World

When you save a 1-2-3 page, it is automatically registered at AOL Hometown. In this context, *registered* means that your 1-2-3 page is kept in a special index that visitors to Hometown can search. Registering a page also entitles you to additional storage space on Hometown. You'll see a page notifying you of your new page's Web address, which will look something like this:

```
http://hometown.aol.com/screenname/myhomepage/
heritage.html
```

Note

When you create a page with a 1-2-3 Publish template, any digital picture you select is uploaded when you preview your page by clicking Preview My Page at the bottom of the template. Your page and pictures won't be made available to others until you click Save My Page.

Instead of `screenname`, the address will contain *your* screen name, of course. Also, `heritage.html` is the filename of a page created with a genealogy template; other templates have different names. Make a note of the address so you can share it with others. Send your friends an e-mail asking them to visit your page, or put the address on your business cards or in the annual family newsletter. Now anyone can visit your home page by just typing the address of your new page in a Web browser, regardless of whether he or she is an AOL member.

Whenever you stumble across an AOL Hometown page you especially like, you can tell a friend about the page by clicking the Send link next to the small envelope icon at the top of every Hometown window. After the e-mail form appears, just type one or more recipients' e-mail addresses in the Send To box, type your message, and click Send. The link automatically appears in the message, and the recipient of the message can click the link to visit the page (his or her browser opens with the page displayed). Take advantage of this easy way to notify your friends when *you* create a Web page; just open your own page and use the Send link to e-mail your page's address to your friends.

When your page is published, you receive official notification right away by e-mail. The message, which includes lots of useful information about AOL Hometown, is worth saving. Click the message's heart icon in the upper-right corner to store the message in your Favorite Places folder, where it will always be available from the AOL Favorites menu.

The Least You Need to Know about Graphics Formats

Every one of your digital pictures is stored in a file. Files have different formats. In general, a file format indicates what type of file you're dealing with.

You can easily spot a file format by eyeballing a filename. In the digital-picture file `daffy.jpg`, the JPG extension — the letters to the right of the period — tells you that you're dealing with a JPG file (pronounced jay-peg), one of the standard graphics formats used for images on the Web. The extension of a file entitled `dizzy.gif` lets you know that you have a GIF file (pronounced giff) on your hands, another popular graphics format for Web use. What's the difference? JPGs are used for photographs (with more complexity and lots of colors). GIFs are used for simpler pictures like icons and cartoons. On "You've Got Pictures," files are automatically stored as JPGs.

Most graphics software lets you save files in a variety of formats (including GIF and JPG) for use in many different programs and on the Web. Graphics software that lets you create projects usually has specialized formats for those projects that can be used only in that program (PhotoSuite's PZP, for instance). Make sure to save the pictures that you want to use on AOL Hometown as either GIFs or JPGs.

Step Up to Easy Designer

Easy Designer (AOL Keyword: **Easy Designer**) gives you more control of layout, formatting, and content than 1-2-3, so you can use it to add all those great digital pictures you've been salting away on your hard drive. When you're all done, your Easy Designer pages, just like your 1-2-3 Publish pages, are stored in AOL Hometown and can be viewed by anyone with access to the World Wide Web. Figure 3-3 shows a page being edited within Easy Designer.

Figure 3-3. This 1-2-3 page is being edited in Easy Designer. You can also create a new page in Easy Designer by choosing File➪New.

How is Easy Designer different from 1-2-3 Publish? Unlike 1-2-3, Easy Designer lets you do the following:

▲ Add as much text and as many images — including digital pictures — as you want, as long as they can all fit, of course.

▲ Move the text and images anywhere you want on the page.

▲ Format and style your text and digital pictures.

▲ Link any text or picture to another page in order to create an organized presentation of multiple pages — a true Web site.

As with 1-2-3, Easy Designer pages are automatically registered with Hometown when you save them. At that point, anyone with a browser and Internet access can view them.

Tip

If you use Easy Designer to tweak a page that you created with 1-2-3 Publish, you can add many more links anywhere on your page. With Easy Designer, you can also create a site, which is a set of linked pages about some theme.

Tip

After you know your page's Web address, anyone with Web access can use the address to view your page!

Cross-Reference

To edit an existing page, such as a page started in 1-2-3 Publish, click the Open an Existing Page link (under the Return Here heading) and then follow the steps outlined in "Editing a Published (Saved) Easy Designer Page," later in this chapter.

Creating a New Page with Easy Designer

To get started with Easy Designer, use AOL Keyword: **Easy Designer**. The keyword brings up a Hometown page that, in turn, lets you call up Easy Designer. When starting Easy Designer you must first choose whether to create a new page or to edit an existing one. Clicking the Create a New Page link lets you create a new page based on one of Easy Designer's many templates, with placeholders for your pictures and text. To create a new page based on an Easy Designer template, follow these steps:

1. Click the Create a New Page link (found under the Start Here heading).

2. Click the big Click to Get Started button. The Select a Template dialog box appears, as shown in Figure 3-4. Select the template category and topic that most closely match your needs. (If you already have Easy Designer open, choose File⇨New to select a template.)

3. After selecting a template, click Next.

4. Select a page layout for your template from the available options, which are shown in Figure 3-5. A layout is the overall arrangement of text and pictures on a Web page. In this step, your layout choices are indicated by several small images. Notice the complexity of the pages relative to 1-2-3 Publish. Easy Designer templates use multicolumn text, multiple images per page, and other visually engaging arrangements.

Choose the page layout that best suits your material and otherwise appeals to you, but don't worry about getting locked into a particular layout. With Easy Designer, you can later move elements around on the page, add new elements, and delete elements.

5. Click Next.

6. Choose a color scheme for your template from the available options. A color scheme defines a combination of colors designed to work together: background color, text color, and a pair of colors for your visited links and unvisited links. If you click a scheme's name in the left side of the Select a Color window, you can see how the scheme looks in the right side. Click OK, and on the next (final) page click Let's Go.

After selecting a layout and color scheme, your template appears, and you can start adding your own digital pictures, links, and text. For example, the templates contain images that you can replace with your own. Find out more about working with pictures and text to a template in the sections, "Using Digital Pictures in Easy Designer" and "Editing Text in Easy Designer," coming next in this chapter.

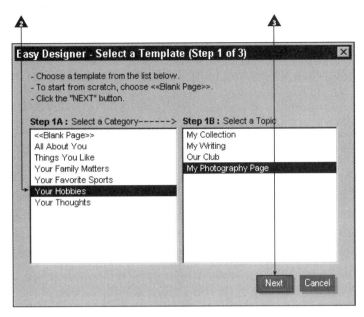

Figure 3-4. Select an Easy Designer category and topic, and you're ready to create your own page.

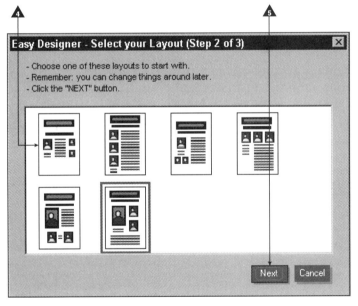

Figure 3-5. After you choose a layout, you can change it any way you wish.

Instead of choosing one of Easy Designer's templates, you can choose Blank Page. You'll be taken to a window with buttons at the top but without the content. For instructions, see the "Editing Text with Easy Designer" and "Using Pictures in Easy Designer" sections.

With your page displayed in Easy Designer, you can at any time click the Color button on the toolbar to change the color scheme or create a custom scheme.

A *visited link* is a link that someone viewing the page has clicked already; an *unvisited link* has yet to be visited. On the Web, unvisited and visited links are usually displayed in different colors to help your users avoid revisiting pages and quickly identify pages they haven't yet visited.

In Easy Designer and 1-2-3, you can't do the pixel-by-pixel editing that improves the appearance of an image. PhotoSuite, the software used extensively in Part II, gives you that kind of control of image appearance.

3

AOL Hometown: Putting Your Images on the Web

Using Digital Pictures in Easy Designer

When you use an Easy Designer template, you'll usually want to replace the template's images with your own. In Easy Designer, this is an example of editing an image — changing its location, changing its size, or swapping the existing image with one of your own or with another provided by AOL. To edit the images on your template, do the following:

1. Select the digital picture you want to replace and click the Modify button on the Easy Designer toolbar. Alternatively, just double-click the picture to edit it.

The Easy Designer Picture Gallery window appears, as shown in Figure 3-6.

2. In the Picture Gallery, click the Upload Picture button.

3. In the Upload Picture window, click the Browse button and navigate to the folder on your hard drive containing the picture you want. The picture you select appears in the Easy Designer Picture Gallery window, as shown in Figure 3-7.

4. Select the picture and then click the Upload Picture button. Be prepared to wait a few moments (or minutes, depending on your connection type and speed) as your picture wends its way from your computer, through the networks, and on to AOL's servers. Soon, you'll see your digital picture in the Picture Gallery. Pictures you upload are stored in My FTP Space and can subsequently be retrieved from there, as discussed in Chapter 2. Make sure the Resize This Picture to Fit Object check box is selected to prevent high-resolution images from filling up your Web page.

5. Click OK to insert the picture into your page.

If, when you return to Easy Designer, a picture appears on top of another object, Easy Designer warns you with an Overlap message. Just click and drag the new picture away from the other picture or text block. Or, resize the object by selecting it and dragging a corner toward the object's center. You can't save a page with overlapping elements.

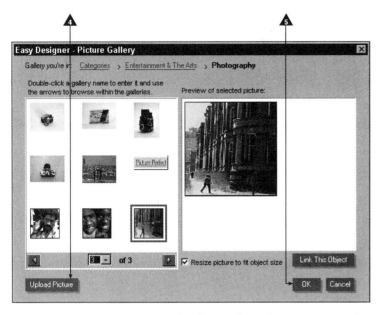

Figure 3-6. Easy Designer's Picture Gallery lets you choose the picture you want from either your hard drive or the Easy Designer clip-art collection.

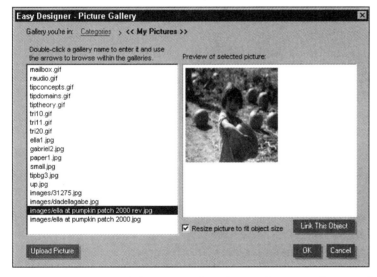

Figure 3-7. A photo uploaded to Picture Gallery. Photos in the Picture gallery are online in the <<My Pictures>> category, ready for you to use.

Editing Text in Easy Designer

When you create a new page with a template, boxes that contain placeholder text indicate areas where you can add your own text, including headlines and paragraphs. Easy Designer allows you to move those boxes around and change their shapes, and you can use the Text Editor to enter and format the text that appears on your page.

The first thing you'll probably want on your Web page is a headline: big text announcing the Web page's theme. To add, remove, or edit text in any text box on your page, follow these steps:

1 To retrieve a saved Easy Designer page, go to AOL Keyword: **Easy Designer**. Click the Open an Existing Page link under the Return Here heading. Wait a moment while Easy Designer loads, and choose the page you want to edit from the list of files displayed in My FTP Space.

2 On your template, double-click any box that contains text. For example, in a headline box, you see something like `Type a headline here`. The Easy Designer - Text Editor window appears, as shown in Figure 3-8.

3 In the main box of the Easy Designer - Text Editor window, delete the placeholder text by selecting it and pressing the Backspace key. Then add your own words and tweak them until they're just right.

4 If you like, use the formatting toolbar at the top of the window to modify your text. Try experimenting with the toolbar's options to add emphasis to your words and sentences. You can use the buttons to do the following:

- Add bold, italics, or underline styling to existing text.

- Align the text along the right or left side or in the center of the template's text box.

- Change font color and size.

5 To link some text (so that it becomes clickable), select a word or a few words and click the Link This Text button. The sidebar, "Linking to Other Pages," describes exactly how you can add a link.

6 Click OK when you're done using the Text Editor and ready to return to Easy Designer. You can open the Easy Designer - Text Editor window and change your text again at any time.

7 Click Preview to see how your page looks with the new text. Your page comes up in the AOL Hometown (Web) window. Click Back to Easy Designer to continue editing. Repeatedly preview your work until you are happy with it.

8 Click Save to make your page available on AOL Hometown. A message window informs you when your page has been saved (online), and it includes your page's Web address.

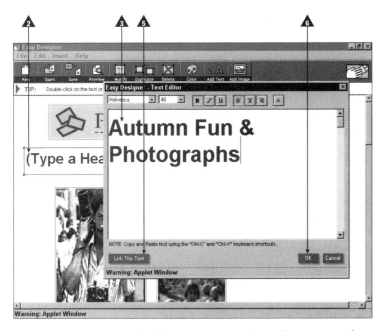

Figure 3-8. Easy Designer's Text Editor gives you control over the appearance of your text.

In addition to editing placeholder text and moving existing text boxes around the page, you can add your own text box anywhere you have room on your page.

In Easy Designer, click Add Text. Up comes the Text Editor, where you can say what you have to say and style your text as you want to style it. Click OK when you're done. The new text appears on your Easy Designer page, ready to be moved, resized, and edited. With all these possibilities, consider creating figure captions for your digital pictures and adding "pull quotes" (as in a magazine) for your personal comments.

You change the shape of a text box by simply clicking any side or corner and dragging in the direction you want. To center the title of your page, clicking the Center button in the Text Editor is not enough. That action merely centers text in the text box. You need to center the box on the page, as well, by clicking and dragging until it is visually centered on the page. A somewhat more precise method of centering on a page is to create a text box as wide as the Easy Designer window; select some text in the Text editor, and click the Center icon on the Text Editor's toolbar. The problem with this method is that you lose a fair amount of space on your Web page by centering a headline in a very wide box.

When you resize an image, you can easily distort the picture's aspect ratio — the relative lengths of the height and width. Drag the top side of the picture down, for instance, and the picture appears flattened, like a pancake; move a side to the left or right, and the picture pulls like taffy. To avoid such distortions, right-click the picture after you've re-sized it and choose Maintain Aspect Ratio from the pop-up menu. If you'd like to restore the picture to its original size, you can do so from this menu, too, by choosing Restore Original Size.

By resizing the text box, you can create long skinny columns of text and create other effects.

Editing a Published (Saved) Easy Designer Page

To edit an Easy Designer page, as with a 1-2-3 page, you first retrieve the page. Here's how it's done:

1 Go to AOL Keyword: **Easy Designer**. After the Easy Designer screen appears, click the Open an Existing Page link under the Return Here heading.

2 From the Open Existing Page box that appears, select the filename of the page you want to edit and then click Open. The page opens in the Easy Designer window, which has the same buttons and works the same whether you're creating a new page or opening an existing one.

3 Edit any element on your page by using the following techniques:

- **Click** any text block or picture on the page (picture, text, horizontal bar, and so on) and then use the mouse to drag the element around the page or resize it. (See "Using Digital Pictures in Easy Designer," earlier in this chapter, for more on using your mouse to move and/or resize elements.)

  Note: After you click any element to select it, you can also use the handy Modify, Duplicate, or Delete buttons on the Easy Designer toolbar for some quick editing. Clicking the Modify button opens either the Text Editor or Picture Gallery, depending on which element you selected. Clicking the Duplicate button makes a copy of the selected item (useful if you want to use the same horizontal graphical divider several times on the same page or repeat a tiny image to serve as dots in a bullet list). Clicking the Delete button simply gets rid of the selected object.

- **Double-click** the element to edit it using Easy Designer's Text Editor or Picture Gallery, as described in the sections "Using Digital Pictures in Easy Designer" and "Editing Text in Easy Designer," earlier in this chapter.

- **Right-click** any block of text, digital picture, or other element, and you can modify, duplicate, or delete it using the context menu that appears. (Buttons controlling these simple functions are also available on the Easy Designer toolbar.)

4 Add any new text to your page by clicking the Add Text button on the Easy Designer toolbar. Type your new text in the new text box that appears and then click and drag the box into position. You can resize the text box by clicking any side or corner and dragging in the direction you want.

5 To add a new image to your page, click the Add Image button on the Easy Designer toolbar to access the Easy Designer Picture Gallery. From there, follow the steps outlined in "Using Digital Pictures in Easy Designer," earlier in this chapter.

6 Click Preview to see how your page looks in AOL Hometown with the changes you just made. Click Back to Easy Designer to edit some more. Preview your work until you are happy with it.

Click Save to make your page available on AOL Hometown. A message window informs you when your page has been saved (online), and it includes your page's Web address. Note that when your 1-2-3 page opens within Easy Designer, it appears just as you left it last in 1-2-3.

Linking to Other Pages

Both the Text Editor and Picture Gallery window give you the ability to link your words or pictures to another Web page. This means that someone viewing your pages can click some text or a picture to jump to a related page.

- To link a picture, double-click the image to edit it in Picture Gallery (Figure 3-7). Click the Link This Object button in the lower right of the Picture Gallery window. You need to type the Web address of the page to be linked to. When your page is published, someone clicking the picture will jump to the page whose address you entered. Here's a tip: Use this technique to link a small version of a picture (a *thumbnail*) to a large version of the picture. The thumbnail images allow users to view only the pictures they want to see — and allow you to provide the higher-resolution pictures that you would not otherwise use directly on a Web page. That is, readers choose what they see and then get a higher-resolution of that image. You can, of course, provide multiple versions of a picture, in the same manner as "You've Got Pictures."

- To link text, double-click the block of text you want to use in order to bring it into the Text Editor. Use the Text Editor just as you used the Picture Gallery. With the block of text displayed in the Text Editor, select a bit of text, and click the Link This Text button. Again, you need to provide the Web address of the page you want to link to.

Editing *Any* of Your Pages

Want to correct a typo or add a link? After you publish your 1-2-3 or Easy Designer page, you can make changes at any time. From *any* page of the AOL Hometown site, first click the Edit link in the top-left corner of the screen. In the Edit My Pages window that appears, you see a list of all your AOL Hometown pages, whether you created them in 1-2-3 or Easy Designer.

Cross-Reference

For instructions on uploading both thumbnails and original-sized pictures, see Chapter 2.

Tip

If you want to edit a published page and know your page's address, then you can use the address to open the page and click the Easy Designer link at the bottom of the page. You are then taken to the opening Easy Designer page where you choose between the two links: Create a New Page and Open an Existing Page. Choose the latter, select the Web page from the list of files, and edit.

Tip

On every Easy Designer page, you can include AOL Instant Messenger Remote (AIMR). AIMR allows your visitors to send you e-mail, add you to their Buddy Lists, send you an instant message, and take part in a chat discussion (not necessarily related to the topic of your site). Add AIMR by choosing Insert⇨AIM Remote. To use AIMR, your visitors must have AOL Instant Messenger, a free program available to AOL and non-AOL members at www.aol.com/aim.

Select the page to be edited (if more than one page is listed) and click Edit. Your page appears within the program (1-2-3 or Easy Designer) used to create it. Make your changes and click Save when you're done. You can also edit a page while using Easy Designer. Just click the Open button to select another page to view and edit.

Sharing a Page with Your Group

Groups@AOL, profiled in Chapter 4, gives AOL members the tools to build small communities on the Web for friends and colleagues. In fact, you can join one of these communities only if you are invited to do so. Think of a Group as a permanent chat room that exists on the Web and has a variety of communication and publishing tools — mailing lists, message boards, Group photo collections, and a jointly created list of favorites (favorite *anythings* — restaurants, books, Web sites, and so on).

Add your new page, whether created with 1-2-3 Publish or Easy Designer, to the favorites section of your Group. You can find your Group (or create a new one) at AOL Keyword: **Groups**. When you're in a Group, click Favorites and enter your page to share with others. Chapter 4's section on Groups can get you started.

Uploading Pages Created with an HTML Editor to AOL Hometown

Web pages are created using a relatively easy-to-learn computer language called *HTML,* which stands for HyperText Markup Language. HTML files contain both content (words and pictures) and *tags* — special instructions for browsers, like Netscape Navigator and the AOL browser, on how to *display* the content. When you browse the Web, all you're doing is downloading HTML files from an Internet computer to your own computer.

How HTML Is Created

When you use 1-2-3 Publish or Easy Designer, the HTML is automatically created for you, behind the scenes. It's there, but you don't access it directly to make your pages.

When you use an HTML editor such as Netscape Composer (see Figure 3-9), you can also create just the effects you want for your Web page without worrying about the underlying HTML — just as in Easy Designer. And an HTML editor allows you to take advantage of HTML's far-reaching capabilities.

Unlike Easy Designer, HTML editors like Composer give you the option of directly accessing the HTML code, allowing you to create more sophisticated effects if you know HTML and other scripting languages such as JavaScript and Cascading Style Sheets. If you know HTML and style sheets, there is no limit to what you can create.

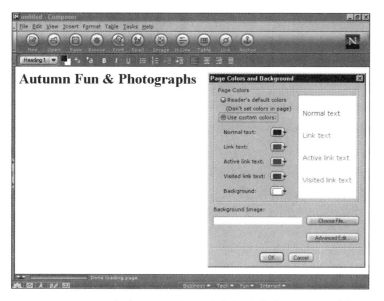

Figure 3-9. Composer, the free HTML editor included with the latest version of the Netscape Navigator browser. The menus give direct access to tables, backgrounds, and formatting, and you can always edit the automatically generated HTML directly.

Using FTP to Upload Web Pages

To publish a page made with an HTML editor, you can use the free space that AOL offers each AOL member who publishes pages at AOL Hometown. This space is called My FTP Space and was mentioned earlier in this chapter in "Choosing the Right Tool." *FTP* is short for File Transfer Protocol and is the heavy-duty means of moving files around the Internet. When you use 1-2-3 Publish or Easy Designer, you're using My FTP Space, but all the uploading takes place automatically, so you don't have to give the process a second thought. Manually uploading files to My FTP Space requires, well, a little more attention.

Here's how to upload a page you created with an HTML editor to My FTP Space:

 Create the page using your HTML editor, and save it on your hard drive. HTML pages have a file extension of HTM or HTML.

 Go to AOL Keyword: **My FTP Space**. In the window that appears, click the See My FTP Space button.

 You'll see a window like the one shown in Figure 3-10, which shows *my* uploaded files; yours will show your uploaded files, or no files if you've never used AOL Hometown.

Tip

After saving a page, you can continue editing other pages. With Easy Designer still open, click New on the toolbar to start a new page; you'll be prompted to select a template or work with a Blank Page. Check out the steps in "Creating a New Page with Easy Designer." Or, use the Open button to edit another 1-2-3 or Easy Designer page you worked on and saved earlier.

Tip

The Netscape Navigator 6.0 browser includes a free, full-featured HTML editor called Composer. To download the browser, start at AOL Keyword: **Netscape**, click Download at the top of the Netscape page, and follow the instructions to download and install the browser and all its tools. When using Netscape, you can access Composer by clicking the tiny pencil-and-paper icon in the lower-left corner of the Netscape window.

Find It Online

If you want to learn basic HTML or acquire more advanced Web skills, start at Build Your Web Page (AOL Keyword: **Web Page**).

3

AOL Hometown: Putting Your Images on the Web

Click the Upload button, and a new window appears. In the Remote Filename text box (see Figure 3-11), first type the name that you want your file to be called when it's online and then choose a transfer mode (either ASCII or Binary). ASCII format is used when uploading text and HTML files. Binary format is used when uploading graphics, such as JPG or GIF files. When done, click Continue.

 In the Upload File box shown in Figure 3-11, click Select File. Browse to the file on your hard drive and double-click it.

 Back in the Upload File box, click Send to upload (copy) your file to your online storage space.

After the file has been uploaded, its Web address will be:

`http://hometown.aol.com/screenname/yourfile.html`

Instead of `screenname` and `yourfile`, the address will contain your screen name and the name you gave your file.

A Web page uploaded to Hometown in this way is not yet registered with Hometown and thus is not searchable or included in a Hometown community. For all that, you'll need to add the page to Hometown as described in the next section.

Using FTP Software to Move Web Pages

You can use special file-transfer software to upload many digital pictures at a time directly to your own storage space on AOL Hometown. To get this software, go to AOL Keyword: **Software**. On the Shareware tab, follow this path (double-clicking along the way): Internet Tools⇨Internet & Web Utilities⇨Home Page Publishing Tools. Click Shareware. Scroll down until you find WS_FTP and click. Read the instructions for downloading the software and follow them if you want to get and install this free, useful program. Help using this program is available at Hometown's Help area (under Building & Uploading Home Pages).

Before accessing My FTP Space using third-party software, you need to give the software some information about your AOL account. When creating an FTP profile in order to use AOL, provide the following tidbits of information:

- Host address: members.aol.com

- Host type: Auto detect

- User ID: anonymous

- Password: yourscreenname@aol.com

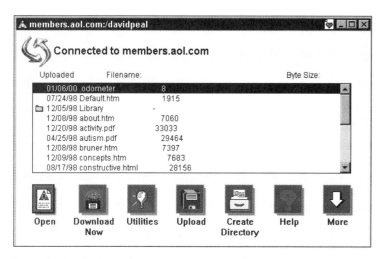

Figure 3-10. AOL Keyword: **My FTP Space**, your online storage space.

Figure 3-11. Specifying a file to upload to My FTP Space, and giving it a remote filename that will be used to name the file on the Web.

Adding Your Pages to a Hometown Community

AOL Hometown resembles a vast settlement with many small towns. Any page you create with 1-2-3, Easy Designer, or other Web-editing software can be included in a well-focused community of people with a shared interest or concern.

Each *community* in AOL Hometown is contained in a larger *subcategory,* and each subcategory in a dozen or so larger *categories,* each focused on a big theme like Hobbies & Interests, Family & Home, or Women's Interests. Subcategories within the Hobbies & Interests category, to take an example, focus on subjects such as Collecting and Genealogy. Within the Collecting subcategory, you can find communities such as Figurines and Model Trains.

You can upload any kind of file to My FTP Space, not just HTML files and digital pictures. For example, I often make available specific Word documents and PDF (portable document format) files for others.

Chat and message boards help keep Web communities together. From the AOL Hometown Help page, look for the Talk About It link.

Make sure you register at least the index.htm page of your Web site; presumably, this page has links to all your other pages. That way, people who find your site on AOL Hometown start on the main page. If you want all your published pages to be searchable in Hometown, click Create at the top of any AOL Hometown page to reach the Create & Manage Pages screen and then click Add All. You can increase visits to your Web site by making all the pages searchable, because this increases the likelihood that people seeking your information can find it.

For you, this organization by categories and subcategories has two benefits:

▲ It provides a more or less obvious home for your own creations, where *others* can readily find them.

▲ It makes finding other folks' pages easy. You can simply browse from category to subcategory, using the convenient Search & Explore box on AOL Hometown's main page.

Every AOL screen name is entitled to 2MB of storage space on AOL Hometown. Adding a single page, as described here, earns you another 2MB per screen name, and adding *all* of your pages stored on My FTP Space is worth 12MB per screen name. To make all of your pages searchable, click Create at the top of any AOL Hometown page. On the Create & Manage Pages window, click Add All. With 7 screen names per account, that makes for 84MB per account!

Adding a single page to an AOL community is easy:

1 After you have created a page and uploaded it to My FTP Space, click the Create link at the top of any AOL Hometown's page. (You upload your page either automatically, by using 1-2-3 or Easy Designer, or manually, by using another HTML editor and FTP.)

2 Click Add. A list of all your files (1-2-3, Easy Designer, and other) appears. Actually, this is just a file listing of the pages you have stored automatically or manually in My FTP Space. Choose the page (filename) you want to add by clicking in the circle next to the page name.

3 Click Next. You can now type a short description of the page, which gives folks in Hometown some idea of what your page is about and why they should visit it.

4 Click Next. Select the appropriate category, subcategory, and community for your page, using the next three pages.

   After selecting an appropriate community, your page is added to the community you selected.

You can add each page to a maximum of five Hometown communities. Just repeat the procedure to add a page to other communities. From the Create & Manage Pages page (available from any AOL Hometown page by clicking Create), you can also edit descriptions of pages to make them more easily searchable or to revise them as your page evolves (and good Web pages tend to grow).

Although you can add only five pages to specific communities, "adding all" your My FTP Space pages to AOL Hometown makes them all searchable, as described in the next section.

Finding Other People's Pages in AOL Hometown

As you create your own pages, other AOL members are creating Web pages devoted to *their* jobs, kids, hobbies, beliefs, and who knows what else. Finding pages on any topic goes to the heart of Hometown's purpose — finding engaging content and congenial people. You can search AOL

Hometown pages for key words or phrases — words used in people's descriptions of their own pages. Or, you can search for pages created by a particular person.

The AOL Hometown home page (AOL Keyword: **Hometown** or hometown.aol.com) puts these search techniques at your fingertips. Simply use the Search & Explore box on the opening AOL Hometown page to look for pages by a certain person (or screen name) or on a specific subject. Just as in any search engine, you type in a few words describing your interests, press Enter, and then see a list of pages that contain your search words. Click any page to jump right to it. In addition to searching, you can also browse AOL Hometown by burrowing through categories, subcategories, and communities.

Wrapping Up

"You've Got Pictures," the focus of the previous chapter, is a soup-to-nuts home for your online digital-picture activities, a place where you can store, manage, and share them. AOL Hometown, likewise, provides you with an online home for creating, storing, and sharing Web pages. Together, these two comprehensive free services are indispensable when you begin to explore digital projects. Although you do the majority of your project work offline — using graphics software and a printer — "You've Got Pictures" can be a source of the pictures you need in projects, and Hometown can give you the chance to put your projects on the Web.

If you are not an AOL member, you will be asked to sign into Hometown.

To make room for a page to add to a Hometown community, you have to delete one of the five already in communities. To do so, click Edit from any AOL Hometown page. In the Edit My Pages window, you see a list of the five pages. Select one to delete and click the Delete button. Use View to remind yourself of what the page looked like.

4

A GUIDE TO ONLINE RESOURCES AND SERVICES: PROJECTS, PICTURES, AND DIGITAL IMAGING

IN THIS CHAPTER

▲ Conducting a search with AOL Search

▲ Shopping for cameras, scanners, and more

▲ Creating a Group on AOL

▲ Finding and sharing ideas and photographs online

▲ Joining online communities

Chapter 4

A Guide to Online Resources and Services: Projects, Pictures, and Digital Imaging

When learning about new cameras or printers, making a product choice, acquiring new skills, viewing what others have done, or getting ideas for your own projects, you can find countless online destinations to support, entertain, and inform you. This chapter profiles some of the most useful, general-purpose online resources about digital imaging and related subjects.

Using AOL Search

One major resource is right at your fingertips: the Search feature of AOL 6.0. Simply type some words (called *search terms*) that describe what you are looking for in the Search box on the AOL 6.0 toolbar. The more specific your search terms, the better the results, at least most of the time. If, for example, you want to search the Web for coloring pages that you can print for children to color, possible search terms might be *coloring kids.* Graduates of within-the-lines drawing who want to move on to freehand drawing or making cartoons can do a search for *drawing lessons kids* or something similar. You don't have to use common words like *for* or *the,* which are usually ignored.

Sometimes, searching for a *phrase,* a series of words that must be together in a certain order, can improve your results. To search for a phrase, such as *"wax paper"* or *"League of Nations,"* put quotation marks around the phrase to keep the words of the phrase together. (When using quotes, you can include common words if they are part of the phrase you're looking for.) By looking for a phrase in a search for activities involving wax paper, you can avoid pages that focus only on wax or paper and don't have anything to do with wax paper.

The first few results of the *coloring kids* search are shown in Figure 4-1. The Web Sites tab lists pages drawn from a hand-selected database of more than two million Web sites, plus all AOL areas. The broader Web Pages tab, shown here, draws from a larger but unscreened list of Web sites only. The Web Pages tab turns up useful results, but parents should bear in mind that AOL doesn't review such sites, so some sites in your results list may not be family-friendly.

At AOL Keyword: **Search**, click the Help button to learn all about the search options at your fingertips on AOL.

Many sites (like AOL Keyword: **CNET**) are so big that you can search within them for specific information.

Figure 4-1: Use AOL Search to find online destinations on specific topics.

AOL Decision Guides

Digital imaging is a consumer paradise these days, with so many new products coming on the market in so many different areas. In addition, all such products are definitely becoming easier to use, and most of them are coming down in price as well.

Get closer to the paradise, however, and the terrain can be confusing to navigate. Many graphics software products are updated more than once a year. Digital cameras from a variety of different vendors are continually improving, too. Printers, software, papers: The choices change week by week.

AOL's Decision Guides (AOL Keyword: **Decision Guides**) cut through the hard work of shopping for digital-imaging software and hardware. If you aren't sure where to begin your search for the right product, follow these steps:

1 At Decision Guides, you first choose a product category, such as digital cameras, printers, or scanners.

If you already know which items you want to compare, you can bypass the Q&A feature on a Decision Guide's main screen by clicking the Compare button directly beneath it and entering the brand names of the products you're interested in.

ZDNet can be reached directly at www.zdnet.com. You can broaden your CNET searches to ZDNet or Web searches by using the links at the bottom of the page with your search results. Look in the Didn't Find What You Were Looking For section on that page.

CNET retains its older product reviews. To avoid using old reviews, check the dates on reviews and look for the latest review of any new product you are considering.

In an actual Decision Guide, such as Digital Camera Match (Figure 4-2), click Q&A to answer a series of questions about the features that matter to you, such as price, resolution, vendor, and so on. (Figure 4-3 illustrates the kinds of questions you are likely to be asked.)

 When you're done answering questions, the Decision Guide displays products from its database that match your preferences, with price, model, and vendor information.

You can click items on your results list to find out more about a particular product. For example, you can click a camera to see a description and specs. You are given the option of comparing several recommendations feature by feature; click the Compare with Another Digital Camera link to see a list of your results, with check boxes used to indicate which ones to compare. Your results will include links to the specialized online computing retailers who carry the products churned out by the Decision Guide. You can also shop for the chosen cameras at one of the larger vendors represented at AOL's online mall, Shop@AOL (see the section "Shop@AOL" later in this chapter). The Decision Guide rates the products matching your preferences. A 100% rating merely means that the product matches every one of your stated preferences.

CNET's Digital Photography Center

CNET, the content provider for AOL's Computer Center channel, is devoted to everything related to personal computers, consumer electronics, software, printers, scanners, digital cameras, and more. Since acquiring another computing empire, ZDNet, CNET offers nearly comprehensive information about consumer technologies and products. Whatever you don't find in CNET may be in ZDNet, which offers comprehensive product reviews, editorials, tutorials, and shareware downloads. CNET searches can automatically be broadened into ZDNet searches.

You may want to head straight for CNET's Digital Photography Center, shown in Figure 4-4. To get there, use AOL Keyword: **CNET**, go to the Electronics Reviews section, and click Digital Photo. (Alternatively, you can use the Photography Center's address, `photo.cnet.com`.) The Digital Photography Center includes its own guide to selecting a digital camera. Unlike AOL's Decision Guides, described earlier in this chapter, which match products to preferences, CNET's guide is based on reader comments and rankings, as well as professional editorials and product reviews. Follow the Perfect Your Images link to access the Digital Photography Center's guide to graphics software (with reviews and prices) as well as useful guides to scanners.

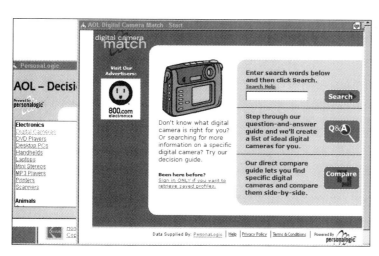

In 2001, Sesame Street's Elmo gave his first-ever on-line chat at AOL's Kids Only Jr.

Figure 4-2: AOL's Decision Guides help you choose the right camera, printer, or scanner for your needs and budget.

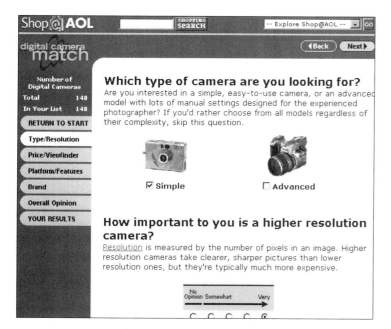

Figure 4-3: Decision Guides work by asking for your preferences in a series of multiple-choice questions (answer by clicking a check box or radio button). Each Guide matches your preferences with the products in its database, displaying the results and letting you compare products and link to online vendors.

Digital (and Other) Project Ideas

A case can be made that old-fashioned quilting parties, stamp clubs, and other communities of hobbyists have found a new home — online. The following list contains a few places to start when you need ideas for crafts and projects. Do an AOL Search (see "Using AOL Search," earlier in this chapter, for some tips) for anything you don't find here.

▲ For traditional handicrafts, start at AOL Keyword: **Crafts**, which has many links to AOL and Web destinations devoted to quilting, scrapbooks, jewelry, and other crafts. If any of these activities seem decidedly undigital, remember that you can also photograph your hand-made crafts and share the digital pictures at AOL Hometown on your own Web page. (See Chapter 5 for an activity that can help you create a Web site for your collectibles.)

▲ From AOL Keyword: **Crafts**, link to the craft-related areas on Moms Online and Better Homes & Gardens. Each has numerous hands-on projects, and many of those projects are appropriate for kids.

▲ If you use software programs such as Print Shop, Printmaster, or KidPix, you may want to familiarize yourself with the online projects at Express It (www.expressit.com). You can download digital pictures from "You've Got Pictures" for use with these projects (see Chapter 2 for the details on using YGP). Not all services here are free.

▲ About.com (www.about.com) is a Web-based mini-world with more than 700 online communities (called sites), each devoted to a different theme, including:

- **Graphics Software** (graphicssoft.about.com): Includes reviews and discussions of different types of graphics software, if you are in the market. (Note that not all reviews are up to date.) Look for the Photo Projects and Gifts section, which contains original articles on caring for photos and making things from digital pictures.

- **Kids' Exchange** (kidexchange.about.com): Includes original content and activities of direct interest to kids, such as jokes, music, sports, hobbies, and more.

- **Arts/Crafts Kids** (kidsartscrafts.about.com): Includes original articles, community features, and links to kids-specific content.

- **Arts/Crafts Business** (artsandcrafts.about.com): Covers the business side of the craft world, including tips for those interested in turning a hobby into a small business.

▲ SesameStreet.com's Workshop area (www.sesameworkshop.org/parents/activity) has plenty of family craft activities, which you can search by activity type, activity theme, and material used (for example, pipe cleaners and sequins). With a bit of imagination, digital pictures can be incorporated into these projects. Many of these activities can now be accessed through AOL, as part of the new Kids Only Junior area (AOL Keyword: **Kids Only Junior**).

▲ Less commercial, yet very rich in ideas and creativity is Bry-Back Manor (www.bry-backmanor.org). Come here for simple printing activities with pages to color, word games, flash cards, and seasonal puzzles for young children and children with special needs.

▲ Print Central's Projects area has a variety of ideas and things you can print, as shown in Figure 4-5.

Figure 4-4: CNET'S Digital Photography Center (photo.cnet.com).

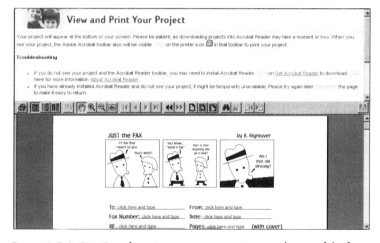

Figure 4-5: In Print Central's projects area, you can print several copies of this fax cover sheet.

Don't overlook the impressive Arts Activities and Crafts Index at About.com. Search the About site if you can't find the index right away.

4

A Guide to Online Resources and Services

Digital Photography

In a white-hot area like digital imaging, the number and variety of online resources can be somewhat overwhelming. AOL's new Digital Photography area (AOL Keyword: **Digital Photo**) is designed to help you figure out the basics and links you to essential online resources. The area's main screen is compact and organized into tabs. The Scanners tab, shown in Figure 4-6, offers links to many of the scanning resources available on AOL. Click another tab such as Printers for similar information. Destinations include several mentioned in this chapter, including Shop@AOL, AOL's Decision Guides, and CNET's Consumer Guides, which compile reviews, specs, and prices. You can also find useful tips, tricks, and tutorials.

Groups@AOL

Groups@AOL (AOL Keyword: **Groups**) provides a wired home on the Web for the close-knit communities in your life, regardless of where people actually live. Imagine a Group formed by an extended family, a neighborhood organization, or a Brownie troop — under the guidance of a parent, of course. Online, members of an AOL Group can

▲ Stay in touch by using its own mailing list.

▲ Hold meetings or just shoot the breeze by using chat tools based on AOL Instant Messenger.

▲ Maintain a Group bulletin board.

▲ Compile a joint collection of digital pictures.

▲ Create lists that rate favorite books, movies, restaurants, Web sites, and so on.

An AOL Group is private. Any AOL member can create one, but membership is pretty much by invitation only, to keep the Group focused and familiar. The owner of the Group can invite people to join regardless of whether they're on AOL, and can also make any group member a coowner, with comparable powers of inviting people. If it sounds exclusive, bear in mind that, in the real world of the Net, you can't join many mailing lists without someone's permission, and Internet Relay Chat, an old form of Internet chat, has always given a channel's owner a lot of control over who can join and what goes on. Similarly, a Group "owner" is just the person who starts the Group.

What do digital pictures have to do with Groups@AOL? Every Group can have a photo on its main page. In addition, every member of a Group can share digital pictures with the Group by creating group photo collections. Anyone can upload pictures, where they'll be instantly available to others. Each Group has 12MB of storage space for its images, and this space is *in addition* to the space that individual AOL members receive to store digital pictures with "You've Got Pictures" and the space that comes with posting Web pages to AOL Hometown. For complete instructions for creating and managing Groups, visit AOL Keyword: **Groups**, and look for the Help link.

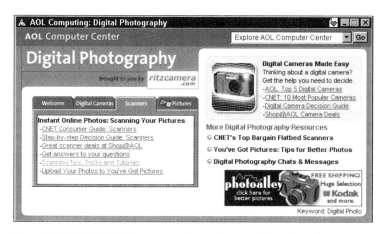

Figure 4-6: AOL's Digital Photography hub provides essential product information.

Figure 4-7: Groups@AOL: A Group's home page. Notice all the tools and services on the left-hand side of the window — all for the exclusive use of your Group.

Photo Communities on AOL and the Web

AOL and the Web have many places where you can see other people's digital pictures and where you can post your own. Here is an overview of such communities.

The Digital Photography area on AOL (AOL Keyword: **Digital Photo**) includes lists of the top-5 products in several categories, including scanners, cameras, and digital cameras.

AOL is currently creating comparable Public Groups, or community centers. They will have community features comparable to a private Group's, but will be open to anyone.

In "You've Got Pictures," which is covered in Chapter 2, a collection of digital pictures is called an album, but in Groups@AOL a collection is called . . . a collection.

Places to Share Your Pictures

▲ **Photo Library:** This new AOL area pulls together many file libraries where you can upload your digital pictures and download others' pictures. Pictures are arranged in big categories such as Scenic Shots, Family & Friends, and Animal Kingdom. Go to AOL Keyword: **Photo Library**.

▲ **American Greetings:** Run by the well-known greeting card company, this site, which you can find at AOL Keyword: **American Greetings**, includes an Online Greetings section and allows you to send a wide variety of cards for free. Click Personalize Your Greeting to add a digital picture to your online card. You must, of course, have the picture's file on your hard drive, which is easy to do by downloading a picture from "You've Got Pictures," as described in Chapter 2.

▲ **Grandstand:** Grandstand is all about sports, and each of the several dozen Grandstand communities is devoted to a specific sport (both the kind you watch and the kind you take part in). Most communities have at least one library of digital pictures. You can download and view pictures of live action and sports heroes, or upload pictures of your softball team or kids' Tae Kwon Do lessons. Begin exploring this area at AOL Keyword: **Grandstand**.

▲ **Pet of the Day:** Nominate your budgie for this honor at AOL Keyword: **Pet of the Day**, but make sure the digital picture is available in JPG or BMP format (see Chapter 2 on these formats). You can also link directly to a pet template at 1-2-3 Publish, which is covered in Chapter 3, and create a Web page devoted to your budgie in a couple of minutes. A celebrating pets activity is in Chapter 5. Also, take advantage of the link to the American Greetings' Cards-for-Pets area.

▲ **Photo Story:** If you have a series of photos that you think others will enjoy, show your creative side and covey a personal story at AOL Keyword: **Photo Story**. Just upload four to six pictures and describe what happened. See Chapter 5 for a photo story activity.

▲ **Graphic Challenge Arena:** Part of the AOL Graphics Arts Community, this area accepts only digital pictures of "artistic merit and technical quality." The Challenge area (AOL Keyword: **Graphic Challenge**) doesn't hold contests but does offer the opportunity to share your best digital pictures with graphic artists, including scans of your best prints.

▲ **Using Pictures:** If you're looking for new places where you can use your digital pictures and projects, go to AOL Keyword: **Using Pictures**. From here, you can go to places such as Love@AOL (online photo personals), AOL Classified ads, AOL Hometown, eBay (where you can provide photographic illustrations of things you want to sell), and "You've Got Pictures."

▲ **Family Photo Contest:** From time to time, AOL Parenting holds photo contests based on seasonal themes. If you've taken the perfect family photo, keep checking AOL Keyword: **Family Photo Contest** for an opportunity to submit it.

Places to View Others' Pictures

The communities in "Places to Share Your Pictures" usually give you the opportunity to see others' work as well as post you own. The following destinations feature professional or semi-pro work; you can simply enjoy these images or look for inspiration. Think of the Web as the world's largest photo gallery.

▲ **Gallery:** Follow the links at AOL Keyword: **Gallery** to see notable photos of current sports, news, and entertainment events.

▲ **Pictures of the Day and Week:** Check out the professional, often compelling news shots from the past week or so at AOL Keyword: **Pictures of the Week**, as shown in Figure 4-8.

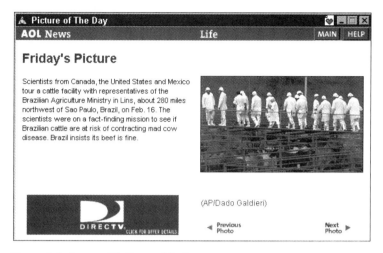

Figure 4-8: A recent AOL Picture of the Day.

▲ **Time.com's Daily Photo Essays**
(www.time.com/time/daily/photoessays): Includes some extraordinary photographs of both day-to-day life and major events playing out continually around the world. Figure 4-9 shows one of a series of photos from a recent photo essay on an oil spill off the Galapagos Islands.

Figure 4-9: From a recent Time.com photo essay. Return here regularly for new essays.

On AOL, a *library* is a collection of digital pictures for uploading and downloading by any AOL member. Usually the libraries can accept only those files that have a standard graphics format, such as JPG, GIF, and BMP. These letters — known technically as a file's *extension* — are a file's last three letters (after the period).

AOL Keyword: **Art Jam** takes you to a group experiment in digital story telling. In your own projects, you can narrate stories.

Put up a series of pictures on AOL Hometown and ask friends to narrate them; you can later post the narrations on the site. Chapter 3 shows how to make a site.

AOL's Graphic Arts community has a large collection of digital images and clip art that you can download. At AOL Keyword: **Graphics**, click the Features tab for the links you need. The community's home on the Web is members.aol.com/graphic%20arts.

▲ **Photo Alley's Pro Galleries and Photo Feedback:** In the Pro Galleries at AOL Keyword: **Photo Alley**, you can find the work of several dozen contemporary professional photographers. Photo Feedback gives you the chance to submit digital pictures for the consideration of and feedback from other photographers.

▲ **Photo.net's Gallery** (`www.photo.net/gallery`): This gallery is one of the very best places to view others' photos, and photo.net stands out for its active, experienced, and opinionated community. The site is described more fully in the next section.

▲ **Time-Life Photo Sights** (`www.pathfinder.com/photo`): Presents more generic themes (for example, animals, people, sports), and again can be tremendous fun for kids to browse and reflect upon.

Photography Destinations on the Web

If you are an avid photographer at any level of expertise or a newcomer to digital cameras, you are likely to find value in the following online resources. Each can help you refine your photographic skills.

▲ **Kodak's Taking Great Pictures** (`www.kodak.com/US/en/nav/takingPics.shtml`): Many photographers bookmark and return repeatedly to Kodak's Taking Great Pictures site, which is part of Kodak's Digital Learning Center. This essential guide for taking good pictures helps you compose your photos more naturally, emphasize your subject, use the flash effectively, and manage difficult lighting situations. The tutorials on light and composition can take you to the next step in your growth as a photographer (or just help improve your vacation slides). Links take you to every useful corner of Kodak's indispensable site.

▲ **Kodak's eMagazine** (`www.kodak.com/US/en/corp/magazine`): Includes feature articles about photographers, in-depth articles about photography techniques, and an excellent archive of tips.

▲ **Photo.net** (`www.photo.net`): This long-time favorite of photography lovers includes Philip Greenspun's online book, "Making Photographs," with its chapters about understanding light, choosing cameras, getting the exposure right, and more. Greenspun, the site's creator, has expertise in many areas, which he is willing to share. Listen in on the lively community that has grown around the site, with message boards, chat, opinions, auctions, and the like. Photo.net includes its own collection of stock photos as well as links to other collections.

▲ **Photo Alley:** For learning about digital photography, Photo Alley (AOL Keyword: **Photo Alley**) is a good place to start. Its Digital Resource Center has dozens of original articles about digital photography, a glossary, technology backgrounders, essays about specific cameras, and more than 100 how-to articles.

▲ **About.com's Photography site** (`photography.about.com`): Includes original articles and links to noteworthy related sites. I especially like the links to pictures of notable photographers of the last 100 years (for inspiration and the sheer pleasure of seeing their work). About's how-tos and articles on useful subjects like building a photo Web site can help if you're making your own pages with Easy Designer (see Chapter 3).

Pictures and Albums Web Channel

Like the Digital Photography area on AOL, described earlier in this chapter, the Pictures and Albums page on AOL serves primarily as a set of links to other places. (To open this area, go to AOL Keyword: **Web Centers** and click Pictures and Albums.) On the Pictures and Albums page, the left-hand column takes you to the AOL Decision Guides and Kodak's Guide to Taking Great Pictures (both described earlier in this chapter), as well as other useful resources, especially for shoppers. The main column down the center of the page takes you to places where you can view exciting sports, fashion, and other photos. At the bottom, look for links to major photo-related sites like National Geographic and Camera Review. Make this Web Center a Favorite Place, so it can serve as a hub for your Web ventures in photography.

Print Central

AOL's new Print Central (AOL Keyword: **Print Central**) is a new choice on the AOL 6.0 Print menu. As shown in Figure 4-10, Print Central pulls together several major services:

Figure 4-10: To go to AOL Print Central, choose Print⇨Print Central. The Projects, Tips, Supplies, and Services buttons take you to the major areas within Print Central.

AltaVista's Picture Finder (not to be confused with AOL's viewing software called Picture Finder, covered later in this chapter) allows you to search high-quality photo collections for particular subjects. Search accuracy appears to be good. Do not use any photograph from this site in your own work without seeking the permission of the copyright holder, however. See AOL Keyword: **Copyright** for more on this issue.

In class or at home, a sequence of photographs can make a great "story starter" for kids. The Time Photo Essays can also introduce children to foreign places and complex situations, as well as cute dog pictures.

Kodak's related site called Special Situations & Subjects has tips for photographing fireworks, sports, rain, and other tricky subjects (www.kodak. com/global/en/ consumer/ specialSituations/ index.shtml).

▲ **Projects:** I also discuss this area earlier, in the section "Digital (and Other) Project Ideas."

▲ **Supplies:** This area is a convenient place to buy inks and supplies for printers from the large vendors.

▲ **Tips:** Because the work and projects that you do with cameras and scanners is likely to involve your printer sooner or later, AOL includes tutorials, tips, and troubleshooting about these projects, in addition to general printing tips. Tips and tricks help you make the most of printers, digital cameras, scanners, and supplies; just click the convenient tabs to get around.

▲ **Printing Services:** This Print menu choice (also available from Print Central), features business-related services from Kinko's, including document printing, binding, and shipping. Included at Kinko's are project ideas for use in preparing professional brochures, résumés, calendars, and more.

In the Projects area, under Comics & Columns, Print Central includes a crossword puzzle to give both your printer and your head a daily workout. These puzzles require Adobe Acrobat to view on-screen and print out. This software (called a *plug-in*) comes with AOL 6.0, but if you ever need a more current version (or a version for a different platform, such as the Macintosh), just go to www.adobe.com/products/acrobat to download a free copy of Acrobat.

Picture Finder

AOL's Picture Finder lets you view your digital pictures and make overall changes in color, orientation, contrast, and size. Online or offline, Picture Finder is available by choosing File⇨Open Picture Finder from the menu bar. In the Open Picture Finder window, use the Look In box to browse to the folder with your digital pictures and click the Open Gallery button. Picture Finder displays small, thumbnail-sized images of all the digital images in the folder, six at a time, as shown in Figure 4-11. (A *gallery* consists of all pictures in the supported formats that can be found in a single folder.) To see an individual image, just click it, and the image appears in a new window, where you can edit it (Figure 4-12).

The Picture Finder tools apply changes to the entire photograph, except for cropping, which (by definition) lets you remove those parts of a picture that don't add anything to your subject, (see Figure 4-12). These quick changes can improve photographs that weren't exposed perfectly, and such changes can spare you the sometimes cumbersome work of using image-editing software. Here are some common problems you may find in your pictures and solutions that the toolbar offers:

▲ If you placed the picture the wrong way on the scanner (which is easy enough to do), rotate the picture (first button from the left, as shown in Figure 4-12).

▲ Use the cropping tool to remove anything in the picture that distracts from or competes with your subject. Many people use the cropping tool (fifth button from the left) to make quick changes to a picture's composition that can create a much stronger image.

▲ For those shots that are blurry or stark, increase or decrease the contrast (sixth and seventh buttons from the left).

▲ For dark indoor shots or overly bright beach shots, increase or decrease the brightness or contrast (third and fourth buttons from the right).

▲ To emphasize the abstract pattern over the subject matter (as in a leaf where you want to emphasize the pattern of veins), remove the color to create the equivalent of a black and white photo (last button on the right).

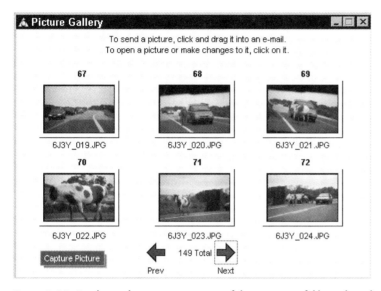

Figure 4-11: Use this window to get an overview of the images in a folder and to select an image to edit.

Figure 4-12: Use AOL's Picture Finder to rotate and resize your pictures, crop them, mirror them, make them black and white, and adjust their brightness and contrast. On the left is a picture from Figure 4-11; on the right, the picture is cropped, the contrast heightened, and the color darkened.

Whenever you like an AOL area or Web site enough to want to return there, click the heart shape in the upper right-hand corner and, in the little window that appears, click Add to Favorites. Then, you can easily find the site in your Favorite Places folder, which is available directly from AOL's Favorites menu or by choosing Favorite Places from the Favorites menu.

Hewlett-Packard's own set of projects, supplies, and tips can be found at Printsville (`printsville.hp.com`).

The Revert button at the bottom of Picture Finder enables you to go back to the last saved version of an image, removing all changes made since then, not just the last change. When you work with graphics in any program, remember to edit *a copy* of the original (and not the original itself), because you cannot undo any changes that you have saved.

Play around with the Picture Finder until you are comfortable with all the buttons. While becoming familiar with its features, consider enlarging pictures before editing them, using the Zoom In/Out button (fourth from the left). For special effects, play with the Flip buttons (second and third from the left), which do just what they say.

Shop@AOL

At some point you may want to expand your capabilities by buying a digital camera, a new printer, special-purpose printer paper, a new version of your software, or more memory for your camera. Making do can inspire creative thinking, but with so many products coming down in price and packing more features, why not avail yourself of the best equipment if you can readily see the differences in what you do? Also, new software, cameras, and other equipment often work more reliably than older versions of the same products.

Shop@AOL, shown in Figure 4-13, consists of hundreds of online retailers gathered in one online Web destination. Shop@AOL has your favorite stores and brands; it's like an online factory outlet. You can visit it by choosing AOL Services⇨Shop@AOL from the toolbar in AOL 6.0 or by using AOL Keyword: **Shopping**. In either case, an AOL screen lets you search for a specific product or browse a category of the Web-based stores that make up Shop@AOL. Select a category and sub-category from the left side of the screen, and you are whisked off to Shop@AOL on the Web.

In bringing together hundreds of stores, AOL is able to provide services across Shop@AOL, including the following:

- ▲ **Mall-wide product searches:** At AOL Keyword: **Shopping**, the AOL screen provides a search box in which you can type the name of a product. The Shopping Search Results Web page lists all the Shop@AOL vendors who sell either the product or accessories for the product. The best you can do by way of comparison shopping, for now, is to do a rough comparison of individual vendor's prices.

- ▲ **An A-Z directory of individual stores and departments:** The list is available at AOL Keyword: **Shopping**; click A-Z Directory. For your digital imaging needs, check out the Electronics & Photo department, which includes Photo & Video, shown in Figure 4-13. When you find a department you especially like, make a note of its keyword so you can go directly to it; each department's keyword is printed in the lower-right corner of its opening page (for example, AOL Keyword: **Photo & Video**).

- ▲ **A high level of customer service:** To ensure quality service, AOL offers its own guarantee and has created a network of Certified Merchants.

- ▲ **Store ratings:** From the Customer Service area (available from AOL Keyword: **Shopping**) and directly on the Web (onlinestoreratings.com/merchants/category.adp), you can check the ratings of all online vendors represented on Shop@AOL, as compiled by independent market researcher Elrick & Lavidge.

- ▲ **Quick Checkout:** This service works like an online wallet and speeds up the checkout process.

- ▲ **Good deals:** You can find bargains advertised daily on the opening page of Shop@AOL as well as on the opening pages of each department.

In addition, Shop@AOL's many retailers are usually searchable (within the store) and often have their own Help and Service areas. Here are some Shop@AOL areas of special interest for people getting started in digital imaging:

▲ **Photo and Video (in the Electronics & Photo department):** Figure 4-13 shows the opening page of the Photo & Video area, which promotes current specials and links to leading vendors within the area, such as AOL Netmarket, Circuit City, and Ritzcamera.com.

▲ **Printers, Software, and Accessories (in the Computers department):** This area is the place to find scanners and printers.

▲ **AOL Netmarket:** A separate vendor, AOL Netmarket provides a useful series of Buyers' Guides. Purchasing here requires registration. As at many supermarkets and drugstores these days, registering entitles you to good prices.

Figure 4-13: Visit big stores, find your favorite brands, and avoid traffic at Shop@AOL.

To find out what each button in the Picture Finder editor does, move you mouse over the button and wait a moment (don't click!). A text bubble displays the button's function.

Want to share a picture you are editing? Click Insert in Email to open the Write Mail window. The picture is inserted into the message body. Type a message, add an address and subject, and you can send the picture to anyone on AOL.

At AOL Keyword: **Shop Direct**, you can access AOL's own store, where you can browse the various sections and buy any number of popular consumer electronics products. Clicking the Digital Imaging tab at the top of the screen takes you to the Digital Imaging section, which features good deals on many digital imaging products, including printers, scanners, cameras, and software. The Digital Imaging section also has links to information about the "You've Got Pictures" service.

YGP's Newsletter, Contests, and Message Boards

"You've Got Pictures" (AOL Keyword: **Pictures**) offers a simple way of converting your film pictures into digital pictures and storing them in one online place, where they can be shared. "You've Got Pictures" offers a variety of ways to get more out of digital pictures:

▲ The Picture This! newsletter, shown in Figure 4-14.

▲ The Picture Poll (AOL Keyword: **Picture Poll**) lets you express an opinion on a weekly question.

▲ The YGP message boards and the Photo Studio chat room are both available from the main YGP screen at AOL Keyword: **Pictures**.

May I Help You?

No matter what you are doing — using the AOL service, working with "You've Got Pictures," preparing a Web page for AOL Hometown, or looking to buy a new digital camera — a resource on AOL can help you do the job right. Here are some places to answers to your questions:

• For general help, start at AOL Keyword: **Help** (also available by pressing F1 at any time in AOL or by choosing Help⇨AOL Help). Help is available in many forms, depending on your question (billing, account, and so on) and preference (help from a screen or help from a person).

• For help with "You've Got Pictures," start with AOL Keyword: **YGP Help**.

• For help using and navigating AOL Hometown, go to AOL Keyword: **Hometown** and click the Help link, which is available on every Hometown page.

• For help using Easy Designer (Chapter 3), open the application (AOL Keyword: **Easy Designer**) and use the Help menu.

• For shopping assistance at Shop@AOL (described in this chapter), look for the Customer Service button at AOL Keyword: **Shopping**.

I have written two other AOL Press books that may be of help as well: *Your Official America Online Internet Guide*, 4th edition, and *Your Official America Online Guide to Pictures Online* (Hungry Minds, Inc.). Both of these books are available at AOL Keyword: **Bookstore**.

Figure 4-14: The Picture This! newsletter is available online and in your mailbox.

Wrapping Up

Return to this chapter whenever you need online support to help you understand and select equipment, figure out how to use equipment, find project and crafts ideas, or get inspiration from the work of others. To learn what others are doing and ask questions, pay a visit to AOL's photo-sharing communities, or create and publicize an AOL Group, as described in "Groups@AOL," earlier in this chapter. If you can't find what you need in this chapter, use AOL Search to locate help online.

Note

The community features for "You've Got Pictures" are currently gathered at AOL Keyword: **Photocommunity**. AOL is currently building a photography Community Center, with many of the features of Groups@AOL.

Tip

The Picture This! newsletter, shown in Figure 4-14, is a weekly newsletter devoted to digital photography and "You've Got Pictures." The newsletter features photo ideas, tips for using "You've Got Pictures," information about photo contests, and links to other people's photos. At AOL Keyword: **Newsletters**, open the Arts & Entertainment category. To subscribe to the newsletter, put a check by Picture This! and click Save.

PART

II

DIGITAL PROJECTS FOR EVERYONE

IN THIS CHAPTER

▲ Doing what you do, but better: From paper airplanes to coloring

▲ Encouraging young writing with picture stories

▲ Tapping higher-level skills with memory cards, picture games, and jigsaw puzzles

▲ Just having fun with warps, filters, and crazy composites

▲ Creating personalized school supplies, such as binder covers and bookmarks

▲ Getting creative with cartooning

▲ Saving money and getting personal with your own cards, notes, and invitations

Chapter 5
School's Out

Parents who are setting up a computer for children often have a tough time knowing where to start. Educational software can seem so . . . educational. Sure, such software can be appropriate for younger kids, but it often fails to go beyond the most basic skills. As for game software, many parents consider it a waste of time or at best an alternative to TV, even when it purports to be educational. As for the Internet, it can seem formless and perhaps a little scary.

For Kids Only — Not!

Where can parents start, especially with kids who are not quite ready for keyboarding, complex screens, and fancy mouse work? This chapter provides examples of kid-appropriate activities that involve computers. It includes intrinsically fun, often useful, and developmentally sound activities for pre-K and grade-school kids. Often enough, the activities involve adults and can interest everyone in the family. You can even modify these activities for different purposes or to include more than one person.

Several activities in this chapter offer new possibilities for perennial creative pursuits such as coloring. Online, for example, you can find about a zillion coloring pages to simply print and let a kid color. As the coloring activity shows, you can take a digital picture of a familiar person, place, or thing, and then convert the image into something kids can color. In addition, graphics software also provides the tools kids need to make, store, and share comics.

Kids can do some of the creative activities in this chapter in conjunction with other activities. The special effects sections in particular offer loads of tips for applying filters, warping images, and swapping parts of different pictures. The skills related to making *selections* can be used in everything from making paper doll cutouts to creating T-shirt designs.

Some of the creative activities in this chapter support traditional childhood pastimes like making paper airplanes and designing masks for Halloween and other occasions. In each case, computers offer new creative opportunities.

Certificates and stickers (special sections are devoted to both) give parents some tools for praising and rewarding kids. Just as important, kids can use these things to celebrate each others' achievements and to decorate their doors and walls. Certificates, ID cards, and signs can be crucial to the functioning of any young child's club. Although transitory sporting events don't often result in friendships that outlast the sports activity itself, sports cards can add something lasting to after-school sports programs. Anything tangible can remind kids of each other. A little more practically, sports cards help everyone learn all the kids' names at the beginning of the season.

A few of the activities, like making bookmarks and binder covers, may seem, to kids, boringly school-oriented. You parents may need to get kids revved up here. Consider for example that a bookmark can personalize books for the beginning, struggling, or diffident reader, as well as the young bibliophile. Making binder and spine covers can be sheer fun and also help kids stay on top of the pile of papers they must cart home from school each day.

Cross-Reference

Chapter 6 contains activities for older children and adults, and you can find activities for the home business in Chapter 7.

Games Kids Play

Graphics software and digital pictures also open up new possibilities in the world of games. One activity in this chapter shows how to build kids' short-term memory by creating pairs of picture cards, placed face down, which they turn up one at a time, trying to remember the location of each pair of matching pictures. In another activity, kids see only part of a digital picture and guess what's in the larger picture. Finally, one of my favorite activities is the picture story, where kids form stories based on a sequence of pictures. Pictures can inspire reflection, serve as tremendous story-starters, and get kids writing.

One familiar game introduced in this chapter is the jigsaw puzzle. This activity makes special use of digital pictures and introduces a Web site to which you can upload your favorite pictures, and then convert them into jigsaw puzzles whose parts can be dragged around.

Lastly, many of the activities in this chapter aren't just for kids. A college student can put together binder covers, use the greeting-card activities to invite friends to a party, or send special cards to stay in touch with family back home and scattered friends. The memory-game cards can be used for learning vocabulary words in a foreign language. And signs can be used to promote a new business or alert neighbors of a lost cat.

In short, don't get hung up by the precise step-by-step procedures. The activities throughout Part II can all be adapted and tweaked to suit your needs.

Airplanes, Paper

Things that fly have a special appeal for kids, right through high school. They ask themselves: "What keeps something as heavy as an airplane in the air?" and "What makes them go so fast?" They want to learn more, and somehow they want to take part in the experience of flight. Welcome to the world of paper airplanes.

Everyone can make a paper plane, right? Not quite. Everyone can make a *boring* airplane — a plane that, well, anyone can make. Online you can find dozens of paper-airplane designs that you probably have never thought of. The planes look cool and have novel aerodynamics.

To make a paper airplane with your computer:

1 Print the step-by-step blueprint from a site like Paper Aeroplane World, Alex's Paper Airplanes, or any of your choice (See Figure 5-1).

2 Using a paint program such as The Learning Company's KidPix or Disney's Magic Artist, open a blank page to hold the design to be used in the plane. (You can buy this software online or at your local computer store.)

3 To match the blueprint (Step 1) to the design (Step 2), use your paint program to draw a line (indicating a fold) down the middle of the page you designed. Detailed folds are more challenging to draw for kids, but consider adding them when you revise and reprint your design (Step 7).

4 Use patterns to fill in the basics of your design, such as the KidPix *background* shown in Figure 5-2.

5 Apply clip art (small pictures, called *stickers* in KidPix), such as the birds.

6 Add text, wherever you want.

7 Print the design on an 8½-x-11-inch sheet of paper. Kids can be encouraged to do more on their own by creating a pattern in KidPix, Disney Magic Artist, or similar graphics program. They can design airline logos, apply a pattern (such as a flock of clip art birds) to an entire sheet of paper, or simply let their minds take wing. Also consider decorating both sides of the paper. Just feed the paper, when completely dry, into the inkjet so that the other side is printed.

8 Now fold! To turn your decorated paper into an airplane, follow the instructions on the blueprint that you found in Step 1.

9 If parts of your design, such as text or clip art, appear in awkward places after you fold your airplane, you may want to experiment with your design so that your plane looks just right. Try moving elements to certain parts of the plane, and then print and fold again. Younger children may want to decorate their planes with stickers created with an inkjet printer. Stickers can include a logo or a digital picture; see "Sticker Fun" later in this chapter for ideas. Younger children are also happy to color their planes after the planes are printed; getting the design just right in software can be frustrating.

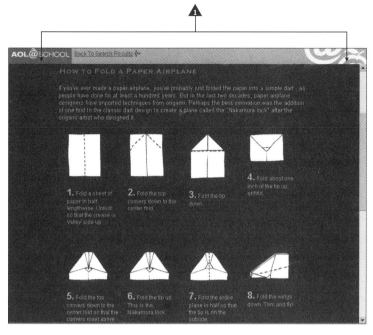

Figure 5-1. Print the blueprint for any airplane you find on the Web. This page, which contains excellent tips for plane-builders, comes from the Exploratorium's Web site, where you can also learn how to make paper.

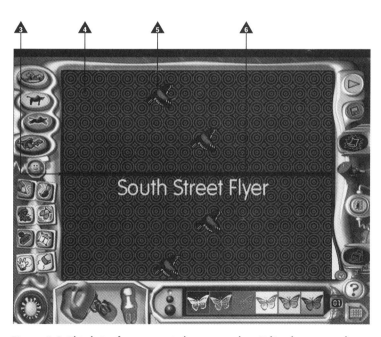

Figure 5-2. This design for a paper airplane was made in KidPix, but any graphics program with painting tools will do.

Note

A preoccupation with planes is a good way for kids to test hypotheses, such as "What will happen if I fold the wings up?" "Down?"

Find It Online

One place (of many) to start your hunt for paper-airplane designs is Alex's Paper Airplanes in the UK (www.paperairplanes. co.uk). Another is Paper Aeroplane World (www. paperaeroplanes.com). The Exploratorium's site (www.exploratorium. edu/exploring/ paper/airplanes. html) includes ideas for going beyond the familiar paper airplane.

Tip

For many reasons, not every child (or adult) can make every plane. Avoid planes that frustrate kids and then (because of their complexity) often don't work. The more steps, the harder. Also, make sure kids are using a ruler when they make planes. That, plus not rushing, can easily produce better results.

Binder Spines and Covers

At a certain point in school, kids start bringing home heavy binders. Adults who find themselves back in the classroom also need large binders, and a businessperson can collect binders, too, with vendor catalogs, customer information, and so on. Binder covers and spines, which slip into binders' clear protective covers, can identify one binder from another and can also individualize them. Kids may want to add pictures of Pokémon figures or sports images. Adults may just want to identify the subject and their own contact information.

Here's how to design your own binder spines and covers:

1 Using a graphics software program such as PhotoSuite, shown in Figures 5-3 and 5-4, start by creating a new document. For PhotoSuite, choose File⇨New⇨Project (not *Photo*) from the menu bar. The New Project dialog box appears.

2 First, type the dimensions for the project you are working on in the appropriate text fields of the New Project dialog box and then click OK.

You are automatically transferred to the PhotoSuite Compose mode, where you make projects. A tall document is displayed.

3 To add text, click the Add/Edit Text button in the left pane. Click in the new document (the tall white box) to create a text box. Type your text in the box on the left, using the Font box and styles to format your words. Click the Return button when you're done.

4 Now you can return to the project area and use the text box, which contains your words. Note how your mouse cursor changes shape as you move it over specific parts of the text box. When the cursor is shaped like a hand, you can move the box as a whole. When it is shaped like an X, you can click a side or a corner of the box and drag it to resize the box. When the cursor is shaped like a circle formed of two curving arrows, as shown in Figure 5-4, you can rotate the box.

In this example, I enlarged the text by stretching the box, and rotated the text to be read on its side. Click the Return button when you are done to accept your changes.

5 To add photos or clip art, click the Add Photos or Add Props button in the left pane. (*Props* is just the term PhotoSuite uses to refer to items in its clip art library.) With photos, select the source of the photo — more than likely the hard drive on your computer — and then to find the picture use the dialog box that appears. When you find it, double-click the image to insert it into the project area. As with text, you can move, rotate, and resize a photo's box.

For props, choose a prop category from the drop-down list. To place a prop on your project, click and drag it to your spine or cover. Figure 5-4 uses a soccer ball prop.

6 Save the file by choosing File⇨Save, and print it on heavy paper by clicking the Print button at the top of the screen and choosing the options you want in the left pane. When you're ready to print, click the Print button at the bottom of the left pane.

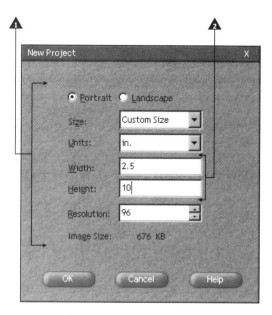

Figure 5-3. Choosing File⇨New⇨Project takes you to this box. Change the unit of measurement to inches and provide the dimensions for the object you want to make.

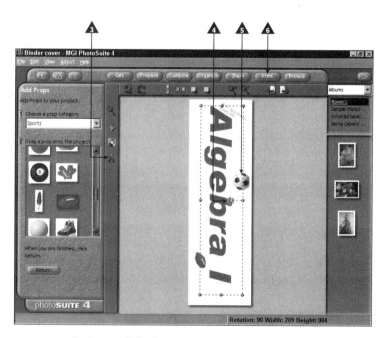

Figure 5-4. This homemade binder spine is ready to be printed. It includes rotated and styled text and two of PhotoSuite's *props*, which are clip-art images.

Find It Online

AOL's Print Central, which is available from the AOL 6.0 Print menu, contains ready-made binder covers (go to Projects⇨Kids Space). Just download the covers and print them. You can also download and print the supplied stickers and apply them wherever you want. Place the stiff spine and binder cover into the plastic sleeves that protect your binder.

Tip

Graphics programs measure things in points, a typesetting unit equivalent to about 1/72 of an inch. Make sure your dimensions are set in inches and not points. Under Units, in the New Project box, select inches. For Size, select Custom size to make the tall document pictured opposite.

Cross-Reference

For more about PhotoSuite's props, see "Comics" in this chapter. For more about selections and cutouts, see "Crazy Effects," also in this chapter.

Bookmarks

Don't fold down the corners of those pages; make yourself a bookmark! While you are at it, make one for your mom, dad, and best friend. You can never read too many books or have too many bookmarks. A bookmark is basically a tall rectangle with a design, printed on heavy paper. You can make one in many programs, but I use PhotoSuite, because of its many choices.

1 Open PhotoSuite and click Compose to access the Compose mode. Buttons appear in the left pane of the screen, allowing you to choose the type of project you wish to make. Click Cards & Tags⇨Bookmark from the list that appears.

2 A variety of colorful bookmark templates appear in the work area to start you off. Select a template by double-clicking it. The template opens in the Compose work area, where you can now add text, props, and cutouts to complete your bookmark.

3 To add new text, click the Add/Edit Text button and then click the bookmark to create a new text box. In the left pane, type over the words saying, Put your text here! Select a font from the drop-down box and a style (plain, bold, or italic) by clicking the appropriate buttons. To change the color of the text, click the color palette. Choose a color that contrasts with the background so your text is readable when printed.

4 Jazz up your bookmark with *props,* which is PhotoSuite's term for clip art. Click the Add Props button in the left pane and then choose a prop category from the pull-down list that appears on the left. To place a prop on your project, click and drag it to your bookmark.

5 To use one of your digital pictures, click Add Photos in the left pane and navigate to your photo on your computer or in another source, such as the PhotoSuite Library, a digital camera, or a scanner. If your picture is on your hard drive, click the Computer button and select the image you want by using the Open dialog box. Click Add. When you are finished, click the Return button.

6 To print your bookmark, click the Print button on the navigation bar. In the left pane, choose the options you want. Then click the Print button at the bottom of the left pane to start the actual printing. Cut out your bookmark and *voilà,* you're ready to read in style. For a longer-lasting bookmark, print it on heavy paper.

If you are making bookmarks for other people, make sure to personalize them with an appropriate text message by using the Add/Edit Text feature. If you have a small business, consider making bookmarks to give your customers, including, of course, your contact information and a picture of your work.

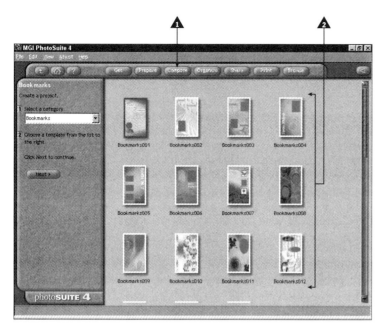

Figure 5-5. Selecting a bookmark template in PhotoSuite. Most PhotoSuite activities provide a series of templates in this fashion, giving you a visual overview of your choices. With most templates, you can usually change any aspect you don't like.

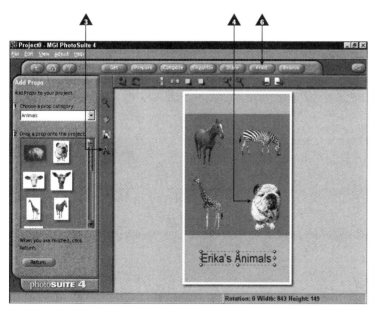

Figure 5-6. Adding animal props to a bookmark template in the Add Props area. Consider using kids' pictures on their bookmarks to give them (perhaps) extra pride in reading.

Laminate your bookmark to make it waterproof. You can have bookmarks laminated at most photocopy shops.

If you would like a bookmark with a solid background, use the blank bookmark template. Double-click the template, and in the left pane, create a solid color background by clicking Paint and Draw⇨Flood Fill. When finished, click the Compose button on the navigation bar and update the project with changes when prompted.

For a cool set of bookmarks, use the five column comic strip template by clicking Compose on the navigation bar and then clicking Create New Project⇨Photo Layouts⇨ Comic Books. Drag a landscape photo from the Library onto the template, and the photo splits into five segments for a coordinated bookmark set.

Certificates

Kids love certificates. Perhaps a certificate is an easy way for kids to reward themselves and their friends in a world of adults and teachers who can seem a little stingy with their praise. At any rate, certificates come in handy on many occasions: to recognize club members, to give every kid at a party something personal to take home, or to reward a child who has just moved up a grade or survived some onerous standardized test. Kids instinctively come up with their own uses, and adults probably have some good ideas as well.

For kids and adults, Print Shop gives you as much control, or as little, as you want. Here's how to make a certificate in Print Shop from scratch, such as the one shown in Figure 5-8. This activity uses Print Shop 6, but the most recent version (11) works almost identically (see "Signs" for a Print Shop 11 activity).

 When you start Print Shop, you first see a window prompting you to choose a type of project to make. For this activity, choose Certificates⇨Start From Scratch to indicate that you want to make all the choices yourself. Click Next.

 Now you must select the certificate's orientation: tall or wide. Figure 5-8 shows a certificate with a wide orientation, which you may also recognize as *landscape* orientation. If you choose a *tall* orientation (also commonly called *portrait*), then one of the short sides of the paper is at the top of your certificate, as when you create an ordinary document.

   In the Print Shop editing window, you see a blank certificate, ready to be created.

 Add a frame by clicking the Frame button on the left-hand toolbar. Figure 5-8 uses a full-pane frame called *African*.

 Add a headline.

 Add regular text explaining the certificate's purpose.

 Now add a digital picture and, if you want, clip art. Print Shop stands out for the high quality and large selection of its clip art.

 When you have your elements in place, move them around by clicking and dragging them. To change what the text says, you can double-click a block of text and edit right in the text box.

 Click the Print button on the Standard toolbar to print a copy of your certificate. Be sure to use good paper, such as parchment or heavy stock.

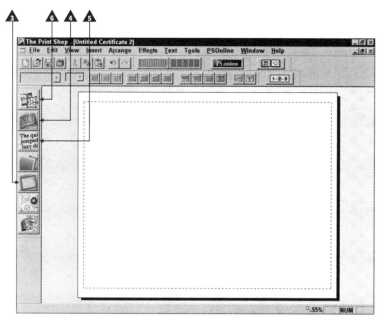

Figure 5-7. Print Shop 6's editing window provides complete control of any project. The buttons on the left let you insert frames, headlines, regular text, pictures, and other elements.

Figure 5-8. This certificate — complete with border, text, and art — took under five minutes to make. Remember that you can vary the combination of elements in almost limitless ways.

In buying software, weigh the trade-off between control (where you do everything) and relying on templates (where the software does everything). Older kids may want more control so they can be more creative. Adults may value their time and just want good-looking results.

When making a specific project with Print Shop, you make an initial choice between (a) Personalizing a Quickstart Layout, where you get all the art and text and then edit or leave them pretty much as they are and (b) Starting from Scratch, which walks you through a few major decisions and then takes you right to the editing window. Using the tools there, you add exactly the elements you want.

Print Shop has been through many versions and comes in several editions. When in doubt about what a button does, pass your mouse over it until a small label appears. For the obscure details, avail yourself of Print Shop's Help, available from (what else) the Help menu.

Cards, Greeting (Microsoft Word)

Shopped for a card recently? The countless cards, from birthday cards to condolences, easily overwhelm yet rarely satisfy. But have you ever noticed that, although the messages change from card to card, the format stays pretty much the same: Cards have a similar size, an opening page and inside (or back) page, and an envelope. With cards so simple, why not make your own? In designing your own card, you have many choices; the first choice is whether to do it all yourself or to turn over the control to your software and printer. This activity and the next look at these options.

You can make simple cards by using a word processor such as Microsoft Word. Cards usually have two pages that a reader is interested in. The *opening page* has a message in large type, like *Happy Groundhog Day,* and a graphic of some sort. The *inside page* usually has room for you to add details for an invitation or write a personal message. Figure 5-10 shows what you want to have at the end: the opening page in the lower right and the inside page, *rotated,* in the upper left.

To make a card in a recent version of Microsoft Word:

1 Choose File⇨New to open a new Word document. Then choose Insert⇨Picture⇨WordArt from the main menu.

2 In the WordArt window, double-click one of the small pictures showing the various types of WordArt. Up comes the Edit WordArt Text window.

3 In the Edit WordArt Text window, type the text for the inner page, which may include party details, driving directions, or a personal message. Press Enter to insert line breaks and play with the font types and sizes. Click OK when you're done to return to the Word document.

4 Choose View⇨Print Layout from the main menu to make sure that you're in Page Layout view. Then click and drag your new WordArt to the upper-left quarter of the page, as shown in Figure 5-10. To resize your WordArt, click and drag the text handles (small boxes).

5 Flip the text by clicking the Free Rotate button on the WordArt toolbar. (When the WordArt is selected, the WordArt toolbar is visible.) Click one of the circles on the WordArt, and rotate the WordArt so that it is upside down.

6 Now, add the text for the card's opening page in the lower right-hand corner. It can be sized and formatted as you would with any text in Word. Or, add a digital picture by choosing Insert⇨Picture⇨From File.

7 When you're done, save your file (File⇨Save) and print it (File⇨Print). Choose the options you want and then click OK to print out your card. Card stock, such as the readily available greeting card paper for inkjets, is the best paper to use for your printouts. Such paper, available from most office-supply stores, comes pre-scored for easy folding, and usually includes matching envelopes.

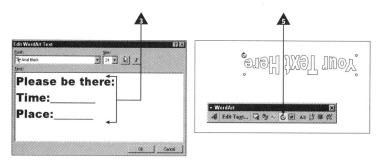

Figure 5-9. The figure on the left shows the Edit WordArt Text window, which allows you to add special effects to text and headlines. On the right, you can see how clicking the Free Rotate button on the WordArt toolbar lets you rotate your text.

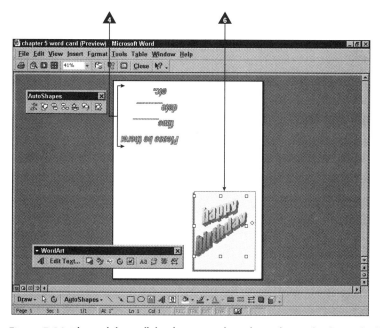

Figure 5-10. This card shows all the elements in place. The inside page has been edited somewhat. Remember that you can edit text and pictures only in Print Layout view (choose View⇨Print Layout).

Tip

Use Word's Drawing toolbar (choose View⇨ Toolbars⇨Drawing) to enhance your card. For example, add a simple rectangle to frame the inside page.

Cross-Reference

If you are attending a party or visiting someone, you may need to bring a gift. The wrapping paper activity is in Chapter 6, where you'll also find instructions for making another party item, a banner.

Note

At AOL's Printing Supplies (Choose Print⇨Printer Supplies from the AOL toolbar), you should be able to find a variety of papers and matching envelopes, including card papers, for your printer.

5

School's Out

Cards, Greeting (PhotoSuite)

Most major graphics software products let you create invitations and other cards, and even provide wizards to guide you through every step. The process is simple, and the results are often as good as store cards. With digital pictures, cards are that much more personal. Most graphics programs offer easy card modules and a set of templates. The finished card in Figure 5-12 shows a PhotoSuite birthday invitation, but you can adapt these software-generated cards to your own purposes, such as thank-you notes or announcements. Here's how to make a card:

1 Find the digital picture or pictures you want to use with your invitation or card. Make sure you have the details, too: where the party or event will be held, when, special instructions (such as costumes required), and so on.

2 In PhotoSuite, click Compose on the navigation bar and then click Cards & Tags⇨Invitations in the left pane. For this invitation, choose Birthday from the drop-down list. A set of birthday card templates appears in the work area.

3 Double-click a template that lets you insert digital pictures. You can tell whether a template accepts pictures by the conspicuous gray area, called a *transparency,* because a picture can go behind the card yet show through the opening, as in Figure 5-11. Click Add Photos, navigate to your digital picture, and double-click.

4 If your photo is on top of the card instead of showing through the gray opening, click the Move Back button.

5 Flip to the inside page of the card. In PhotoSuite, for this card, you do this by clicking the forward arrow just above the card *twice.* Double-click the placeholder text that says Put your text here to move to Text Editing mode. (For more on how this mode works, see the binder activity earlier in this chapter.) Type your text, adjust the text box by clicking and dragging the sizing handles, and click Return in the left pane when you're done. This text, as in the previous activity, will appear upside down and in the upper left-hand corner.

6 Click Print to use your card in a quarter-fold design, so that the picture and message are printed on one side of the sheet, as in the previous activity. After clicking Print, you see your picture and text in the Print Preview window. Click Print at the bottom of the left pane to print a copy of your card. For now, just print on normal paper, using a color (inkjet) printer if possible. Fold the paper to make sure the picture is correctly positioned. Unfold it and hold it up to the quarter-fold card paper. If you need to move the image slightly, return to Print Preview and click Nudge to move it horizontally and vertically a little at a time.

7 Proofread everything. When you proofread, examine color quality, check whether a picture could be better cropped to highlight the subject, and check the picture's position. Make sure the card is perfect before you print on card stock.

8 Children can sign the cards and address the envelopes by hand.

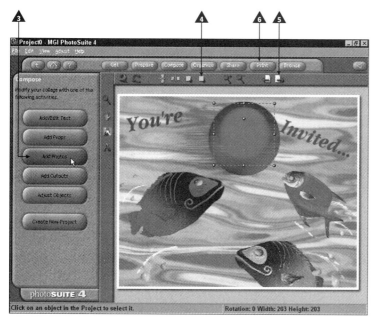

Figure 5-11. You can import a photo into this happy birthday template. The buttons on the left allow you to add your own text, props (clip art), and cutouts.

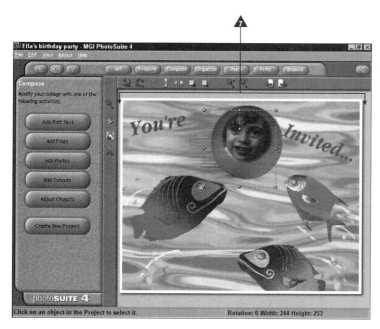

Figure 5-12. The completed card contains the picture correctly positioned behind the template. The bright eyes were achieved with a pixel or two of white, applied with the Effect Brush.

Note

This activity and the previous one involved quarter-fold cards. Half-fold cards are bigger, of course, and require two-pass printing — once for the picture, the second time (on the other side) for the message.

Find It Online

You can purchase half-fold and quarter-fold greeting card paper and envelopes online. From the AOL 6.0 toolbar, choose Print➪ Printer Supplies.

Find It Online

To send electronic cards, start at AOL Keyword: **American Greetings**. Many cards let you add a digital picture and your own text.

Caution

PhotoSuite's text boxes can be temperamental. If you're editing a card in Compose mode with Add/Edit Text selected, a new text box is created every time you click in the project area.

Cartoons

The appeal of comics seems to outlive childhood. *Making* comics is another matter. Many kids take to the hobby in elementary school but don't pursue it, perhaps for want of the right tools. Software can support cartooning in many ways and give kids a taste of the satisfaction of creating engaging stories, complete with heroes, word bubbles, and pictures.

Kids don't need expensive software to create the key ingredients of cartooning: figures, comic fonts, and word bubbles. This activity focuses on the homely but indispensable *word bubble* — where the words appear when a comic-strip character speaks. Even in Microsoft Word, you can readily create a comic, including the word bubbles. Here's how:

 Add the comic art that requires a word bubble to your document. Office comes with clip art; just choose Insert⇨Picture⇨Clip Art to access the Office clip-art gallery. You can just as easily use digital pictures or original drawings from another program.

 To add a word bubble, access the AutoShapes toolbar by choosing Insert⇨ Picture⇨AutoShapes from the main menu. The second button from the right on the AutoShapes toolbar shows the Callouts submenu. Click the button to see the submenu's selection of word bubbles.

 To use a particular bubble from the submenu, simply click it. You won't see the bubble right away. In your Word document, click where you want to place the bubble, and it appears. The word bubble includes a text box ready for you to type the comic-strip character's line.

 Type a couple of lines of text, aiming for conciseness and effect. Continue with another frame (if any); then tweak, save, and print.

You can resize the word bubble and comic figure in any way you want. Just select the figure or bubble, and click and drag one of the handles on the selection box. Text in the word bubble can be edited, styled, enlarged, and so on. Just select the text or picture and use the available editing functions. Microsoft has a particularly readable font called Comic Sans, which you can use for your bubble.

PhotoSuite offers comic book pages with boxes for your figures, text, word bubbles, and so on. Just click the Compose button and click Photo Layouts⇨Comic Books in the left pane. To create a simple word balloon for a digital image, open a picture by clicking the Get button and finding the picture from the appropriate source. Then click Compose⇨Collages in the left pane, click Add Props, Word Balloons. Drag the balloon that you want to use into the work area then you can add text.

Figure 5-13. You can use Microsoft Word to make cartoons with word bubbles. The AutoShapes toolbar includes a set of Callouts, which includes labels and word bubbles. The clip art comes from the Office clip-art collection.

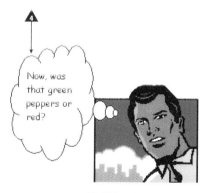

Figure 5-14. A word bubble with text. Notice how the bubble was dragged.

 Definition

Clip art consists of public domain or commercially available images that you can use in your own documents, for noncommercial purposes. Many programs, like Print Shop, come with a large set of clip art. In Microsoft Word, you can access Microsoft's clip art by choosing Insert⇨ Picture⇨Clip Art from the menu bar.

 Find It Online

For a daily quota of the funny papers, start the day at AOL Keyword: **Backpage**, which takes you to a long list of syndi-cated comic-strip authors whose current and recent work can be viewed online.

 Find It Online

For comic fonts on the Web, start with a place like Comic Book Fonts (www.comicbookfonts. com) for downloadable fonts, plus instructions for installing them. Many are free; some have a licensing fee.

Collectibles, Creating a Web Site for

Collecting is about *things* — dolls, coins, stamps, and so on. Because you can photograph things and digitize those photos, your collection can readily form the basis of a Web site. Why a site? It's a safe way to display valuable things, from first editions to old dolls, and it's an easy way to find like-minded collectors. Digital pictures also make buying and selling collectibles much simpler. Young collectors and older ones can do all of this — documenting, sharing, trading — by using AOL's Easy Designer to create a collectibles site, as you'll see in this activity:

1 Go to AOL Keyword: **Easy Designer**. On the opening page, click the Create a New Page link (under the Start Here heading) to create a new page, and then click the big Click to Get Started button.

2 In the Select a Template dialog box that appears, choose the Your Hobbies category and the My Collection topic. Click Next.

3 In the next dialog box, choose a page layout for your template. The thing to remember about templates is that everything can be changed, as you'll see in this example. Choose a page layout to start with, and then click Next.

4 In the next box, you are prompted to select a color scheme for your template. You want a color that complements your images and does not compete with them. Make your selection and then click Next.

Your template appears in Easy Designer, ready for you to start adding your own elements.

5 Now you can start making the page your own, with your own headline, text, and images. For more on adding text and images in Easy Designer, see Chapter 3.

6 Click Preview to see how your page will look on the Web, and click Save to store the page at AOL Hometown, where anyone can view it.

7 To share your page, visit AOL Keyword: **Hometown** and look for the Create link. On the Create & Manage Pages page, click Add to include your page in one or more communities in the Hobbies & Interests category (full procedures can be found in Chapter 3). If you are in the Collectibles business, add your page to the Business Park page and visit the other promotional Web sites there.

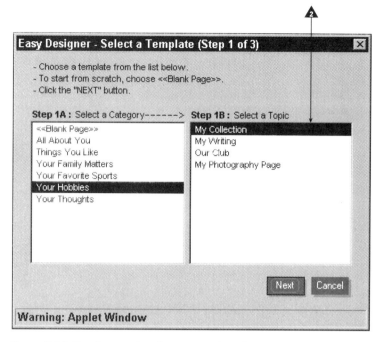

Figure 5-15. You choose an Easy Designer template whenever you start a new page. You can also choose to create a blank page, if you can picture what you want to accomplish in your head.

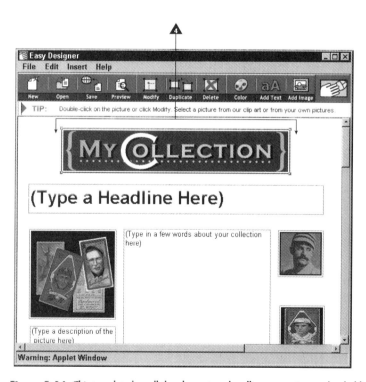

Figure 5-16. This template has all the elements: a headline, text, picture placeholders; you just replace the existing text and pictures with your own and if you want, keep the styling and positioning of the text and the placement of the images.

Cross-Reference

The eBay activity in Chapter 7 provides tips for taking close-ups and posting digital pictures at the eBay auction site (AOL Keyword: **Ebay**).

Note

What you see in Easy Designer is not exactly what you see on the Web. Preview your page repeatedly (click Preview) to see how your page will look to others. Chapter 3 has a full introduction to Easy Designer and AOL's other Web services.

Find It Online

AOL's Antiques & Collectibles area (AOL Keyword: **Collecting**) forms the online hub for many AOL communities devoted to collectibles, such as coins and stamps.

Coloring

For children well into elementary school, coloring develops creativity, fine-motor skills, observation, and concentration. It's also absorbing, of course — a perfect use of those dreary moments when kids just begin to get bored. In addition to shapes and colors (and staying within the lines), kids learn proportion and design while becoming immersed in something creative.

This activity shows how to make coloring pages based on your own digital pictures. I base the steps on PhotoSuite, but many other graphics programs can produce comparable results. An adult needs to help a younger child work through these steps, but as kids get older, they can assume more and more control.

1 With PhotoSuite open, click the Get button at the top of the screen. Buttons appear in the left pane, providing you a choice of places from which to retrieve a picture: your computer (the most common choice), digital camera, or scanner. If your picture is on your hard drive, simply click Computer and select an image using the Open dialog box. Before going any further, save your picture with a new name (choose File⇨Save As).

2 In this step, you remove the color information from your picture to make it easier to raise the contrast and apply the effects required to "colorize" your picture. From the Prepare Photos menu on the left, click Touchup⇨Touchup Filters. From the Touchup Filters menu, choose Fix Colors from the drop-down list.

3 Drag the Saturation slider scale all the way to the left (-100). In place of a color picture, you now have a black and white one!

4 Click Apply and then click Return to keep your changes.

5 Now, to cartoonize your black-and-white photo, click Special Effects⇨Effects from the Prepare Photo menu on the left. From the Category drop-down list, choose Artistic and from the Effect drop-down list, choose Cartoonize.

6 Put a check in the Preview check box. Click Adjust Effect Settings and choose a color level — High, Medium, or Low (often the best choice). With Preview checked, you can see the effects of each of these choices on-screen. When you like the results, click the Apply button in the left pane. The effects are applied to your picture. Click Return.

7 Send the cartoon to your printer by clicking Print at the top of the screen. In the Print Preview window, you can alter the number of sheets to be printed so that you give kids a chance to approach an image in different ways. You choose your printing options in the left pane, and click the Print button at the bottom to send your image to your printer. Normal paper is fine.

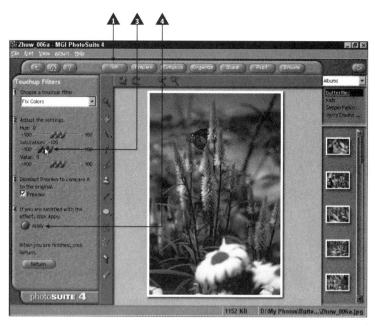

Figure 5-17. Change the original digital picture from color to grayscale in PhotoSuite. This view shows the Fix Colors Touchup Filter.

Figure 5-18. The Cartoonize special effect has been applied to the grayscale photo, which is now ready for coloring both on-screen and on paper.

Note

When your picture opens, PhotoSuite switches automatically to the Prepare Photo mode, where you can edit it.

Tip

Most graphics software lets you adjust the contrast. After removing the color from your picture in Step 3, you might want to click Touchup⇨Touchup Filter, and then use the Brightness & Contrast filter to turn up the contrast, creating some dramatic photo effects along the way.

Find It Online

You can find many coloring pages (to be printed and colored) at the Kids' Exchange (kidsexchange. about.com) under Coloring. For *on-screen* coloring, Coloring.com (www.coloring.com) offers more than 100 simple pictures for children.

5

School's Out

IDs, Fun

Kids love to pretend, and what better way to do so than with proof that they are someone else? They also like to do adult things like wearing their parents' shoes or pretending to drive. For elementary-aged kids, IDs can be the essential adult-like paraphernalia of organized play. This activity shows how to use the Fun ID templates in PhotoSuite to make a variety of official-looking identification badges.

1 Open PhotoSuite and then click the Compose button on the navigation bar. (Compose is the PhotoSuite mode in which you create projects.) In the left pane, click Fun Stuff⇨Fun IDs.

2 Many colorful ID templates give you a starting point for your ID badges. Double-click a template, and the template opens in the project area.

3 To add your personal data, click the Add/Edit Text button in the left pane. Click in your ID card to add a text box or select a text box that contains placeholder text. In the left pane, type your text into the field, select a font from the drop-down box, and add a style (the bold button is in bold, the italic button is in italics, and so on). To change the color of the text, click the color palette and pick a color that contrasts with the background so your text is readable. When you are done, click the Return button.

4 To add your photo to the ID card, click the image placeholder to select it. A selection box appears. Click the Add Photos button to select your photo from your computer or another source, such as digital camera or scanner. If your picture is on your hard drive, click the Computer button and select the picture by using the Open dialog box. Click Add.

- To widen or lengthen a photo, click and drag the appropriate middle handles.
- To enlarge or reduce a photo proportionately, click and drag the appropriate corner handles.
- To move a photo within the template, simply click somewhere in the photo and drag it to a new position.

5 To save your ID card project, click the Share button on the navigation bar and click Save in the left pane. This is the same as choosing File⇨Save.

6 Click Print on the navigation bar, choose your options on the left, check how the ID looks in Print Preview, and then click Print at the bottom of the left pane. From the Category drop-down list, select a business card design. Click Fill Placeholder (Fit within Placeholder crops off part of the ID image). Click Next to preview your cards and then click Print. Now you and your child can enforce the law, withdraw money from a bank, or join a mission into space.

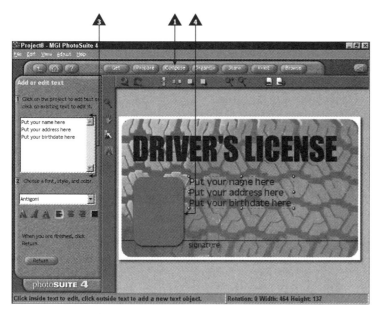

Figure 5-19. Add personal data to a Drivers License ID in the Add Text area.

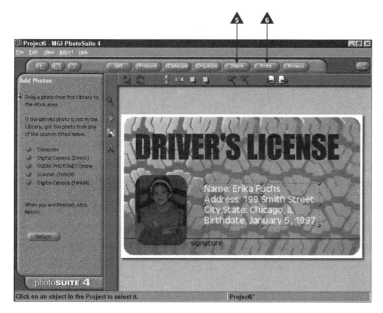

Figure 5-20. Play governor and add a photograph to a Drivers License ID in the Add Photos area.

Tip

To print a sheet of blank IDs, choose the Print Multiples selection on the Print menu in the left pane and select a template.

Tip

For a longer-lasting ID, use heavier paper, mount your plain paper ID on cardboard, or laminate your ID to make it waterproof.

Caution

In PhotoSuite, you can easily spend a good deal of time editing, only to forget to click Return (or Apply) when done. Your changes don't take effect until you say you're done.

Tip

To make a batch of similar ID cards quickly, choose a template, edit the ID, and then print it. Just change the photo and text on each individual ID, and then print again without saving or starting a new project (or save the customized changes under a new name).

Jigsaw Puzzles

Among the blessings of the digital age is the electronic jigsaw puzzle. Now you can play these *e-puzzles* right on your computer. Online, you can find plenty of e-puzzles showing everything from lighthouses to teddy bears, some of which you can download for offline use. You can also make puzzles from your own pictures. This activity shows how to make an online e-puzzle from your own digital picture at Shockwave.com.

 Visit the Shockwave site (www.shockwave.com). Choose Games from the main menu and then follow the links from Puzzles to Jigsaws and finally to PuzzleMaker. The program may take a minute to download. When the Launch button turns black, click it to begin.

 Click the prominent Import button on the New Puzzle screen. In the dialog box, navigate to the picture on your hard drive. Digital files can come in the standard graphics formats (JPG, GIF, BMP, and PICT); JPG happens to be the "You've Got Pictures" format. Click Open.

 The next step is to decide how you want to display your puzzle. Your options include special effects such as emboss and the following basic controls:

- **Zoom:** Use the left or right arrows to make more or less of your photograph visible. Watch the selection box to determine how the puzzle fits in the area.

- **Rotate:** Flip your pictures so they are right-side up (or for a challenge, make them upside down). Each time you click Rotate, the image rotates 90 degrees.

- **Stretch or Crop:** Stretch makes your picture fit the puzzle mat by altering its height or width, distorting the dimensions. Crop cuts off a portion of the image to make it fit, retaining the right proportions.

- **Shape and Number of Pieces:** Changes the complexity of your puzzle.

 When your configuration is complete, click Make Puzzle. After the puzzle is created, it appears scrambled on your screen, ready to play. Use your mouse to move the pieces of the puzzle. When you have a match, you hear them snap together. If you give up, choose Options⇨Solve Puzzle from the main menu to have the program complete the puzzle for you.

 When you're done, you can just quit, play again, or try another puzzle. If you like, you can also save the puzzle (choose File⇨Save Puzzle from the menu bar) or even send the puzzle to someone else by e-mail, using the form shown in Figure 5-22 (choose File⇨Send Puzzle). The recipient receives a Web address that links directly to your online puzzle in PuzzleMaker.

Figure 5-21.: Setting the characteristics of a new puzzle in Shockwave.com PuzzleMaker.

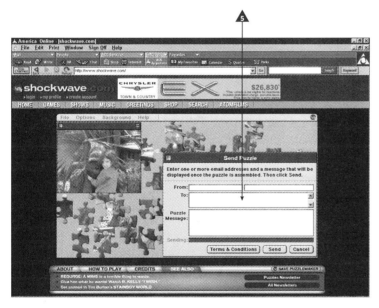

Figure 5-22. Playing, saving, and e-mailing a puzzle in Shockwave.com's PuzzleMaker.

Tip

PuzzleMaker suggests using a monitor setting of at least 16-bit color for best appearance. To change your monitor settings in Windows, choose Start⇨Settings⇨ Control Panel⇨Display. In the Display Properties box, click the Settings tab. Under Colors, select High Color 16 bit and then click OK. You don't have to restart your computer.

Note

If you plan to use PuzzleMaker frequently, you can download Shockmachine, a Shockwave application available at www.shockwave.com that lets you use PuzzleMaker offline.

Find It Online

If your children like doing online puzzles, spend some time at popular sites such as www.crayola.com/ kids/games/ jigsaw.cfm and www.billybear4kids. com/jigsaw-puzzles/ main-page.html.

Masks

Many young children love the occasions when they have a good excuse to wear a mask, whether it's for Halloween or dress-up. Masks, like fun IDs, give a kid a chance to try on a different role. A tiger mask can make a child feel strong, not small; effective, not klutzy. In this activity, you make a mask based on a digital picture of an owl included with PhotoSuite. You can make your masks out of any digital picture, of course. Consider using a digital picture of a familiar person's face, a raccoon's eyes, a superhero, and so on.

 As with many PhotoSuite projects, you start this one with a digital picture. Click Get and then, in the left pane, click Computer (or other source of your picture). In the Open box, find your picture and double-click it.

The picture opens up in the Prepare Photo mode of PhotoSuite. Make sure that the face fills as much of the picture as possible. The owl picture shown in this example was included in the Jerry Downs photo album that comes with many versions of PhotoSuite.

 To select and cut out the part of the picture to be used for the mask, first click the Cutouts button on the Prepare Photo menu. The Cutouts toolbar appears to the left of your picture. Click the Elliptical Selection Tool button on the Cutouts toolbar.

 Click one corner of the intended selection (the mask) and drag to the opposite corner. Double-click the picture when you're done and then click Make Cutout⇨Copy to the Clipboard.

 From the menu bar, choose File⇨New⇨Photo to create a new file. In the New Photo box that appears, type the dimensions and printer orientation you want. (In my owl example, I kept the suggested dimensions, 5 x 6.7 inches or 640 x 480 pixels, but changed the orientation to *landscape,* or wide.)

 Paste your picture into the new file's work area by positioning your cursor there and pressing Ctrl+V. The cutout of the owl face appears in the white box. You need to click and drag the picture to the upper left and then resize it so that it assumes the dimensions of the face of the person who will be wearing it (this is a trial and error process!).

 Print the picture on pliable paper. Click the Print button on the navigation bar, choose your options in the left pane, and then click the Print button at the bottom of the left pane. If the mask is too large or small, return to Step 5 to resize it appropriately.

 You or a child can now take scissors and hole-punch in hand to add an interesting shape, cut-out eyes, holes for the ears, and a string or elastic band to keep the mask in place. Color, decorate, and have fun!

Younger kids can have fun making a mask with a program like KidPix, though in this program, creating a design from scratch is easier than importing a digital picture.

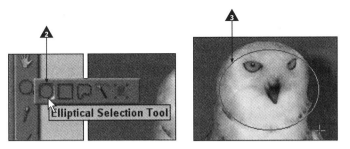

Figure 5-23. The Cutouts toolbar (on the left) is always available when you are in the Prepare Photo mode. On the right, you can see the Elliptical Selection tool in action.

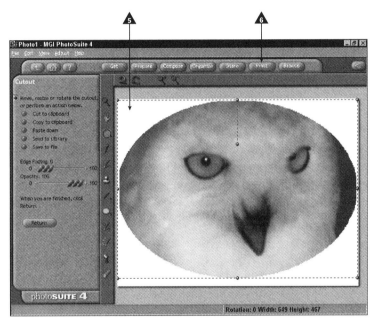

Figure 5-24. Paste your cutout into a new file to make your mask.

Cross-Reference

Related activities in this chapter include "Sticker Fun," "IDs," and "T-Shirts."

Find It Online

Children's book author Jan Brett has created masks based on the characters in her book, *Gingerbread Baby* (www.janbrett.com/gingerbread_baby_masks_main.htm).

Note

What to do with a cutout after you've clicked Make Cutout? You have several choices in the Cutout menu on the left. *Cut to Clipboard* removes the selection from the digital picture, leaving a hole. *Copy to Clipboard* keeps the original picture in place and makes a copy of the selection that you can paste elsewhere. *Send to Library* makes the cutout available during your current PhotoSuite session. *Save to File* makes the cutout available later.

Tip

Try using materials other than paper. Print your mask on a piece of sticker paper and use it with a paper bag or paper plate. For a cloth mask, print the mask design onto transfer paper and then iron it onto the cloth.

Memory Game

After they learn to count, learn some rules, and learn to take turns, kids start playing cards — baseball cards, trading cards, board games with cards, and so on. Cards seem nicely adapted to small hands, and each card usually has only one thing on it, minimizing distractions. Memory games strengthen a child's short-term memory, which in turn helps their long-term memory.

One great memory game for kids involves an evenly numbered set of cards, arranged face-down in a grid (for example, 2 cards x 3 cards). Every card's face has a picture or symbol, which it shares with only one other card. The objective is to pair up matching cards. Players turn over only one card at a time, and the only way to pair cards is to recall the matching card's location. The larger the grid, the more to remember and the harder the game becomes. Using a word processing program like Microsoft Word, creating a set of memory cards is easy. Here's how:

1 In Word, choose File⇨New from the main menu to create a new document.

2 Choose View⇨Toolbars⇨Drawing to access the Drawing toolbar.

3 Click the Rectangle button on the Drawing toolbar. You are automatically switched to Print Layout view, where you see more of the document and can use graphics tools.

4 Click and drag anywhere in your new document to create a 2-x-3-inch rectangular box. The margin rulers on the top and left sides of the screen can help you measure the length and height.

5 This activity requires that each card have an image of some sort. To insert a digital picture, select a rectangular box, choose Insert⇨Picture⇨From File, find the file in the Open dialog box, and then click OK.

6 To position the inserted digital picture in the center of the card (or elsewhere), click and drag the picture. (If Word won't let you click and drag the picture the way you want, double-click the picture, click the Layout tab, and set the wrapping style to In Front of Text.) You'll probably have to resize the picture by clicking a corner and dragging it to the middle of the picture.

7 Select the card *and* image and then click Copy on the toolbar to make a copy of both. Move your cursor to a free area on your page and then click Paste on the toolbar to insert your copies.

8 Print your picture on heavy paper by clicking the Print button.

A few inkjet printers now offer double-sided printing, so you can apply a design to the backs of the cards. For flash cards, you can put the question on one side (such as a picture of a dog) and the answer on the other (the word *dog,* which the child is expected to spell).

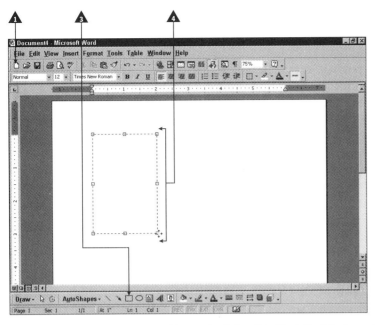

Figure 5-25. Creating a memory card (or any kind of card) in Word. Use Print Layout's margin rulers to make the card the size you want.

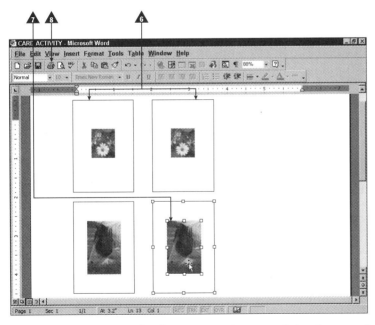

Figure 5-26. You can import digital pictures into a document and place them on cards.

Cross-Reference

Of related interest is "Sports Cards," which is also in this chapter.

Find It Online

You can find many card-related activities at Bry-Back Manor (`www.bry-backmanor.org`). The 200+, diverse activities at this simple, creative site can be printed out, played with, and colored.

Note

Word's patterned clip art works well for card designs (choose Insert⇨Picture⇨ Clip Art). If you didn't install clip art with Word (or Office), you will need to fetch the art from the CD.

Panoramas

Imagine being able to capture the entire horizon in one photograph. Even if your camera doesn't have a panoramic setting for wide photos, you now can create them after the fact by joining, or *stitching,* photos into one continuous photo. Stitching works by joining pictures at the places where they overlap. A panorama can be quite effective when you want to capture a wide natural landscape, a large group of people, or a sports event. Any situation in which your subject just doesn't fit into the frame has panoramic possibilities. When you take the series of photographs, use a tripod to keep the camera at the same level.

This activity shows you how to prepare a panorama with a tool that is integrated into PhotoSuite 4.0's Platinum version. Many digital cameras come with software that enables you to create a similar effect.

1. With PhotoSuite open, click the Prepare button on the main toolbar. Click the Stitching button.

2. Choose a stitch type or orientation: Wide (for horizontal panoramas such as the horizon shown in Figure 5-28) or Tall (for vertical scenes such as tall buildings and trees). Make your choice, and click Next.

3. Retrieve your photos from one of the sources listed on the Stitching menu (Computer or Scanner, for example). When you are finished, click Next.

4. Click and drag your photos around the work area until pictures with shared subject and similar orientation are adjacent. You can also flip photos horizontally and vertically, as well as rotate them right and left by using the tools that appear at the top of Figure 5-27. When you are finished sorting, placing, flipping, and rotating the photos, click Next.

5. To ensure greater accuracy, select your camera type or the lens focal length that most closely resembles the one you were using. This enables PhotoSuite to optimize the stitching process and display a recommended number of photos to stitch. If your camera isn't listed in the drop-down box, you can create a custom setting or download new camera settings from the MGI Web site. After you are finished, click Next.

6. Manually align your photos by dragging them, or if you click Auto Align Photos, PhotoSuite aligns them. When you are finished, click Next.

7. Select your stitch options and watch the preview of your panorama displayed in the work area. Click Blend Photos to make the stitch look more natural. Click Next.

8. Click Crop to crop the stitched panorama and then click Return. Save and name your new panorama by clicking Share on the navigation bar and then Save in the left pane.

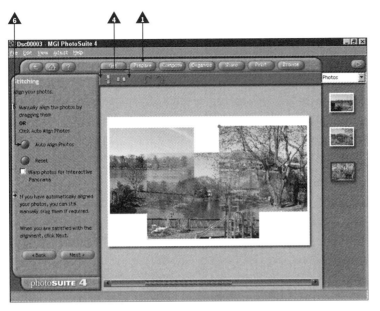

Figure 5-27: Arrange photos and stitch them together as a panorama in PhotoSuite 4.0.

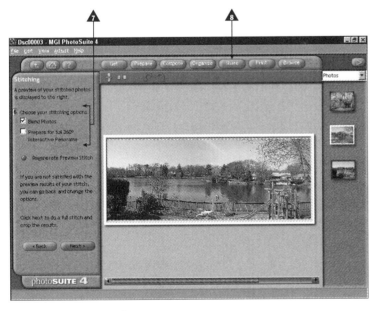

Figure 5-28: A preview of your panorama.

Note

The stitch feature in PhotoSuite works best when the original photos overlap by at least 30 percent. More overlap (as much as 65 percent) gives PhotoSuite even more to work with. In other words, when taking photos, include from one to two-thirds of the previous scene in each photo.

Tip

You can make your favorite panorama into an interactive Web page in PhotoSuite 4.0 (Platinum). Users can then explore a panorama by clicking around it, as if they were standing in a room and turning around to see everything that's there. Please consult the PhotoSuite on-screen help for more information about interactive panoramas.

Find It Online

A free tool for creating panoramas for Web pages is available at www. albatrossdesign.com/ products/panorama. The latest ADG Panorama Tool generates, allows you to edit, and publishes 360-degree interactive panoramic compositions for the Web.

Paper Dolls

The Web brings new choices and ideas to the rainy day pastime of making paper dolls. It also provides numerous patterns to print and design; these patterns can be printed again if they tear or another child wants one, too.

To create paper dolls based on characters familiar to your child, follow these steps:

1 In PhotoSuite, bring in the digital picture you want to use for the doll. Click Get, choose the source for your digital picture — your computer or scanner, for example — and then select the image. The image appears in the Prepare Photo mode.

2 Use the Freehand tool — available from the vertical toolbar between the work area and the left pane — to trace the outlines of the figure you want to use for your doll. When you're done, double-click and then select Make Selection. In the Cutouts menu, click the Send to Library button. This selection is now available from the PhotoSuite Library.

3 Choose File⇨New⇨Photo from the menu bar to create a new, blank file into which you can paste the cutout. In the New Photo box, click Portrait, change the units to inches, type **5** in the Width text box, and type **7** in the Height text box. Click OK.

4 With the new file (a white box) in your work area, open the PhotoSuite Library if it isn't open now (click the triangle in the upper-right corner, and choose Photos from the drop-down menu). When your cutout appears in the Library on the right, drag the cutout to the work area.

5 Your cutout is unlikely to be perfectly selected, and the edges may appear ragged when you zoom in. You can either fix the figure on-screen or trim it with scissors after it's printed. The latter is much easier, but if want to fix it on-screen: in Prepare Photo mode, click Touchup⇨Touchup Brushes. On the Touchup Brushes menu, choose Normal from the drop-down list, a brush size under 5, an opacity of under 100, and a white paint color. Before you start, zoom in by clicking the Plus icon. Brush alongside the figure, neatening up the border, and adjust the brush size and opacity as you go.

6 Now things fall into place. Print the figure on heavy stock and cut it out. Kids can color the clothing or use the figure to trace out clothing, making sure to add those clip-on tabs. You and your child may have to devise your own base, if you want the doll to stand up.

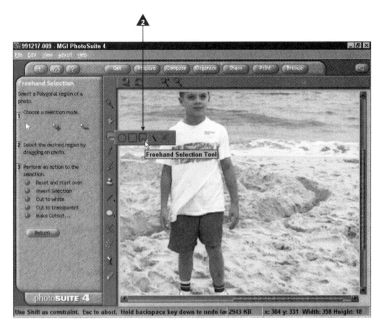

Figure 5-29. Start by bringing a digital picture into PhotoSuite and make a selection to cut out the figure. With all selection tools, be prepared to retrace your selections until you get a feel for the tool.

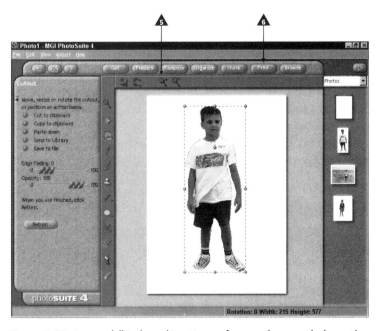

Figure 5-30. A paper doll in the making. You can fix somewhat ragged edges with a touchup brush or by trimming them after they're printed. Using scissors is a lot easier than using on-screen touchup brushes.

Definition

A *selection* is a part of a digital image selected for special editing, for use in another digital image, or as the basis of a new image, as in this case. Selection tools are discussed in the "Special Effects: Composites" activity. The Freehand selection tool (in PhotoSuite, Paint Shop Pro, and others) lets you cut out just the part of a picture that you want.

Cross-Reference

For more details on how to make a cutout, see the "Special Effects: Composites" activity in this chapter.

Definition

Opacity refers to the extent to which an effect (such as a touchup brush) covers up the underlying image. At 100 percent, the image is covered up completely. At less than 100 percent, you can create a softer effect to blunt the jagged edges you often get with cutouts.

Find It Online

Kids Domain (www.
kidsdomain.com/kids/
links/Paper_Dolls.ht
ml) has a good index of
paper-doll designs. Graphic
Greetings also has a sizable
directory (www.
graphicgreetings.com
/printablespaper
dolls.htm).

Pets, Celebrating with a Web Page

Pets can claim a good chunk of their owners' budget, space, time, and affection. They can also provide company for the elderly and teach kids responsibility and compassion. If your children would like the world to know how important their pets are to them, help them create their own Web page featuring their pets. Here's how it's done:

1 Go to AOL Keyword: **Easy Designer**. The main Easy Designer page appears.

2 Click the Create a New Page link (under the Start Here heading).

3 Click the big Click Here to Get Started button.

4 In the Select a Template dialog box, choose the Meet My Pet template (currently in the category called Things You Like). Click Next.

5 Choose a page layout for your template. A layout specifies where the text and picture elements go on a page. Later, you can always add your own pictures and move them around. Click Next.

6 A box asks you to select a color scheme for your page. Consider a color that goes well with your pet's feathers, fur, scales, and so on. Click Next to see your template.

7 Add your own elements. To use a picture of your pooch in place of a picture in the canned template, select a picture to replace and click Easy Designer's Modify button to open the picture in Picture Gallery.

8 Click Upload Picture.

9 In the Easy Designer - Upload Picture dialog box, click Browse and double-click the picture you want from your hard drive. Back in the Upload Picture box, click Upload Picture. Be prepared to wait a few moments as your picture wends its way to AOL's computers. Soon, you'll see your pet's picture in the Picture Gallery.

10 Click OK to bring the picture into your Web page. If you see an Overlap warning on the picture, resize the picture by dragging a corner so that it doesn't overlap another object.

11 Save your page when you're done (use Easy Designer's Save button).

12 Back in AOL Hometown, add your page to one of the Family & Home communities devoted to pets, as explained in Chapter 3. At AOL Keyword: **Hometown**, click Create. On the new page, click Add and select a page. Follow the prompts from here on.

Figure 5-31. Easy Designer's Pet template allows you to swap out the existing pictures and use your own in their place. The cute, dopey pooch with the birthday hat, on the left, is the first to go.

Figure 5-32. To begin transforming a template into your own Web page, the original pet picture has been replaced with another picture. You can also add any text you want to celebrate your pet.

Cross-Reference

This activity is based on the discussion of Easy Designer templates in Chapter 3. Use that chapter for additional guidance in making and editing pages in Easy Designer.

Find It Online

Pet lovers are well served on AOL. Start at AOL Keyword: **Dogs** or **Cats** or **Pets** (each takes you to a separate area).

Find It Online

If you are searching for a pet, don't forget the adoption services. AOL Keyword: **Animal Adoption** includes general information, as well as access to Petfinder.com's searchable database. For information about pet abuse, go to AOL Keyword: **Be Kind to Animals**.

Picture Games: Parts and Wholes

This activity is inspired by Voices of Youth (www.unicef.org/voy), a UNICEF site that gives kids around the world a chance to discuss day-to-day realities such as war, disease, and nutrition. The Whole Picture area displays part of a photograph and asks kids to figure out the situation that would explain what's going on in the picture segment. The figure opposite shows a child apparently in pain, perhaps at risk of being harmed. A click away is the entire picture, which shows exactly what is going on: The child is receiving a vaccine.

You can have fun with your own Parts and Wholes games, and you can make the game as serious or silly as you want:

1 Start by opening any digital picture in any graphics editor that allows you to edit pictures and to make selections. In this example, I use PhotoSuite. Click Get, and then choose a source for your image, Computer or Scanner for example.

2 Select part of your image. For this activity, try the Freehand tool — available from the vertical toolbar to the left of the work area — because it allows you to make an irregular selection of anything you want. Before starting, look closely at the picture for that part that can reveal something about the picture as a whole but that, on its own, can be interpreted in many ways. Using the Freehand tool, trace a shape around the part you wish to cut out.

3 Generally, you'll want to think of the entire shape you're selecting, tracing a shape that ends where it started. When you're done, double-click. Click Make Cutout⇨Save to File, so that the picture can be saved as a distinct file, printed, and displayed with the picture from which it was cut out. When prompted in the Save As box, give the new cutout a name.

4 Print the cutout, and then print the image from which it has been cut. Display one of the images, and do the following: Click Print on the navigation bar, choose Print, view your image in Print Preview, and then click Print at the bottom of the left pane to print the original picture and your cutout. Now print the other image. Show people the cutout and see whether they can figure out what the whole picture shows.

You can vary this activity in many ways:

▲ Take a picture of a mundane object (like scissors) and show a part of it (such as the inside edge of a handle). See who can guess what is shown in the whole picture.

▲ Take a person's picture and apply effects, perhaps using some of the ideas in the "Special Effects" activities (warps, filters, and so on). Now select part of the picture to cut out and have people guess who is shown in the whole picture. Or, change the color balance or apply a filter and make a selection that reveals as little as possible of the larger action.

▲ Create a comic strip consisting of several frames, and leave out a frame. Kids can make their frames independently and then compare results and justify their choices.

Figure 5-33. What's happening? A vaccination!

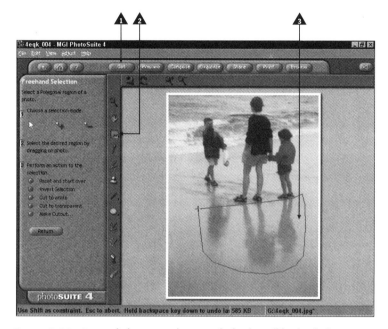

Figure 5-34.: Start with the scene to be guessed. The clue will be the shadow. See any other parts that would be possible choices? Here, you cut the shadow out by using the Freehand tool.

When using the Freehand tool, click to end each segment of your cutout. You'll need many small segments, and many clicks, to define a complex irregular shape. Double-clicking has the effect of joining the points where the selection starts and stops. Usually, you'll want to continue your trace back to where it started, but you terminate it anywhere.

When you save a selection as a file, PhotoSuite saves it as a Portable Network Graphic (PNG) file. Although the PNG standard is becoming an increasingly popular graphics file type for different types of computers, not all software can display PNGs.

For more on selections, see "Special Effects: Composites" in this chapter. For related activities, try "Cartooning" and "Comics" in this chapter.

Screen Savers with Digital Pictures

One screen saver can make your PC's monitor look like an aquarium, with bubbles rising and colorful fish drifting back and forth. Another can simulate the effects of being in space or inside a kaleidoscope. Still others draw continuously changing, colored abstract shapes. From AOL you can download software called Create-a-Saver that lets you incorporate your own digital pictures into a screen saver. This software can be set up to display one digital picture after another, automatically. You decide what pictures to display, with what messages and backgrounds, and how long to display each picture. The software does the rest.

Here's how to get your screen-saver up and running:

1   Visit AOL Keyword: **Create Screensaver**, and follow the on-screen instructions to download and install the Create-a-Saver Lite program.

2   To set up the screen saver program, first choose Start↪Settings↪Control Panel↪Display from the taskbar to access the Display Properties box. In the dialog box, click the Screen Saver tab. Select Create-A-Saver Lite from the Screen Saver drop-down list and then click the Settings button. The Create-a-Saver Lite Preferences dialog box appears, as shown in Figure 5-36.

3   In the top left of the Preferences window, select the folder on your hard drive containing the digital pictures you want to display.

     Note: The digital pictures you want to use must all be in the same folder; *all* a folder's images are displayed in alphabetical order during the slide show. If you don't want to use them all, create a new folder just for the pictures you want.

4   Preview the pictures by clicking individual files in the list just below the file directory. The picture appears just to the right.

     The next three steps explain how to create messages to appear with your pictures. You don't have to add messages, but they can say something humorous or descriptive about your pictures.

5   With the image selected and displayed in the Preview box, type your first message in the Message Across Top box. (This message appears at the top of the image when displayed). Align the text using the three buttons just above the box. Using the first two buttons to the right of the box lets you alter the message's font and color; the third button lets you display several messages, one at a time. For long messages, reduce the font size. Use the Preferences button at the bottom to tell the software how long to display each message if you add several.

6   If you like, type a second message in the Message Across Bottom box and set it up, just as in Step 5.

7   From the drop-down list at the very bottom of the window, choose either a background color or one of about 40 designs against which your pictures will appear. To avoid clashes and to keep the messages readable, I used a light blue background with this screen saver. Click OK when you are done.

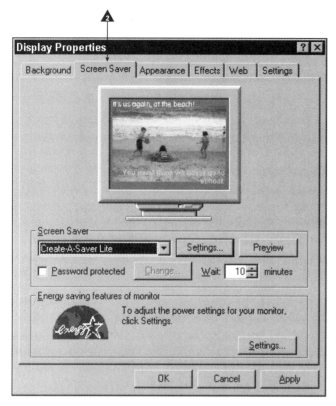

Figure 5-35. The Display Properties dialog box lets you control many aspects of how your computer looks; the Screen Saver tab lets you control your various screen savers.

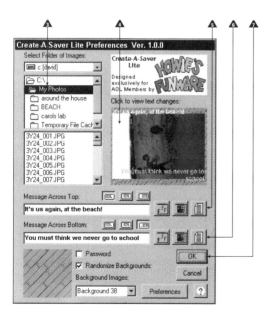

Figure 5-36. Create a nonstop slideshow consisting of your own digital pictures. This complex-looking window has everything you need to choose pictures, create messages, and select background designs and colors.

Find It Online

AOL has its own collection of free screen savers (AOL Keyword: **Screensavers**).

Definition

A *screen saver* is a type of software that shuts off the monitor after a certain period of idleness, and goes blank or displays a moving image of some sort. The original justification was to prevent screen images from being burned into the monitor. Today's monitor technology makes burn-in unlikely.

Tip

To have pictures display in a certain order, assign alphabetized names (such as A*xxx* as the first picture, B*xxx* as the second, and so on).

Cross-Reference

See the "Slideshow" activities in this chapter for variations on the theme of presenting pictures in a sequence.

Signs

Signs are a good way of getting attention and passing on some information. Kids post them on their bedroom doors. Children and adults can use them to jog their memories or to notify neighbors of yard sales, lost dogs, and the like. Nowadays, it's a snap to include digital pictures and clip art in your signs, which can help convey your message.

Like certificates, most signs use a single-page design and a small number of elements, which include text that informs the reader of something. Word processors can make fine signs, but graphics software such as Print Shop, used in this activity, offer a smoother experience and many more choices. The sign in this activity is for kids who do leaf raking:

1 From the opening Print Shop menu, select Blank Pages. From the next page, select an orientation for your blank page. In my example, I chose Tall. You can select signs and work with an existing template, but in this case, try creating a sign from scratch in order to learn about Print Shop's key features. Your blank page appears in the Print Shop window.

2 Create a backdrop to enhance your sign. Click the Panel Effects button, and select Backdrop. From the list of all backdrops, I chose Autumn Leaves.

3 To create some attention-getting text, click the Text/Headline button, and select Insert Headline. In the Create a Headline box, you indicate both the text you want to use and the way it is styled. Click the Customize button to open the dialog box shown in Figure 5-38 for even more control of the type, shape, color, color blend, texture, and position of your text. Figure 5-38 shows a color blend from green to red, fitting the season and purpose. The text is also aligned to a curve, achieved with the help of options available on the Shape tab. Click OK.

4 Repeat Step 3 for the other highly styled text.

5 Click Insert Graphic to add an image that serves as an informal logo. In the Art Gallery, select The Print Shop Art as the collection (source of art) and pick a category. I found this Black Elm leaf image in the Nature/Trees & Plants category. Double-click to insert into your sign.

6 To add simple, informative text, click the Text/Headline button and select Insert Text. A text box is inserted into your sign. You can drag it around, resize it, and type your text directly into the box. Right-click and use the Text menu for all your text-editing options.

7 Tweak all your elements, as necessary. Double-click the headlines to edit them in the box shown opposite; simple text can be edited right on-screen. Double-clicking the black leaf (logo) takes you back to the Art Gallery.

8 When you're happy with your sign, save (File⇨Save) and print it (File⇨Print). Or, just use the Save and Print icons.

Tip

Move your mouse over the top of any button to display the button's name.

Note

For simple text, effects are limited to what's available on the Print Shop toolbar: style (B or bold, and so on), alignment (right, left, and so on), font size and type, and *leading* — the amount of space between lines.

Figure 5-37. Print Shop gives a lot of control over the elements of a sign, including headlines, regular text, and your own pictures. You can find these elements used throughout Print Shop activities.

Cross-Reference

See the sign with tear-offs activity in Chapter 7 for a sign meant to meet the needs of a business.

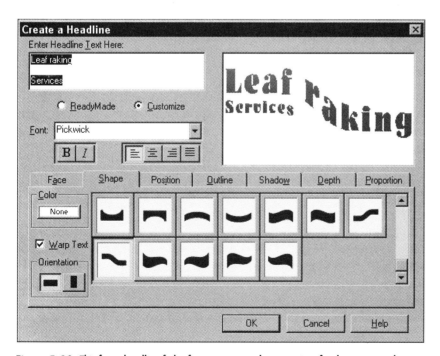

Figure 5-38. This fancy headline fades from green to red, appropriate for the season and sign.

Slideshows with PhotoJam (Shockwave)

A *slideshow* is a series of several digital pictures that are played one after another (yes, like the slideshows you might have suffered as a child or in art-history class). Slides sometimes consist of other content, such as sound effects and text messages. Slideshows can usually be played automatically, and most slideshow software gives you the ability to control how long each slide stays up and what visual effects, if any, accompany the transition between slides.

Macromedia makes free presentation software called PhotoJam, which greatly simplifies the process of making a slideshow.

 Go to Shockwave (www.shockwave.com) and look for a link to PhotoJam. Click the link and follow the instructions for downloading and installing this software. Then open the software by double-clicking its icon, as you would any program.

 In the PhotoJam window, click Create.

 The short menu asks you to select photos for your slideshow. Click Photos and select the folder with your photos. When you run your slideshow, PhotoJam displays one picture after another in that folder, in alphabetical or numerical order.

   Note: All digital pictures must be in the same folder. If you don't want to use all the pictures, use Windows Explorer to create a new folder just for your PhotoJam images, and copy pictures into it.

 Adding music is optional. If you want to play music while your slideshow is going, you need to select a music file (MP3 file). The latest version of PhotoJam includes jazz, rock, and other MP3s for your slideshow.

 Finally, choose a Style from the drop-down list. Slideshow style is simplest, but don't ignore some of the more creative options. The 80s Video style, for example, creates neat transitions between slides. The Art Film style not only gives your pictures an arty twist, but also merges them and has funky transitions.

   Figure 5-40 shows a moment from a Music Video slideshow — missing are the dramatic colors you would see on your computer screen. The Collage style shows many pictures at the same time, for a filmstrip effect.

 Click Watch to see your creation and click Edit to change your pictures, music, or style.

For more fun, consider buying PhotoJam Pro, which lets you create screen savers for your computer, add captions and word bubbles to slideshow images, share your slideshows via e-mail, and even include slideshows on your Web site.

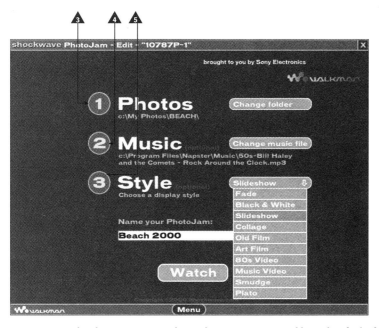

Figure 5-39. The PhotoJam main window makes it as easy as possible to identify the folder containing your digital pictures, select an MP3 file to play as background music, and add awesome visual effects that blur the line between slide and transition.

Figure 5-40. One way to keep people's attention for your next slideshow: A PhotoJam slideshow using the Music Video style.

Find It Online

To learn about digital music and find out how to download and play it, start at AOL Keyword: **Digital Music Center**.

Cross-Reference

Chapter 7 looks at the PowerPoint presentation software and includes tips for creating a professional slideshow. The difference between fun slideshows and business presentations is that business presentations require more work and tend to be more predictable.

Definition

Albums in PhotoSuite help you organize your photos so that you can keep track of them and readily use them within PhotoSuite. Pictures in the album don't have to be in the same folder. Like slideshows, albums are created in Organize mode. Albums help you manage projects requiring several pictures. For more, see the album activity in Chapter 6. In "You've Got Pictures" (Chapter 2), an album is primarily a set of pictures meant to be shared.

5

School's Out

Slideshows with PhotoSuite

Some full-featured graphics programs come with a slideshow feature. Even programs intended for a younger audience such as KidPix, IBM's Make a Masterpiece, and Kai's PhotoSoap let kids create slideshows with their own creations (made with the software, of course). Kids can pick up the elements of multimedia literacy in the process.

PhotoSuite enables you to put together engaging slideshows, using digital pictures, in a few quick steps. To do this activity, you must first have created an album, which you can learn to do in Chapter 6. Every slideshow gets its pictures from an album; unlike many programs, PhotoSuite's albums can be drawn from many different folders.

1 In PhotoSuite, click Organize on the navigation bar. On the Organize menu, skip to the bottom and click Create a Slideshow.

2 In the left pane, choose an album you've already created in PhotoSuite. Thumbnail images of the pictures in the selected album appear in the work area.

3 Indicate which pictures to use from the album. Click Select All in the left pane, or in the work area, click only the pictures you want to use. Shift-click to select several pictures in a row, or Ctrl-click to select several pictures not in a row.

4 Choose a transition from the drop-down list. You'll want to revisit this option when your slideshow is done, to see the effect of using different transitions.

5 When you're done, click the Create button. The New Slide Show dialog box appears.

6 In the New Slide Show box, you can make the following choices: what to call your slideshow, how long to display each slide, how long to make the transition, what color to use for the background (click the Background Color button and choose a color), and whether to scale the pictures to fit the screen (check the box — unless your pictures are so fuzzy you don't want to show them too large). Click OK. Your slideshow now comes up in the Edit Slide Show window.

7 Play your slideshow using the familiar video-style controls at the top. These buttons are used for playing, stopping, pausing, and so on.

From this window you also can add photos (refer to Step 3), change transitions (Step 4), and adjust slideshow settings (Step 6).

8 Your family and friends don't have to watch the slideshow at the unsightly Edit window; click the Full Screen control button to devote all your screen space to the slideshow.

9 When your slideshow has a name, save it (choose File⇨Save). Note that it is saved with the PhotoSuite file extension PZS, so it can be opened and edited only within PhotoSuite (choose File⇨Open).

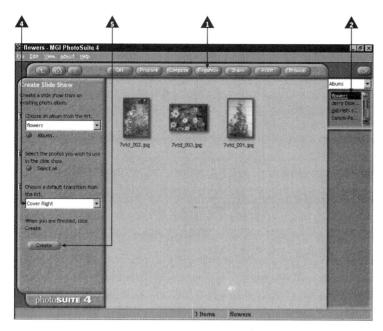

Figure 5-41. Creating a PhotoSuite slideshow involves selecting an album, pictures, and a transition between slides. A blue frame appears around each picture you select in the work area.

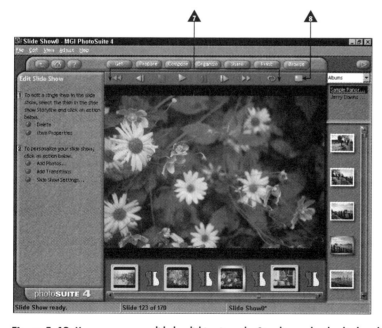

Figure 5-42. You can open any slide by clicking it on the Storyline under the displayed slide. On the Edit menu in the left pane, you can add photos and change transitions. Under Slide Show settings, you can alter the display time and the transition.

Definition

A *transition* defines what happens between the display of one slide and the display of the next slide. Common transitions are *wipes,* which blacken a slide from one of its four sides like a squeegee, and *covers,* in which the new slide overlays the old slide.

Find It Online

For slideshow software downloads and reviews, see About.com's Graphics Software site (`graphicssoft.about.com`).

Special Effects: Composites

A *composite* involves cropping or copying part of one picture and adding it to another. Composites can open up a whole new world of possibilities. Serious photographers use them to turn a bland gray sky into a turbulent one by cutting out the sky from one photo and dropping it into the other. Kids can have fun swapping friends' heads with pets' bodies. You can use your composites with many activities in this book: T-shirts, kids' invitations, personal stationery, and so on. Figure 5-44 shows a composite made from two beach photos.

Here's how to make your own composite:

1 In PhotoSuite, start by retrieving the digital picture *from which* you want to extract a part to use within another digital picture. Just click the Get button, define the source for the image — computer or scanner, for example — and then select the particular image.

2 Use the Edge Finder or other appropriate selection tool — available from the toolbar to the left of the displayed picture — to trace around the area of the picture you want to cut out.

Note: Edge Finder is always available when you're in PhotoSuite's Prepare mode.

3 Click any point on the edge of the part to be selected and then trace around the figure's edge. Each small step creates a long rectangle whose ends cross the figure's edge. Continue tracing the figure until you completely define the area you want cut out.

4 When done, click Finish Tracing. Drag the selection border's handles as needed to improve the accuracy of the selection (Edge Finder is always an approximation). When the selection is how you want it, click Make Selection.

5 From the Cutout menu, click Send to Library to make the selection available for use in another picture. The library is the strip of pictures down the right of the PhotoSuite window; the selection is available in the Photos collection.

Note: If the Library is not already displayed, click the leftward-pointing triangle in the upper-right corner of the PhotoSuite window and choose Photos from the drop-down list. The selection appears at the top of the Photos list from the library's drop-down list (albums, photos, projects, slide shows).

6 Click Compose. Use the Add Photos button or the library to select a picture *into which* you want to incorporate your new cutout.

7 Open the Photos library on the left half of the screen. Find the cutout and drag it onto the picture that you opened in Step 6. Adjust the cutout as appropriate. If you want, use a selection tool to define part of the image where the cutout is to go; use Cut to Transparent to create an opening behind which you can position the cutout.

8 Click Share to save your composite and print it by clicking Print on the navigation bar. In the left pane, choose your printing options and click Print at the bottom.

Figure 5-43. I cut out a selection from this digital picture for use in another picture. The tools shown here are always available in the Prepare Photo mode; from the left, they are Elliptical, Rectangular, Freehand, Magic Wand, and Edge Finder.

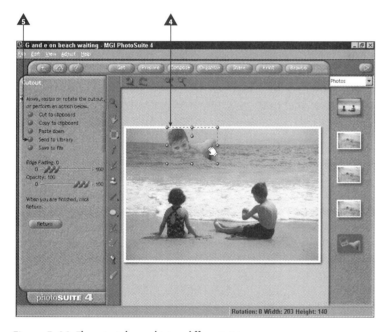

Figure 5-44. The cutout dragged into a different picture.

When making a cutout, zoom in (click the Plus sign above the work area) enough to see what you are doing. Get too close, however, and all you will see are pixels.

Sending a cutout to the Library in Step 5 or saving it as a file means the cutout can be used in several pictures. The PhotoSuite Library is available on the right side of the PhotoSuite screen (click the triangle in the upper right if you don't see the Library).

Special Effects: Filters

Photographers have always used filters — coated glass rings that screw a lens — to do things like screen out ultraviolet light or enhance contrast. Today, anyone with graphics software can create the effects of filters. PhotoSuite's filters include natural effects such as fog and artistic effects such as swirl. In this activity, you apply a filter to an entire picture using PhotoSuite:

 In PhotoSuite, click Get to retrieve a picture to be filtered. Most likely you'll be getting your picture from your computer's hard drive. Find the folder with your picture and then double-click the picture to select it.

 Before altering any picture:

- Save the picture as a file with a different name (choose File⇨Save As). Take advantage of those long filenames to give your picture a descriptive name.

- Let the software enhance the colors automatically. With a picture displayed, click Touchup⇨Enhance⇨Apply. The figure opposite has been enhanced, and I brightened it up by increasing the contrast.

 Click Prepare. In the left pane, click Special Effects⇨Effects.

 Choose a category and then an effect. I applied the Spherize effect to Figure 5-46, which (arguably) enhances the subject's features. Other filters pile on so much effect that the original subject is often unrecognizable.

 Click Share to save your new picture and then print it by clicking Print on the navigation bar. Make sure you like what you see in Print Preview; click Print in the bottom left when you do.

Other Ways to Apply Filters

- **Using *selections* to apply a filter to a part of a picture:** With a picture displayed, select the part of the picture to be changed. Do not click Make a Selection. Instead, click PhotoSuite's Up (or, in older versions, Back) button to return to the Prepare Photos menu. Click Special Effects⇨Effects, and choose a filter from one of the categories. The effect will apply to just the selection.

- **Using Effect Brushes when editing any picture:** In the Prepare mode, click the Effect Brush tool to apply a filter effect with a paintbrush tool, whose thickness, solidity, and opacity you can control. Consider softening backgrounds with one of the blur brushes. Use a brush to daub on moonlight or blur the whole background to emphasize the subject.

- **Using Adobe Photoshop plug-ins (third-party filters):** PhotoSuite can use any plug-in on your computer. In the Prepare mode, click Special Effects⇨Plug-in Effects. Navigate to the folder with the plug-in, and select it. You can download many plug-ins from the Internet.

5

School's Out

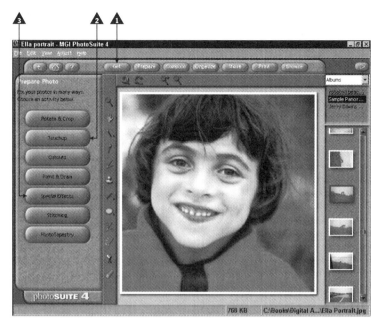

Figure 5-45. Compare this original picture with the one below. After retrieving the picture, click Special Effects⇨Effects to apply a filter.

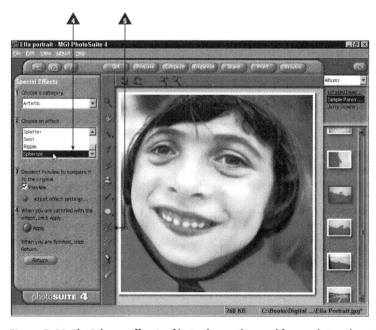

Figure 5-46. The Spherize effect (or *filter*) enhances the round form and gives the picture the silly look of a fisheye lens (very wide angle). Kids love this kind of software, and the software seems to love kids, too.

To apply filters or special effects only to a selected area, don't click Make Selection. Instead, click the Up (in earlier versions, Back) button to find and apply the effects and filters. How do you then deselect the selected area? You have to return to the selection tool used to create the selection, and click Reset and Start Over.

PhotoSuite lets you enhance any picture's overall colors with a single click. Depending on the quality of the original, the tool can make a real difference. To use it, open the picture and then click Touchup⇨ Enhance from the Prepare Photo menu. Check and uncheck the Preview box to see the effects of the enhancement. Click Apply to accept the changes.

PhotoSuite has a second set of filters designed for ordinary touchup work. With a picture displayed, click Touchup⇨Touchup Filters from the Prepare Photo menu. For more about using filters to improve color balance, see the sections on fixing photo goofs in Chapter 6.

Special Effects: Text on Pictures

Text on an image adds information to a photo as well as an interesting compositional touch. You can add text if you are making an ad for your business, for example, or creating a cartoon-style birthday invitation. As hot sauce, you can apply unusual fonts or shadow effects.

Not all graphics programs let you add words to pictures easily; Easy Designer, for instance (Chapter 3), doesn't allow text blocks and images to overlap. If you make your text-on-picture creations in PhotoSuite, however, and save them as JPG files, you can use them anywhere — including on the Web. Here's how to add text to a picture in PhotoSuite:

1 Click Compose. In the left pane, choose a project to create. In my example, I've chosen Collages. Click Other Photo⇨Next.

2 In the New Collage from Photo box, find your digital picture and double-click it.

3 With the picture displayed in the work area, click the Add/Edit Text button in the left pane.

4 Think about *where* you want the text to be. Click the photo in that place, and a text box appears, surrounded by a dotted line.

5 In the left pane — not the actual text box — replace the placeholder text, `Put your text here`, with your own. The text you type appears in the text box on your image.

   Note: To edit the words in an existing text box, click the text box once and make your changes back in the field in the left pane.

6 Choose the font, style, and color by using the controls on the left. Using the marquee box on the picture itself, you can drag the box around, rotate it (to make the text vertical, for example), and resize it. Resize the text box by clicking and dragging one of the marquee's handles or any of the sides (resizing increases the font's size). Click Return in the left pane when you're done.

   Note: To reposition a text box in the work area on the right, click it once and, when the mouse cursor is shaped like a hand, drag the box somewhere else.

7 If you want more than one block of text in your picture, repeat Steps 4 through 6 for each text box you want to add.

8 When you're done, save your creation by clicking Share and then clicking Save in the left pane. If you want to use your picture on the Web, make sure to save it as a JPG.

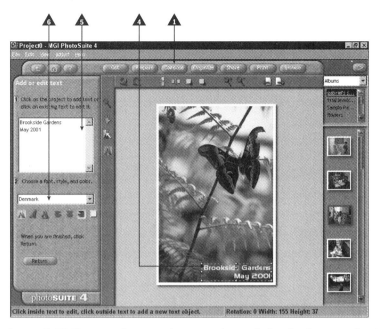

Figure 5-47. The text in this picture documents where and when the photo was taken. The words are positioned over the darkest part of the picture.

PhotoSuite's Paint & Draw tools (available from the Prepare Photo menu) include two ways of applying filters to specific parts of a picture: Filled Shapes and Effect Brushes. Both let you apply Sepia, Tile, and other effects onto any part of a picture, without using selection tools.

To delete a text box, select it and press the Delete key.

PhotoSuite's text tools do not yet have a way to set font size. Instead, changing the size of a text box makes the font size bigger or smaller.

You can improve text legibility in several ways. Choose a simple font family and adjust its size. You can also make the font color contrast with the background and place your text over a solid part of the picture.

In PhotoSuite, to make your new picture a JPG that's usable in any program and on the Web, select JPEG image.

Special Effects: Warps

A *warp* turns a digital picture into taffy, goo, or bubble gum, which you can pull in any direction. Kids of most ages love warping tools; crazy, funny effects can be cooked up in no time. As for adults, warping effects serve no real purpose, which is all the more reason to enjoy them.

In PhotoSuite, you can make warps in two ways:

▲ Interactive warps let you apply warp effects to specific parts of a picture.

▲ Preset warps apply to entire pictures. Such warps include vertical and horizontal warps, as well as bulge and monster warps (see Figure 5-49).

To create a preset warp:

1 In PhotoSuite, click the Get button. Then, in the left pane, click Computer, navigate to the correct folder on your hard drive, and double-click the picture to which you want to apply a warp.

2 PhotoSuite automatically switches to the Prepare Photo mode. Click Special Effects⇨Preset Warps.

3 The short menu of warps includes the Horizontal and Vertical Funhouse Mirrors. Each makes a dramatic impact on your picture. Try each one to see what it does. Click Adjust Warp Settings to fine-tune horizontal and vertical warps. You drag a slider bar left to lessen the effect and to the right to increase it. In Figure 5-49, I heightened the vertical reflection to create a mirroring effect and combined it with horizontal reflections for a kaleidoscopic effect. Click Return when you're done.

4 Back in the main editing window, click Apply and then click Return when you're done.

This easy procedure turned a so-so picture shot on a gray, cool summer day into an interesting composition that makes the day more memorable. Why let a so-so picture spoil an otherwise good memory?

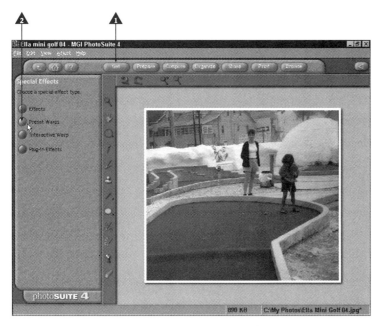

Figure 5-48. The original picture, the weather, and the setting were less than memorable.

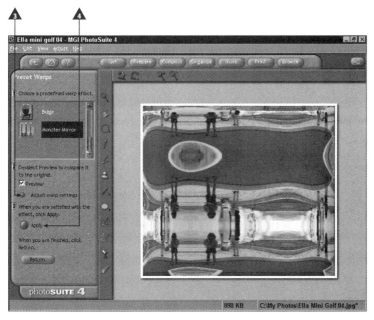

Figure 5-49. The Monster Mirror warp transformed this digital picture into a kaleidoscopic image that still captures the miniature-golf theme. Note the stronger vertical than horizontal reflections. Monster Mirror makes pictures abstract in no time.

Note

PhotoSuite's Preview check box (in the Monster Mirror dialog box) is a valuable feature you see throughout PhotoSuite. It lets you quickly see the effects of a single feature, such as the ones applied with the horizontal and vertical controls here. It also helps you quickly gauge whether you want to use an effect. The Apply button captures the effect without saving it. The Return button applies the effects and lets you continue editing using other PhotoSuite tools. Until you save your changes, however, you can undo them by pressing Ctrl+Z.

Tip

Try combining effects, too. After applying a filter to the whole picture, for example, use the Effect Brush to enhance part of the picture. A little bit of any effect goes pretty far.

Sports Cards

For a sports team, cards with each player's photo and stats can help everyone learn each others' names at the beginning of the season. At season's end, cards can be redesigned with photos, memorable achievements, quotes, and so on, so that everyone can remember the experience and his or her new friends. This activity shows how to make sports cards in PhotoSuite:

1. Open PhotoSuite and click Compose. From the Compose menu, click Cards & Tags⇨Sports Cards.

2. Choose a type of template. Blank templates leave almost all the choices up to you, while Finished templates include art and designed text, some of it sports-specific.

3. Replace the placeholder text in any existing text box by clicking the text box in the work area and typing your own text in the appropriate field in the left pane. To add new text boxes, click Add/Edit Text and then click in the work area where you want to place the new text box. In the left pane, type your text and make font, style, and other choices. When finished, click the Return button.

4. To add a student's digital picture, click Add Photos, find the picture, and double-click it. In the work area, select the picture and pull the handles to resize it or move it by clicking and dragging it. When you're done, click Return.

5. Click the Add Props button to add extras such as clip art, drop shadows, and word bubbles. Props can be dragged to the work area.

6. Save your first card by clicking Share on the navigation bar and then clicking Save. Shared projects are now available on the Project menu in the PhotoSuite Library. (Click the left-pointing triangle if you don't see the Library; select Projects from the drop-down list. Repeat Steps 1 through 5 for each player and save subsequent cards with a separate file-name by choosing File⇨Save from the menu bar.)

7. When you complete all the team cards, you're ready to print. Make sure the PhotoSuite Library is open (see Step 6). Open your cards by choosing File⇨Open. Then hold down the Shift key and select all of them.

8. Highlight a card in the Library, right-click it, and choose Switch To from the pop-up menu. The project fills the work area. Click Print on the navigation bar. Then in the left pane, click Print Multiples and choose a template whose rectangular placeholders match a card's orientation (portrait or landscape) and intended size (such as Avery 3256). Click Fill Placeholder as the placement method so the picture fills the whole space. (In Figure 5-51, a single image fills all the placeholders on a page.) Click Next.

9. Make sure the paper orientation is correct and select the number of copies you want to print. Click Print in the left pane. Be prepared for a couple of trials on ordinary paper before using heavier stock or laminated paper. After the printing orientation and figure-placement is right, print on card stock, just like baseball cards.

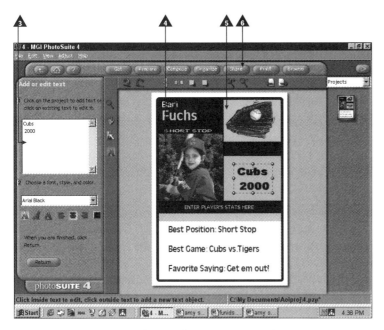

Figure 5-50. Customize a trading card for a sports team in PhotoSuite.

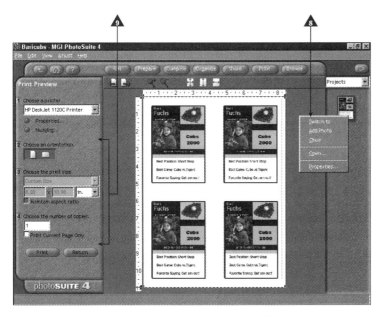

Figure 5-51. Preview your trading card before printing in PhotoSuite.

Note

Some cards have a second "page" (the other side of the card) where you can put additional pictures, props, and text. In Compose mode, you'll see right and left arrows above and to the right of the work area; use these arrows to go back and forth between the two sides of the card. In printing a two-sided card with Print Multiples (to get several cards on a sheet), select and print one side of the card. Using the same sheet, select and print the other side of the card. With some experimentation using regular paper, you can print so that the front and back line up. In printing a two-side card with Print (once), you print both sides on the same sheet; they're "hinged" so you can cut them out as a unit and simply fold into a two-sided card.

Tip

In the Print Preview window (Step 9), click Nudging to move a picture slightly to the right and left, or up or down.

Note

Trading cards can be fun in lots of other group situations, too, such as family reunions, school clubs, camp, after-school activities, and birthday parties.

Sticker Fun

For kids, stickers can be dentist-office trophies, school rewards, property labels, and name tags. These trophies wind up on helmets, windows, and bathroom walls. Although you can buy stickers easily enough, homemade ones can convey a special message or personal touch. What could be more fun for kids than seeing a picture of their face or favorite toy on a sticker?

This project shows how to make stickers from your digital pictures. The activity requires printable sheets of precut labels, available in office-supply stores or on AOL. (Choose Print⇨Printer Supplies from AOL's toolbar for more info.) The activity assumes that you have digital photos, parts of photos (called *selections*), or digital art ready to go. Sticker-making on its own is just a printing activity; the things kids *do* with the printed stickers is what counts.

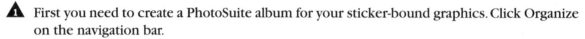 First you need to create a PhotoSuite album for your sticker-bound graphics. Click Organize on the navigation bar.

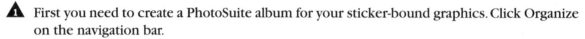 In the Organize menu on the left, click Albums. When the Master Album dialog box appears, click New to create a new album and call it *Stickers*. Click OK to return to the Organize window.

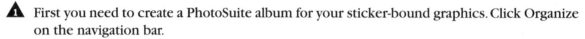 Click Add Photos to select digital pictures to put in your new album for use on your stickers. Hold down the Shift key and select multiple pictures in a sequence (or use Ctrl to select pictures in no particular order). Click Add when you've selected all the graphics files you want. Thumbnails of the images appear in the work area.

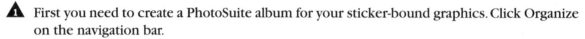 Click Print on the navigation bar and click Print Multiples to indicate that you want to print several stickers per sheet.

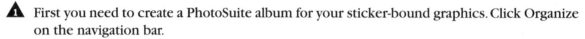 Choose the company that made your labels (Avery, Kodak, or Package Prints) and then choose a template that matches your label size and configuration. Click the Fill Placeholder option and click Next.

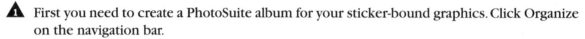 When printing albums, selecting One Image Per Page repeats a single image in each placeholder. To put a different image on each successive sticker on a sticker page, as shown in Figure 5-53, select the images to be printed and then select One Image Per Placeholder. Click Next.

In the Print Preview window, you can now preview your printed page.

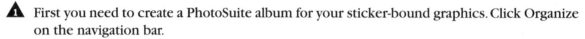 Make sure the paper orientation is correct and select the number of copies you want to print. Insert the label paper into the printer and click Print in the left pane.

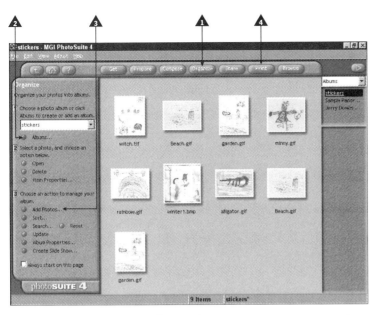

Figure 5-52. Create your sticker album in PhotoSuite.

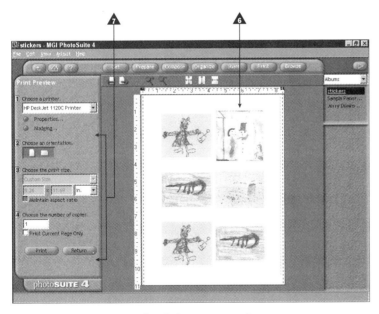

Figure 5-53. Preview your stickers before printing in PhotoSuite 4.

If you aren't sure how to insert the paper, place a mark on a piece of regular paper and do a test print, using the mark as reference to determine which side the printer prints on. Running a sticker sheet through the printer more than once can cause stickers to curl off and harm your printer.

For a collection of printable stickers online including notebook, locker, book, and ABC stickers, visit www.kiddonet.com and click Printables. AOL also has a selection of My Property stickers, which you can find by choosing Print⇨Print Central⇨Kids Stuff from the toolbar.

A *placeholder* is the rectangular area in label templates indicating where an image will go. In Print Multiples, when using a template, Fit within Placeholder means that a picture's proportions are retained inside a placeholder, so a panorama appears "long" even in a square placeholder. Fill Placeholder causes the picture's proportions to be adjusted so that an image entirely fills a placeholder.

Stories with Pictures

A story, real or imagined, has simple elements: a setting, a couple of thinking creatures, and a problem to solve, if only to make the story start, go somewhere, and stop. In telling stories, kids give shape to their imaginations. By raptly listening to others' stories, they can get a handle on everything from their own murky feelings to abstract concepts of love, evil, and loyalty. Stories help kids learn about these things without any lecturing from their parents, and kids can remember stories easily. Adding digital pictures can make the sequence and moral even more memorable.

This activity shows how to use a word processor (such as Microsoft Word) and your digital pictures to create your own stories. You can collect your stories in a binder or share them on the Web. This activity assumes the child is telling the story to an adult who is typing it; older children can do more of the work themselves.

1 With Microsoft Word open, choose File⇨New from the menu bar to open a new document.

2 Separate the page into two uneven columns by choosing Format⇨Columns from the menu bar and selecting the Left preset design (second preset from the right in the Columns box). In the Number of Columns box, type **2**. Check the Line Between option to create a line between the columns. Click OK to return to your document. You don't see the columns until the text needs to wrap within the column.

3 To see your work better, zoom in by choosing View⇨Zoom and choosing a higher percentage.

4 With your child, make up a title and type it at the top of the left column. Type your child's name below it. Highlight these lines and increase the font to 16 points with the Font Size box on Word's Formatting toolbar. (If you don't see the toolbar, choose View⇨Toolbars⇨Formatting.)

5 Have your child select photos that relate to his or her story. Your child may want to use photos from a recent event or trip. Insert them in sequence below the title in the left column. You insert the digital pictures one at a time by choosing Insert⇨Picture⇨From File and navigating to the picture's location. You can use AOL's Picture Finder to review pictures on your hard drive. If your child wants to use clip art, you can add that too by choosing Insert⇨Picture⇨Clip Art and selecting a piece of clip art from Word's gallery.

6 Choose File⇨Save from the menu bar, or click the Save icon, to save the document when you are done inserting pictures.

7 Have your child describe the events that occurred in each of the photos. The story can be narrated to you or typed by the child in the right column. Save the file regularly.

8 Use Word's Formatting toolbar to liven up the document. Change the font, as well as the font's size and color. Play around with all the cool characters available by choosing Insert⇨Symbol. Most of all, focus on the story and elaborate it.

9 Choose File⇨Print from the menu bar to print your finished document.

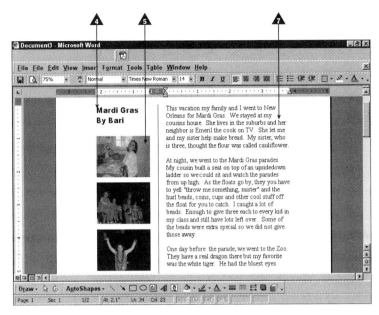

Figure 5-54: A photo story created in Microsoft Word.

Columns will appear only after you choose View⇨ Print Layout.

Several kids can tell a story together, with each kid in turn adding a picture and text that develops the previous kid's contribution.

Do your pictures tell a story? Find out at AOL Keyword: **Photo Stories**. Just send four to six photos and an accompanying description of the events depicted in the photos, and you might be featured in AOL's Picture This! newsletter. To subscribe, go to AOL Keyword: **Newsletters**, search for Picture This!, put a check by the newsletter, and click Subscribe.

T-Shirts

What makes a better gift for a grandparent, a birthday, or Mother's Day than a T-shirt with someone's smiling face on it, preferably a kid's? This activity shows how to make a T-shirt. You need a good-quality photo, an inkjet printer, graphics software, an iron-on transfer available at your local office supply store, and a regular iron. Print a picture onto the transfer and then iron the transferred picture onto the T-shirt.

❶ In PhotoSuite, click Get to retrieve a photo from one of the available sources such as your computer or scanner.

❷ The image you choose probably has elements you don't want on your T-shirt. To select just the area you want transferred, use the Freehand Selection tool — available from the vertical toolbar to the left of the work area — to trace around the part of the image you want.

❸ When you are done tracing, double-click the image to make a cutout and then click Make Cutout⇨Send to Library. Your cutout now appears in the Library under Photos. If the Library is not visible, click the leftward-pointing triangle in PhotoSuite's upper-right corner.

❹ To add a background to the image you want to transfer, first click Compose on the navigation bar and then in the left pane, click Fun Stuff⇨Backgrounds. Select a background that suits your fancy. Drag your cutout from the PhotoSuite Library onto the background, resize it, and position it.

❺ Personalize your T-shirt with a caption. With the picture still displayed in Compose mode, click Add/Edit Text. Click the spot in the work area where you want the text box and then type the text for your caption in the Add/Edit box in the left pane.

❻ Iron-on transfers require that all text and images be printed in reverse, as you're looking at them in a mirror. Why? When the transfer is ironed onto the shirt, the image appears backwards if it's printed normally. To create a mirror image in PhotoSuite, select each photo or text box individually with the mouse and click the Flip Horizontally button at the top of the work area. When all have been reversed, make any positioning adjustments you need to make.

❼ Save your project by clicking Share on the navigation bar and then, in the left pane, clicking Save. Do a test print on plain paper by marking one side of the paper to identify which side your printer prints on. Click Print, preview your picture, and click Print at the bottom of the left pane. When you like the results, insert the transfer paper (for example, Avery 3271) into your printer. Complete the activity by ironing the transfer onto your T-shirt, closely following the instructions that came with your transfer paper.

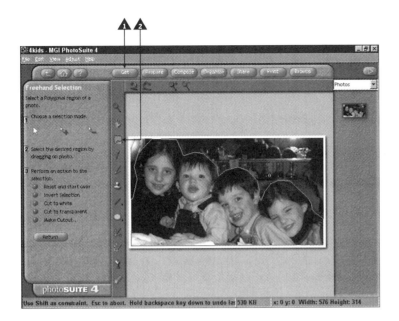

Figure 5-55. Creating a freehand cutout in PhotoSuite to eliminate the background around the subject.

Figure 5-56. The final T-shirt image has an abstract background, and the text and image are reversed.

Note

For a good-looking image, follow the resolution guidelines, which are available in Chapter 2. For good resolution, use a megapixel camera. For pictures of lower resolution, consider printing pictures at a smaller size on your transfer sheet.

Find It Online

For blank, brand-name T-shirts, sweatshirts, and tank tops in many colors and sizes, visit www. t-shirts.com. For iron-on transfers and other inkjet craft materials, visit www.invent-it.com.

Note

If your software lacks a Reverse option, check your printer's preferences for a Mirror, Reverse, Flip, or Back Print option. If your printer doesn't have this option or it doesn't work, use a software package that allows you to flip the image and text horizontally.

6

FOR THE WHOLE FAMILY

IN THIS CHAPTER

▲ Celebrating your family with scrapbooks and family trees

▲ Showing off your pictures with frames

▲ Sharing kids' pictures with posters, magnets, and mousepads

▲ Fixing those photo goofs and enhancing composition

▲ Keeping track of it all with albums and to-do lists

▲ Throwing parties with banners, posters, and gift wrap

▲ Staying in touch with personalized stationery and labels

Chapter 6
For the Whole Family

The activities featured in this chapter tend to be more practical than the kid-oriented activities in the last chapter, but a sharp line can't easily be drawn between them. You can be as creative as you want with the activities in the next few pages, and these activities can be fun for older folks as well as kids, singles, and seniors. The bottom line is plain old usefulness, from which just about anyone can benefit.

Keeping Track of Things

Many activities in this chapter help you keep track of things. Starting with digital pictures, you will find out how you can create software albums for your digital pictures so that you can, in the future, quickly search for and retrieve them. Albums also simplify the use of sets of pictures in a single activity such as making a screen saver or family tree.

You will also find ideas for bringing order to a collection of CDs and discover a program for creating a searchable database with your favorite recipes.

Everyone has to keep track of time — schedules in particular. PhotoSuite, the software featured in many activities in this book, has many attractive templates you can use to create monthly calendars with pictures of pets, family members, mountains, and anything else you like.

For keeping track of things on a more day-to-day basis, you could simply print some of the attractively designed, generic to-do lists available on the Projects tab of AOL's Print Central. This chapter's personalized to-do list activity shows how you might design an activity schedule for a child who is just learning such things. You can readily adapt the activity to the needs of the senior citizen who must take medications at set times each day.

Family Matters

The activities in Chapter 6 are household-oriented, and several focus sharply on the family itself. If you're single, you can use these activities to study your family origins or stay in touch with distant relatives.

Delving into genealogy is a highly popular pastime for many people. Programs like PhotoSuite simplify the process of making photo pages for family trees. They also provide templates for quickly designing scrapbook pages, so you can commemorate family events. Both family trees and scrapbooks have an important role in introducing young folks to whiskered and corseted ancestors.

Why not create a home for your family on the Web? There, it simply doesn't matter where everyone actually lives. Groups@AOL, which I cover in Chapter 4, provides one way of building such a homestead. Creating a newsletter on the Web, too, can be a tremendous way for families to actually talk to each other on a regular basis, as you'll see in this chapter. What a concept.

The photo goofs activities explain how to improve the pictures you use in all these projects. Remove those dust specks and bump up the contrast on those grayed-out pictures. The photo goofs activites also show you how to *crop*, or remove edges of a photo to improve its composition.

Communicating with Pictures

Digital pictures and graphics software give life to the old art of letter writing. In one activity, you can learn how to make personalized letterhead, featuring a favorite digital picture, perhaps of a loved one or favorite place. Digital pictures also make outstanding postcards; find out more in the "Postcards" activity. Oh, and you'll find out how to make return address labels.

Digital pictures make good gifts. In this chapter, find out how to make your own mousepads and refrigerator magnets for yourself or others. After you create your gift, make personalized wrapping paper in a special activity at the end of this chapter.

Several activities, finally, can help you celebrate events, family and otherwise. You can use banners and posters for homecomings, births, special birthdays, promotions, retirements, and multiple-digit anniversaries.

6

For the Whole Family

Albums for Organizing Digital Pictures (I)

With so many ways to *get* digital pictures — "You've Got Pictures," a scanner, a digital camera, stock photography, clip-art collections — keeping track of them all can become a chore in itself. "You've Got Pictures" stores all your online pictures in albums for easy retrieval and sharing. Offline, many graphics programs use albums to help you organize pictures.

Such albums are not primarily intended for sharing, but for helping you keep track of pictures. Albums also help you store information about individual pictures for later reference. This activity uses PhotoSuite to show you how to create a new album; the next activity shows how to enter details about specific photos in that album.

1 Start by clicking Organize on the PhotoSuite navigation bar.

2 Click the Albums button in the left pane to open the Master Album window. Click New from the toolbar on the right, and name your new album in the dialog box that appears. Click OK first in the New Album box and then in the Master Album box.

3 To add photos to the album, click Add Photos in the left pane. The Add Photos menu comes up in the left pane, giving you a menu of places where you can find and fetch pictures — from your computer, digital camera, or scanner. Most likely, your pictures will be on your computer. An album can have pictures from many different sources, including different folders on your computer.

4 When you click any source — Computer, Digital Camera, and so on — the Add Photo to Album box comes up. Use it to select one or more pictures at a time from any folder, and click Add after each selection. You can add more than one picture at a time by holding down the Shift key (for sequential pictures) or Ctrl key (for pictures in no particular order) and then clicking the pictures you want. The Preview window on the right shows the picture — if you are selecting only one. New pictures added to your album display in the PhotoSuite work area.

5 Click Return in the left pane when you are done adding photos.

Albums can be displayed in two ways on PhotoSuite. To show thumbnails (small pictures) of an album in the work area, click Organize and select the album's name from the drop-down list. From the album library on the right side of your screen, thumbnails for each album can be displayed vertically at any time. If the library is not displayed, click the left-pointing triangle in the upper-left corner of your screen, select Albums from the drop-down list, and select the specific album from the list just below the drop-down. Double-click (or drag) any picture from the library into the work area to see a larger version of the image.

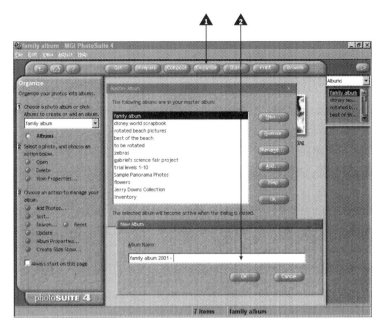

Figure 6-1. Use the album feature in PhotoSuite to organize your photos into meaningful categories or groups of photos that are easy to locate and work with.

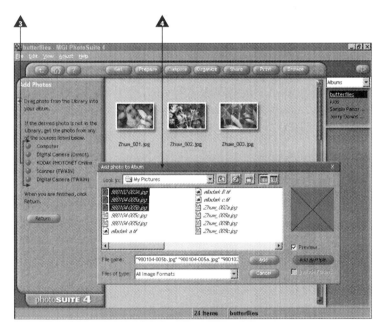

Figure 6-2. The Add Photos menu and the Add Photo to Album dialog box put your photos where you want them.

Note

A single album in PhotoSuite can include digital pictures in many different folders on your hard drive.

Note

In addition to "You've Got Pictures" albums (for sharing) and PhotoSuite's (for organizing), there's yet a third type of albums — the more familiar kind, for displaying wedding pictures. Click Compose and then click Create New Project⇨Photo Layouts⇨Photo Albums to put together a traditional photo album.

Tip

Keep your original digital files. Choose File⇨Save As to give modified files a different name. That way, you can always go back to the original if you need to. Consider using a Zip disk or rewriteable CD (called a CD-R) to store files rather than fill up your computer's hard drive. The "CD Labels" activity shows how to make labels for your discs.

6

For the Whole Family

Albums for Organizing Digital Pictures (II)

What good is a great organizational scheme if you can't find anything? PhotoSuite provides an opportunity to collect as much or as little data as you want about every picture in every album — who took the picture, with what camera, when, who's in the picture, and so on. All this information is kept in a database that you can search at any time to help you retrieve photos. To collect such information:

1 Click Organize, select an album, and drag a picture from the PhotoSuite Library (on the right) into the workspace. If the Library is not displayed, click the left-pointing arrow, choose Albums from the drop-down list, and click the album's name.

2 With the picture highlighted, click Item Properties in the left pane. The Item Properties dialog box appears. The drop-down box lets you describe almost 20 aspects of every picture, including who's in the picture, who took it, where, when, and what's going on in the picture. You can also add a descriptive title.

3 Choose a property for which you want to add information. Properties are listed in the Item Properties window's drop-down menu. They include subject, title, people in photo, place, event, comments, and so on.

4 Type a description. Click Add/Modify when you're done with the property. Repeat for all the properties you want to describe for a picture. Enter as many or few properties as you want.

5 To describe another picture, click Next.

6 Click OK when you are done.

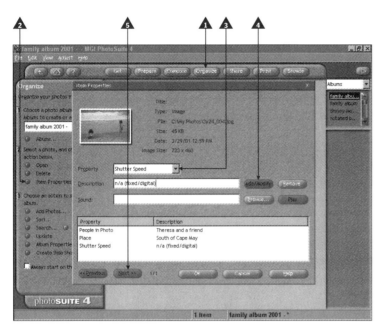

Figure 6-3. The Item Properties dialog box lets you describe a wide range of photo characteristics. These properties can then be used when you search for specific pictures.

Tip

If you enter the specific properties for each photo in an album, or at least the important ones, you can later search for pictures using a specific word in that property's description. With an album selected, use the Search button on the main Organize menu.

Note

The information you enter for an album is stored in a PhotoSuite format and will not be usable if you use the pictures in an album in another program.

Tip

Be as specific as possible in your titles and descriptions. Use standard wording such as Storm July 2000 so that you can later retrieve a subset of pictures within an album.

Banners

Some messages are so important they need to be shouted. Banners and posters are a great way to make your message stand out, even at a distance. Whether the occasion is a birthday, bake sale, or new store hours, a banner can help you make your point.

A banner usually spans the length of several pieces of letter-sized paper. For that reason, use a program that allows you to create a multipage project on one screen and then breaks it up for you when printing (a process known as *tiling*). The Learning Company's Print Shop has this capability and was used to make the Happy Anniversary banner you see in Figure 6-4. To make your own banner, adapt this procedure to your own needs:

1 Start Print Shop and highlight Banners in the project category menu that appears. Click Next.

2 You can choose either the Personalize a Quickstart Layout option or the Start from Scratch option. In this example, I chose Start from Scratch to create exactly the design I wanted. Click Next.

3 In the next screen, choose a wide orientation (rather than tall) for the banner layout.

4 To customize the banner text, replace the placeholder text (*Banner*) by highlighting it and typing your message.

5 To add some color, click the Panel Effects button on the toolbar and then click Backdrop. In the Select a Backdrop dialog box that appears, choose a background appropriate for your design. (In this example, I chose Balloons.)

6 To personalize your banner, you can import a digital photo by choosing Insert⇨Import from the menu bar.

7 To add an additional text box, first choose Insert⇨Text Box from the menu bar and then place your mouse where you want your text to appear. Click and drag to draw the text box. When you're done drawing, double-click in the new text box and type your text.

8 Before printing, save the file by clicking the Save button on the toolbar. Be sure to give your file a descriptive name in the Save As dialog box that appears.

9 To print, click the Print button on the toolbar, choose the options you want in the Print dialog box, and then click the dialog box's Print button. To do a test print of just the first page, click the Which Tiles button from the Print dialog box, highlight the first panel, and then click OK.

Figure 6-4. A banner is a great way to mark a special occasion. Make your banner fill the room and display your message loud and clear.

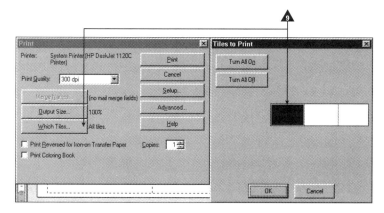

Figure 6-5. The Print dialog box in Print Shop lets you control which pages of your project print and you can change the output size by using a special process called *tiling*.

Tip

After printing your banner, trim off the white borders at the connecting sides, arrange the pages in the correct order, and tape the back of the sheets to join them.

Cross-Reference

For another kind of large project, see the "Posters" activity in this chapter.

Note

If you don't want to print your banner on separate pages and tape them together, you can buy special banner paper for your inkjet printer. This paper is continuous and can be up to 18 feet wide. To print on banner paper, you have to select Banner paper in your printer's Properties box (available whenever you go to print a document in a Windows application). In an HP PhotoSmart, for example, you choose paper in the Setup tab from the Paper Type drop-down list; other inkjets use different names. To buy such paper, check out AOL Keyword: **Shopping** and visit AOL Printer Supplies by choosing Print⇨Printer Supplies from the AOL 6.0 toolbar.

6

For the Whole Family

Calendars

Calendars have always made visually attractive gifts. Now, using graphics software and your own pictures, you can create your own calendars. In this activity, you can make a colorful family calendar by using PhotoSuite. Hang it at work or give it to someone. Kids love making calendars with pictures of friends, family, and pets. Here's how:

1 With PhotoSuite open, click the Compose button on the navigation bar. Buttons appear in the left pane, allowing you to choose the type of project you wish to make.

2 Choose Calendar from the projects list and then select a category (Yearly, Monthly, or Quarterly). Figure 6-7 shows a yearly calendar.

3 Select the category you want, Horizontal or Vertical. Vertical calendars have a tall orientation, like the one shown in Figure 6-7, and Horizontal calendars are wide.

4 Open a template from the selections in the work area by double-clicking the design you like. Most calendar templates have a gray (transparent) patch where you can drop in one of your digital pictures. The template you select appears in the work area, and the Compose menu appears in the left pane.

5 Add a photo by clicking the Add Photos button. Just choose a source for your photo — such as Computer or Scanner — and then retrieve your image.

6 Resize or relocate the photo within the placeholder, as necessary.

For a calendar with a photo background like the one in our example, choose a template with a full gray (semitransparent) background to show as much of the picture as possible, even through the design.

7 Add your own text or props (PhotoSuite clip art). Change the color of the text, if you want, to make it readable on the calendar background. Make the text larger or smaller by dragging the handles of the text box.

8 Save your project by clicking Share and the clicking Save in the left pane.

9 To send your calendar to the printer, click the Print button on the navigation bar and choose the print options you want in the left pane. When you're ready to print, click the Print button at the bottom of the left pane. Consider using good high-quality paper, which is usually bright white or card stock.

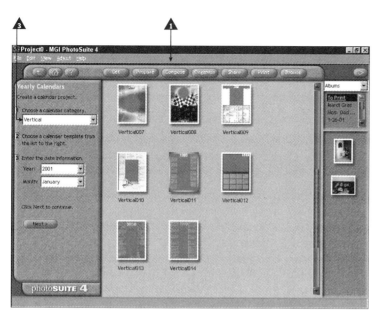

Figure 6-6. The selected template is for a yearly, vertical calendar with a placeholder for a photo background.

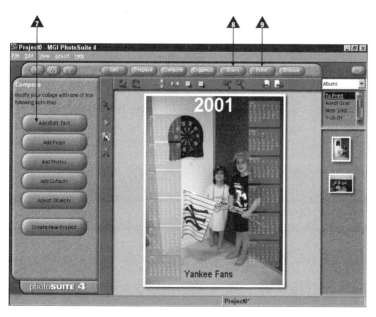

Figure 6-7. This completed calendar for 2001 contains a vertical (portrait) photograph and some text.

For desk calendars that are ready to print and fold, check out AOL Print Central by choosing Print⇨Print Central from the AOL toolbar.

To manage your time online and off, use My Calendar, available from the AOL 5.0 and 6.0 toolbar. You can customize your calendar by adding your personal meetings, dinners, favorite TV shows, and so on.

Calendars make great holiday gifts. Collect special photos throughout the year at family events. Before the holidays, create and bind a 12-month family calendar for the following year.

To resize a digital picture, select the image so that dotted lines surround it and then click and drag any corner or side. To rotate the picture clockwise or counterclockwise, click the circle in the center of the selected area and drag right or left.

CD Labels

With the popularity and falling cost of recordable compact disc players (CD-Rs), discs have become a smart way to store large multimedia files, including digital pictures. Because quality digital pictures run to about 50 to 100 kilobytes (K) per image, you can fit more than 5,000 pictures on a 650MB CD (at 100 kilobytes per image).

To keep your burgeoning CD collection organized, consider creating your own CD labels. You need blank CD labels — available from Avery and other vendors — and you may also want to invest in a CD label maker kit, because such kits come with label applicators designed to help you accurately position labels on CDs. CD label maker kits are available at office-supply stores and on AOL (choose Print⇨Printer Supplies on the AOL toolbar).

To put neat designs on your blank CD labels, do the following:

1. With PhotoSuite open, click the Compose button on the navigation bar. In the left pane, click Business⇨Stationery and choose Media from the drop-down list. Double-click the CD Disk Label 1 template. Each template contains two labels.

2. Each label consists of a gray circular band the size of a CD. To add a picture to this gray placeholder, double-click the placeholder and use the Add Photos menu in the left pane to fetch one from your computer or another source. If the photo appears as a rectangle over the placeholder, select the photo and click Move Back on the toolbar.

3. Click the Add/Edit Text button to add text that describes the CD's contents.

4. To add a background color to your label rather than a full-sized image, double-click the blank CD label to open a small version of it in Prepare Photo mode and then click the Flood Fill button on the toolbar. Click Colorize, select a fill color, and then click the object using the Flood Fill tool. Click Compose to switch back to Compose mode, and click Yes to update your project with the changes you just made. To add information or liven up your design, add text with the Add Text button or use the Add Props button to bring in some of PhotoSuite's clip art.

5. Save your completed label by clicking Share and then clicking Save in the left pane.

6. Click Print on the navigation bar and choose Print Multiples in the left pane. Then choose CD-Label from the Generic category and select Fill Placeholder to have your text and art completely fill the circular template. Click Next.

7. Choose the options you want in the Print Preview menu and then click Print at the bottom of the left pane. Test your creation on plain paper before inserting the more costly CD label paper.

Note

If the label is not centered properly, the CD can be severely imbalanced, which can cause CD-ROM drive damage, especially in newer, higher-speed drives.

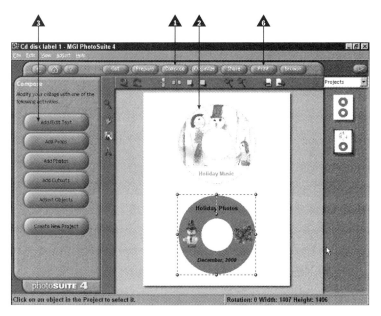

Figure 6-8. A customized CD label helps you find the disk you want and remember what is on it. An illustrated, colorful label can help to organize your CD collection and differentiate between discs containing music, photos, and other sorts of data.

Tip

Use PhotoSuite's CD Insert and CD Tray labels for your CD's jewel case. Just click Compose and in the left pane, click Create New Project⇨Business⇨ Stationery⇨Media.

Find It Online

You can find predesigned templates for some Avery labels, including CDs, at the Microsoft Office Template Gallery (www. officeupdate.com/ templategallery).

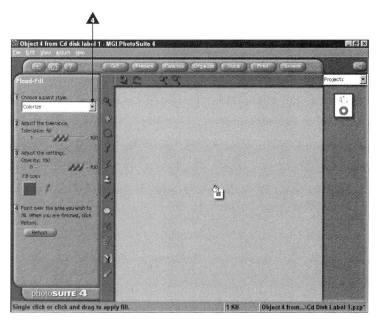

Figure 6-9. To change the background color of the disc label in PhotoSuite, you must switch to Prepare Photo mode and modify the template.

6

For the Whole Family

Family Trees

A family's collective memories often come quietly to rest in shoeboxes, tattered albums, and various other photo cemeteries. A family tree can bring memories to light, however, while giving family members something they can share — especially if the family tree is posted online. Such projects can become elaborate, however, and large software packages and innumerable Web sites are devoted to genealogy. The following PhotoSuite activity takes a more limited approach by focusing on making photo pages for your family trees:

1 With PhotoSuite open, click Compose. From the projects menu in the left pane, click Photo Layouts⇨Family Trees. A series of design layouts for your own family tree appears in the work area. Double-click a design, and your template now appears with gray openings called placeholders.

2 To use one of your digital pictures, first select a placeholder by double-clicking it. From the Add Photos menu in the left pane, choose a source for your digital image (Computer or Scanner, for example) and then retrieve your image.

3 If your photo covers the template when it appears, click the Move Back button on the toolbar once or twice to position the image correctly. Select the next placeholder and continue adding photos until you've added all your images to the project. When you are finished, click Next.

4 Adjust the position of each picture by clicking and dragging the picture as a whole. To adjust the size of an image, click a corner and drag in or out until you have the dimensions you want.

5 If you want to give your family tree a title or add names as captions to your photos, click Compose and then, in the left pane, click the Add/Edit Text button. Type your text in the Add/Edit text box on the left and click and drag the newly created text box where you want it on your family tree. Click Return when done.

To customize any existing text, first click the Add/Edit Text button and select the text box you want to change. In the left pane, edit the text. If you like, change the font type or color and adjust the size of your text box.

6 Click Share on the naviagation bar and save your project.

7 Click the Print button on the navigation bar and choose Print when you're ready to see your work on paper. Choose your options in the left pane and click the Print button at the bottom when you're done.

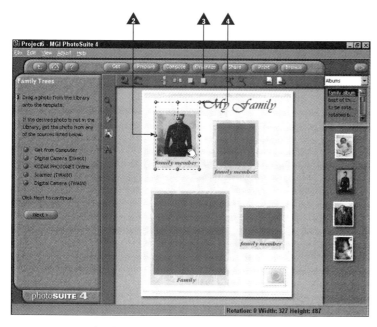

Figure 6-10. Your family tree is a blank slate: Add photos, descriptive text, and a title. Then print it and add it to an album.

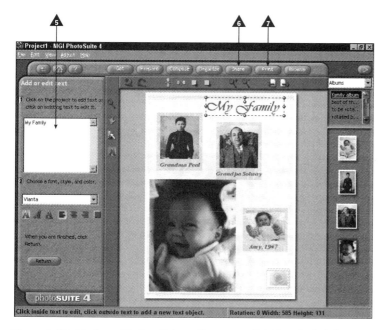

Figure 6-11. Fix the positioning of photos if necessary. Click Move Back if photos are positioned on top of the template, not behind it. Click and drag a photo to move it within its placeholder.

Tip

Before starting this project, select the photos you need and make sure they are digitized. Then organize them on your hard drive for easy access while you work on your family tree.

Find It Online

If you're writing histories and narratives, consider a full-featured genealogy program such as Family-Tree Maker (www.familytreemaker.com).

Cross-Reference

For more information about online resources, see *Your Official America Online Guide to Genealogy Online,* 2nd Edition, by April Leigh Helm and Matthew L. Helm (Hungry Minds, Inc.). You can buy the book at AOL Keyword: **AOL Shop Direct**.

6

For the Whole Family

Frames, Photo

Before printing and sharing your treasured digital pictures, take the time to give them a special background or frame. PhotoSuite offers plenty of stock digital frames but is also flexible enough to let you customize a frame, as in this activity:

1 In PhotoSuite, choose File⇨New⇨Photo from the menu bar.

2 In the New Photo dialog box that appears, click in the Portrait radio button if your photo is tall or Landscape if it is wide. Set the background color for your frame by choosing the shade you want from the Color palette. Click OK to begin editing your frame.

3 To add decorative elements to your frame, click the Photo Sprayer button on the vertical toolbar, which provides you with a cool way of spraying your frame (or any other image) with small pictures of objects such as clocks, steering wheels, or pastries. You can use any design from the Photo Sprayer drop-down list in the left pane or click the Create My Own option.

4 Play around with the Size, Spread, and Opacity settings on the Photo Sprayer menu in the left pane. Click Undo on the toolbar above the work area to remove your last actions one by one. Click Return in the left pane when you're done.

5 To make room on the frame for your actual photo, click Cutouts in the left pane, choose an appropriate selection tool, and then use the tool to cut out a space for your photo. (In Figure 6-12, I used the Ellipse tool.) When you're done, click Cut to Transparent in the left pane.

6 To insert the photo, click Compose and then, in the left pane, click Collage⇨Current Photo⇨Next. (The "photo" is actually the frame you just created; you are now going to use it as the basis of a project.)

7 The Compose screen reappears. To retrieve the photo you want to insert, click Get and, in the left pane, choose a source, such as Computer or Scanner. Adjust the photo's size and click the Move Back icon to send the photo behind the frame if necessary.

8 To save your project, click Share and, in the left pane, click Save.

9 To print a copy, click Print on the navigation bar, click Print (not Print Multiples), and choose the print options you want in the left pane. When you're ready to print, click the Print button at the bottom of the left pane.

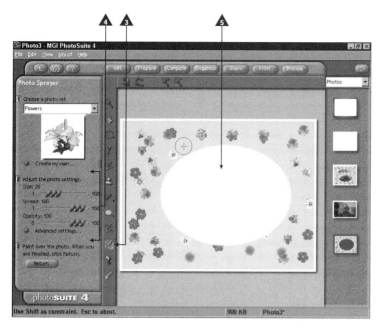

Figure 6-12. This frame is being created from scratch. You can modify the background color, clip art, placeholder, and photo.

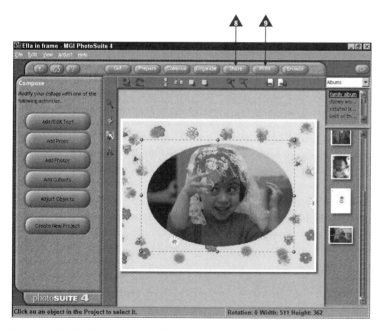

Figure 6-13. The frame and photo begin to take shape. With a little more positioning and perhaps a text label, this picture will be ready to print.

Cross-Reference

If you're comfortable with cutouts, create your own painting objects for the Photo Sprayer and save them as files. From the Photo Sprayer menu, click Create My Own⇨Computer to use your cutouts as paint drops. For more information on making a cutout, see the composites activity in Chapter 5.

Tip

If you want to send your digital pictures to a friend or relative who doesn't have a computer, you can use a "smart" digital picture frame. The unique technology downloads pictures over a telephone line and displays them on a classic looking photo frame. These clever but pricey gadgets are available at many photography stores or online from a vendor such as StoryBox (www. storybox.com).

6

For the Whole Family

Letterhead

If you are one of the few remaining people who still write personal letters on paper and send them in the mail, you now have the equipment to make custom stationery with your own designs, art, and text. You can print only as many sheets as you need and then change the design depending on your mood and recipient. Maybe you'll start something, and letter-writing will catch on again.

Original stationery can add impact to your letters. If you are writing to an aging parent or a kid at college, a picture of your house or garden can be a pleasant surprise to the recipient. And a business can't do without quality stationery for official and courtesy correspondence. In this activity, I use one of PhotoSuite's templates to create letterhead:

1 Click Compose and in the left pane, click Create New Project⇨Business⇨ Stationery⇨Letterhead. The thumbnail images show you your template options. Double-click a template you like.

2 To customize the existing text, first click the Add/Edit Text button and select the text box you want to change. In the left pane, edit the text and, if you like, change the font or color with the formatting options. To adjust the size of your text box or the font size, drag one of the corner handles in the work area.

3 To add a new text item, click the Add/Edit Text button, add a new text box by clicking an open space in the template, and then type your text in the field in the left pane.

4 The background images define the template, and you'll probably want to keep them in place. To add a photo to the template, click Add Photos and then click a source, such as Computer or Digital Camera. Find and double-click an image.

5 Add those final touches that set your letterhead apart. If the PhotoSuite template you've chosen seems too busy, just select an object and delete it by pressing Ctrl+X on your keyboard. If you want more or less of the pictures to come through, adjust the transparency of the background image. Select the background, click Adjust Objects, and drag the Opacity slider to the right and left.

6 Save your completed project by clicking Share and then, in the left pane, clicking Save.

7 Print as many copies as you like by clicking the Print button on the navigation bar and clicking Print. Then, in Print Preview menu on the left, type the number of copies you need. (If you like, you can also change the Print Size option to 4 x 6 in order to make matching note pads, as shown in Figure 6-15.) When you're ready to send your letterhead to the printer, click Print button at the bottom of the left pane.

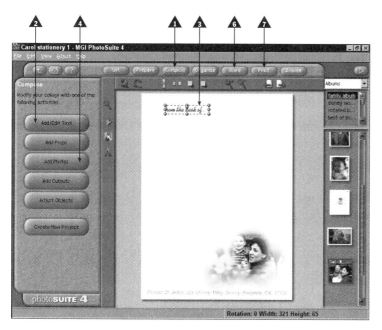

Figure 6-14. Personalized stationery is easy to make by modifying a predesigned template and adding your own information and graphics. This PhotoSuite template is simple yet professional looking and took no time to modify.

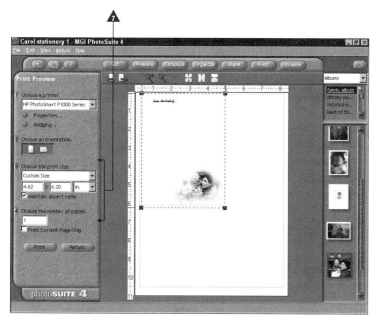

Figure 6-15. In Print Preview, turn your letterhead into note cards by printing them at a reduced size. Make sure the smaller size remains legible.

Tip

Print Shop offers a stationery set that includes matching letterhead, business cards, fax cover sheets, and envelopes.

Find It Online

For a wide selection of fanciful, ready-to-print stationery, visit AOL's Print Central. Choose Print⇨Print Central from the AOL 6.0 toolbar and then click the Projects tab. These designs are certain to get your creative writing juices flowing and create a lasting impression.

Note

Good-quality paper can make your stationery look and feel special. For colored designs like this one, make sure the paper color doesn't clash with the design. Matching envelopes complete the impression. You can find laser and inkjet paper in your local office supply store or on AOL.

6

For the Whole Family

Magnets, Refrigerator

Few people need to be sold on the concept of refrigerator magnets, those handy and usually not quite magnetic-enough items for holding snapshots, shopping lists, event notices, and children's artwork onto the refrigerator door. Making magnets might seem like a technical undertaking: How do you get your pictures onto magnets, you ask? Actually, the process is simple. For this activity, all you really need are a few digital pictures and the new-fangled printable magnetic sheets available at most office supply stores. To make magnets, you can use any program that can display and print digital pictures, but for quality and control of multiple images per sheet, a program like PhotoSuite is necessary.

 Create a new photo workspace in PhotoSuite by choosing File⇨New from the menu bar. In the New Photo dialog box, set the correct orientation: landscape or portrait, and choose dimensions appropriate to a refrigerator magnet — 2 x 3½ inches per side, for example, and up.

 Bring your digital picture into PhotoSuite. (Click Get and, in the left pane, click a source, such as Computer or Scanner.) You may need to resize the picture to fit the workspace by clicking and dragging a corner of the picture.

 Now you're ready to print. Click Print on the navigation bar, and then click Print or Print Multiples.

To make a single 8½ x 11 inch magnet, click Print. View your image in Print Preview, then click Print at the bottom. Cut out and trim the printed picture. Follow your printable magnet paper's instructions, and do a test print first using regular paper if only to make sure you print on the correct side of this expensive paper.

To make a whole sheet of identical magnets (for example, to use as gifts), click Print Multiples. Choose a layout such as Avery C2242 with placeholders that match the size and orientation of your intended magnets. Click Next, and then tell PhotoSuite whether to Fit within Placeholder (to retain image proportions, but leave white borders) or to Fill Placeholder (to fill a placeholder, but cut off some of the picture). Click Next to proceed to Print Preview, where you specify how many pictures to make and (finally) print the sheet. Cut out and trim each picture.

 Cut up the printable magnetic sheets to make your magnets. You can think of these trophies as ways of sharing a picture more than as ways of holding things on the refrigerator.

Attach the magnets to your refrigerator (or any other magnetic surface). Kids love to see themselves on these magnets, and grandparents appreciate the magnets, too.

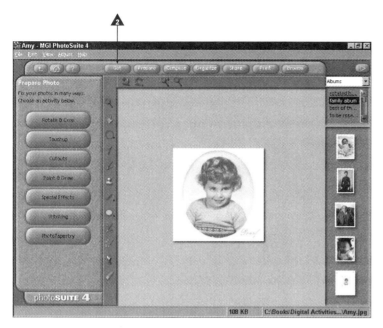

Figure 6-16. Create the image that goes on a magnet. The new box was set to 2 x 2 inches. This 50-year-old photo was cropped but not retouched.

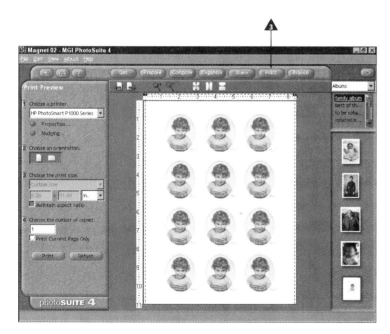

Figure 6-17. The Print Multiples option lets you print the same image over and over on a single sheet.

IBM's EZ Print site (www.ibmezprint.com) has online templates for magnetic business cards. Find out about IBM's line of papers here, too, including IBM Photo Quality Business Card Size Magnets.

Cut magnets in irregular shapes instead of doing complex cutouts. For example, cut out the shape of just the head (or the oval frame, in this activity).

You can find all sorts of designs to print on adhesive-backed magnetic sheets. Just choose Print⇨Print Central from the AOL 6.0 toolbar.

6

For the Whole Family

Mousepads

Why let company-designed mousepads take up desk space when you can make your own customized mousepads? Creating a personalized mousepad for yourself or for family is fun; creating one for your customers, depending on your business, can make a strong impression. For this activity, you need good-resolution pictures, plain white mousepads (available in products such as Invent-It's Mousepad kit), a household iron, and iron-on transfer paper. You can use any graphics software, but the following steps are based on PhotoSuite:

1 Click the Get button, choose the source for your picture (your computer, usually), and then select the digital picture you want to include on your mousepad. Your digital picture appears in the work area, and PhotoSuite switches to Prepare Photo mode.

2 You can print your picture onto a mousepad as-is, but if you do, make sure to enhance it first by clicking Touchup⇨Enhance⇨Return in the left pane.

3 Figure 6-18 uses the Painterly special effects filter (click Prepare, and, in the left pane, click Special Effects⇨Effects⇨Artistic⇨Painterly).

4 Iron-on transfers require that all text and images be printed in reverse. Why? When the transfer is ironed onto the mousepad, the image appears backwards. Thus, you need to start by reversing your original image. To do this, click the Flip Horizontally icon at the top of the work area in Compose mode.

5 Print your image on plain paper as a test. Click Print on the navigation bar, and choose the options you want from the Print Preview menu. Under Orientation, you will probably want to make your image landscape (wide), not portrait (tall). Adjust the dimensions of your picture so that they match the size of your mousepad. Under Choose the Print Size, choose Custom Size and type in the dimensions. Do a test print on normal paper. Make a mark on the paper before printing so you know whether to place the transfer paper face up or face down in your printer. Print again, using a sheet of transfer paper.

Preheat your iron.

6 After the image on your transfer paper dries completely, position the mousepad on top of the transferred image, and trace it lightly in pencil. Use scissors to trim off what won't fit on the mouse pad. Now position the picture side of the transfer against the fabric side of the mouse pad.

7 Follow your transfer paper's ironing instructions closely. Move the iron firmly and continuously in wide circles on top of the transfer paper. Let the paper cool completely before peeling off the paper. Figure 6-19 shows the completed mousepad.

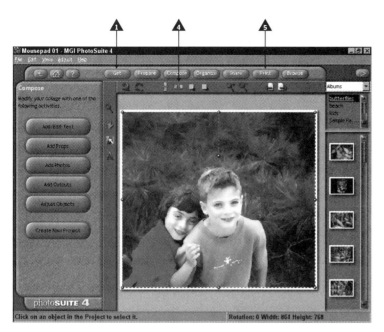

Figure 6-18. This mousepad image is based on a megapixel-plus image taken in sand dunes. It needs to be reversed before it's ready for printing. I added a special effects filter (Painting) in Prepare Photo mode.

Figure 6-19. The finished product.

Caution

AOL Print Central warns: "Caution: Do not use iron-on transfer sheets in a laser printer or any printer that heats the paper. These printers might melt the transfer paper, which could damage the printer."

Find It Online

This Dutch Web site claims to be the "first virtual mousepad museum." It features European organizations and the designs they use on their mousepads. Find some inspiration by visiting the museum at www.expa.hvu.nl/ajvdhek/.

Tip

If you want wrapped, guaranteed, gift-quality mousepads, visit the "You've Got Pictures" store and buy a mousepad there.

6

For the Whole Family

Newsletters, Online

Many families have gotten into the habit of putting together annual newsletters to mail to friends and families at the end of the year. Word processors and programs like Print Shop have simplified the process, so you can focus on what you have to say. Why wait for the holidays, however, when you can use a newsletter to announce big events like a marriage or birth? And why use paper when you can reach your Net-savvy friends year round with a Web newsletter? Putting your newsletter online is easier than it sounds — so easy, in fact, that you may find yourself putting out more editions than you expected.

The following activity uses AOL's Easy Designer to create a Web newsletter announcing a birth, but you can adapt this activity to any event:

1 Go to the Easy Designer main screen (AOL Keyword: **Easy Designer**) and click the Create a New Page link to begin. When the program has loaded, click the big Click to Get Started button. The Select a Template dialog box appears.

2 In the Select a Template dialog box, select the template category and topic that most closely match your needs. Click Next.

3 Select a starting layout by double-clicking the thumbnail image that most closely resembles the number and size of the photos you want to use.

4 Choose a color scheme for your Web page and click OK. In a few moments, you see an AOL Web-page template in the selected color scheme, layout, and theme.

5 To add a picture, click one of the existing photos to select it and then click the Modify button on the toolbar. The Easy Designer Picture Gallery appears.

6 Click Upload Picture and then click the Browse button in the Upload Picture window to navigate to the folder on your hard drive containing the picture you want. Select the picture and then click the Upload Picture button.

7 Back in My Pictures Gallery, make sure a check is in the Resize Picture To Fit Object check box, to prevent higher-resolution images from filling up your entire Web page.

8 Click OK to bring the new picture into your newsletter. Repeat Steps 5, 6, and 7 for other pictures.

9 Back in your template, resize photos so that they fit and look good.

10 The template text must also be replaced. Double-click a text placeholder, and in the text-editing box, replace it with your own words. Click OK when you're done.

11 Click Preview to review your page. Then click Save to store it on AOL Hometown. After the file is saved, your page's Web address (or URL) appears on a special page, and you receive the URL in an e-mail that you can forward.

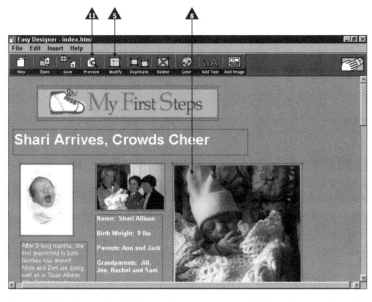

Figure 6-20. A customized Web newsletter announcing the birth of a bouncing baby girl, complete with birth information and photos of the new arrival and her family.

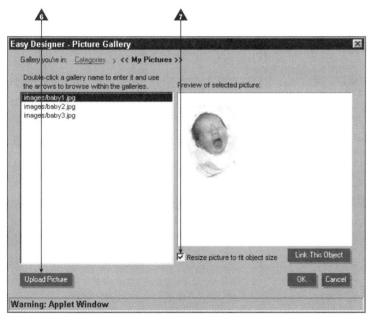

Figure 6-21. Easy Designer Picture Gallery makes selecting clip art or photos from your computer easy. Clicking Category in the upper left gives you access to a large collection of free clip art.

Cross-Reference

See Chapter 3 for complete Easy Designer instructions.

Tip

To simplify things, create an e-mail group with the e-mail addresses of everyone who is to receive your newsletter. Just choose Mail⇨Address Book from the AOL toolbar and click New Group. Give your collection of addresses a name so that in the future you can inform everyone when you make changes to your newsletter. Include a link in your message so that recipients can click directly to your newsletter. (Don't know how to add a link? Click Help in the lower right-hand corner of the Write Mail window.)

Find It Online

For more about making your own page, check out personalweb.about. com.

6

For the Whole Family

Photo Goofs: Removing Red Eye

Pictures can come out imperfectly for about a hundred reasons, and on many of these occasions graphics software offers handy tools that can help you rescue pictures from the trash. The next few activities look at common problems and how to address them with PhotoSuite: red eye, color imbalance, dust marks, and stray objects that distract from the overall composition.

The dreaded red eye — the red circles at the center of the eye in color pictures — occurs because most cameras today have a built-in flash that is very close to the lens. So close, in fact, that the light from the flash travels through the iris of your subject's eye and lights the blood vessels in the back of the retina. This shows up as a red spot on the eye where you would normally want a white highlight. Dogs and cats can suffer from red eye as well. The problem is most noticeable on older compacts and is being eliminated in newer compacts as well as single-lens reflex (35mm) cameras.

Most editing software offers a tool for removing red eye with the click of the mouse. These tools work by desaturating the red in the eyes — making the red in the eyes less intensely colored. Here's how to remove red eye in PhotoSuite:

1 Open the digital picture showing red eye. Click Get and, in the left pane, click the source for the image — Computer or Scanner, for example. Then select the digital picture you want.

2 In the left pane, click Touchup⇨Remove Red Eye. The Remove Red Eye menu appears, and a Touchup brush that you can move with your mouse appears in the work area.

3 Zoom in on the photo by repeatedly clicking the magnifying glass with the plus (+) sign. Zoom out to see the picture as a whole by clicking the magnifying glass with a minus sign.

4 Adjust the size of the Touchup brush by moving the Brush Size slider back and forth. The more you zoom in, the greater the brush size; you want to make the Touchup brush about as big as the red color in the subject's eyes, as shown in Figure 6-22.

5 Click until the red is gone, and then click Return.

6 Save your improved photo by clicking Share on the navigation bar and then Save. If you like, you can make other improvements to your photo as part of your editing session.

Figure 6-22. Removing red eye requires you to zoom in. In the Remove Red Eye menu, size the Touchup brush so that it matches the diameter of the red blob in the subject's eye and then click once or twice to remove the color.

Photo Goofs: Improving Contrast and Colors

All kinds of things can go wrong with a color photograph: dull colors, unwanted tint, low contrast, and either overexposure (too much white) or underexposure (too much dark). PhotoSuite has filters for handling these and similar situations, each with its own controls for specifying the exact effect you want. Often, you will want to use more than one of them. Here are the important filters to know about:

▲ **Fix Colors.** This filter modifies a picture's overall color pattern and lets you alter the major aspects of color: hue, saturation, and value. The Hue slider adjusts the overall colors mix, from purplish through greenish. Saturation adjusts the amount of color, from gray to garish. Value adjusts the amount of gray in a picture.

▲ **Brightness and Contrast.** Dragging the Brightness slider to the left causes your picture to look darker; to the right, brighter. Adjusting contrast is a good way to bring out a full black-to-white range in your picture, but too much contrast can render any picture harsh.

▲ **Gamma Adjustment.** The gamma slider brings out mid-tones; it can brighten or darken a picture without making it look too bright or too dark. Gamma is a good alternative to the Brightness slider on the Brightness and Contrast filter.

▲ **Color Adjustment.** This filter lets you adjust the amounts and combinations of the three basic colors that make up on-screen images: red, green, and blue. Because you are adjusting only one color at a time, you need to give your eye time to adjust to the changes; experts suggest adjusting colors in small increments. For some effects, you need to adjust all three colors to achieve an effect.

The following steps explain how you can use the filters:

 Open your picture by clicking Get and selecting your picture.

 From the Prepare Photos menu, click Touchup⇨Touchup Filters.

- If you have dull overall coloring, use the Fix Colors filter.

- If your photo has an annoying colored tint, choose the Color Adjustment filter. In general, for a green, red, or blue tint, reduce the amount of that color and increase the other two colors by about half as much. For garish tints, it can be helpful to first lower the overall saturation (Fix Colors). A small change in saturation goes a long way.

- If your photo is underexposed or overexposed, choose the Brightness and Contrast filter from the drop-down list. For underexposed pictures, lighten up the image with the Brightness slider and raise the contrast with the Contrast slider. For overexposed (too white) photos, you can darken them.

- When a photo is too blurry, there's not much you can do, but the Contrast slider (Brightness and Contrast filter) or the Sharpen filter may help.

 When you are satisfied with the way your photo looks, click Apply in the left pane to keep your changes and then click Return. Your changes are not preserved until you save the file. Save it with a new name to keep a copy of the original.

Figure 6-23. The original, out-of-focus picture on the top had low contrast and washed-out color. Some improvement was possible (bottom) with the Enhance filter. Then I applied the Sharpen filter and increased both contrast (Brightness and Contrast filter) and saturation (Fix Colors filter). In addition, I cropped the picture to remove the bland sea and improve the composition.

 **Definition**

Here are three terms to know when adjusting colors. *Hue* defines which color, and *saturation* defines how much of that color; desaturating an image turns it into a grayscale image, without any color at all. *Value* affects how white or black a grayscale image is.

Caution

Save a picture with a new name before adjusting or removing a picture's colors. It is difficult at best to restore original color data.

 **Tip**

Riptide lets you make changes to an image's overall brightness, hue, contrast, and saturation. To monitor your changes, you can view your original and the edited version side by side. The software, part of the AOL GraphicSuite 2.0 CD, can be found at AOL Keyword: **AOL Store**, under Interactive Learning (click AOL Learning).

6

For the Whole Family

Photo Goofs: Removing White Dust Marks

Dust from a scanner's surface or an old negative detracts from the quality of digital pictures. In PhotoSuite, you use the Cloning tool to remove such dots. This tool works by applying the color of a neighboring, properly colored pixel to the missing or marred pixel. You can also use the Remove Blemishes tool, which is easier to use but less precise.

To use the Cloning tool, follow these steps:

1 With PhotoSuite open, click Get, choose a source for your digital picture (Computer or Scanner, for example), and then select the digital picture you want to edit.

2 Click Touchup⇨Clone. The Clone menu appears in the left pane.

3 Click the magnifying glass with a plus (+) sign to zoom in on the dust marks in your image.

Cloning requires that you first define the exact location of the pixel from which color will be copied (called the origin.) Then, you define the exact location of the pixel to which you'll apply the color. To set the origin, start by looking at colors surrounding your dust mark. You usually want an origin that's close to the problem pixel, so that they share colors and blend naturally.

4 To clone away the dust, first click the Reset Origin button in the Clone menu and then click the part of your picture that contains the color you want to apply to the dust-pixel. The part you click now appears like the letter x. To apply the origin's color, click the part of the picture you want to fix. If you want the coloring to be as precise as possible, reset the origin frequently while you replace the dust marks with neighboring pixels.

5 If you like, use the slider in the Clone menu to adjust the size of the Cloning brush. I recommend a low setting (2 or 3 for most dust-busting). The Clone menu also allows you to alter the brush's opacity — how heavily you lay one color onto the other. If you choose 100 percent opacity, you completely cover the dust; with a lower opacity, the coverage is less complete but the effect of an imperfectly matched pixel is less jarring. Just move the Opacity slider to the right or left with your mouse to alter the setting.

6 Click Return when you're done, and save the picture when you are sure you want to keep your changes.

PhotoSuite's Remove Blemishes feature removes dust as well as many other irregularities that may mar a picture. Using this tool is easier than using the Cloning tool, because you don't have to set an origin or worry about precision. The downside, however, is that Remove Blemishes can be a little sloppy, reducing the amount of information in your picture. In effect, Remove Blemishes provides you with a brush you can use to cover over a speck or irregularity with colors borrowed from the surrounding area. To use it, click Touchup⇨Remove Blemishes.

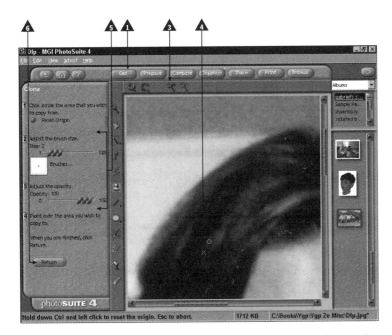

Figure 6-24. This image has lots of dust marks because the scanner surface was dusty. When cloning pictures that vary in color greatly, set the origin close to the dust mark and repeatedly reset the origin as you fix different parts of a photo.

Definition

A pixel is the little colored box from which pictures are made. Every pixel has one color. To see pixels, display a picture and click Zoom In several times.

Tip

Cleaning your scanner is easier than removing one speck of dust at a time from a digital picture. When scanning prints or film, take time to remove all smudges and dust. Use glass cleaner and dust-free paper cloths. Look obliquely at the glass with the scanner light on so you can see all the dust particles. Then use either an antistatic cloth or an antistatic brush (or both) to carefully clean the surface.

Tip

Use the Cloning tool to remove unwanted parts of a picture (such as a garbage can next to a cherry tree) or extend wanted parts (such as a cloud).

Photo Goofs: Improving Composition by Cropping

Cropping means to remove edges of a picture to form, in effect, a new picture that consists of part of the original image. Cropping thus allows you to improve a composition in two ways. You can *remove* the extraneous objects that distract from your subject. Cropping also lets you *improve* the composition of the subject itself. In other words, you can use cropping to enhance composition even if you are not trying to remove anything. Cropping gives you the chance to think about how a picture is framed and how the eye travels within or through the picture. The following steps explain how to crop with AOL's Picture Finder:

1. Open AOL 6.0, and choose File⇨Open Picture Finder from the menu bar. In the Open Picture Gallery dialog box that appears, navigate to the folder that includes the picture to be cropped. Double-click the folder and then click the Open Gallery button. The Picture Gallery appears, displaying thumbnail versions of all the digital images in the folder.

2. In the Picture Gallery, click the thumbnail image of the picture you want to crop. That picture now comes up in the editing window (the window's title bar has the file's name).

3. Click the Zoom In/Out button to see more or less of your picture. The editing window changes size to accommodate the changed picture size.

4. Click the Select and Crop Picture button on the editing window toolbar.

5. To crop, click in one corner of the area to be cropped, drag to the opposite corner of the area you want cropped, and then release the mouse button. If you don't like the area you've defined, click Revert, confirm your intention to revert, and crop again.

6. When you have traced an area you like, click the button showing a pair of scissors (temporarily replacing the button you clicked in Step 4). Clicking the scissors cuts out the rectangular area you defined.

7. If you like the new picture, click the Save button and save it with a new name so that you have a copy of your original. Otherwise, click Revert to start again, or quit.

Figure 6-25. This picture is being cropped to remove the billboard (left) and car (right). The drab sky depresses the entire picture, too. Note the filename in the title bar: It is a random number assigned by "You've Got Pictures."

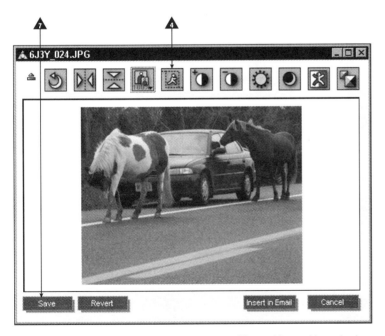

Figure 6-26. The resulting picture is better composed but could use additional enhancement and bumped-up contrast. You can replace the filename with something more meaningful now that the image is worth keeping.

6

For the Whole Family

Postcards

People buy postcards for all sorts of reasons — to remember a place, to share an experience, to acquire a premium version of one's own snapshots, or to get change for the bus. The new digital tools at your disposal give you the chance to make your own postcards. That way, you can personalize your cards and show off your pictures — things the postcard people will never do.

For this activity, you need a digital picture, of course, and postcard inkjet paper, such as Avery 8389. Graphics software is recommended because you use specialty paper. Here, I use PhotoSuite:

1 Click Compose and, in the left pane, click select Create New Project⇨Cards & Tags⇨Postcards. From the drop-down list, select a category such as Travel or Miscellaneous. The Miscellaneous category includes a blank template, so your picture fills the entire card. Double-click a card. For this example I chose a travel template (007).

2 In Compose mode, click Add Photos in the left pane to bring in a digital picture.

3 From the Compose menu, you can use the Add/Edit Text, Add Props, and Add Photos buttons to add new elements. Figure 6-27 shows a text box being added with the photo's date.

4 Click Share on the navigation bar and then click Save in the left pane to save your card.

5 Click Print and, in the left pane, click Print Multiples, because postcard paper comes in sheets of two cards per page. You can send postcards with the same image to many people. That's the idea, of course — a picture everyone can enjoy on one side, and a handwritten message on the other.

6 In the left pane, choose Avery Letter from the Category drop-down menu. A number of different Avery Letter templates appear in the work area. Select the Avery 8389 template, used for creating 4 x 6 glossy postcards. Make sure to select the Fill Placeholder option in the Print Multiples menu to make the image fill the postcard, but remember that this option can crop out part of your picture.

7 Click Next when your postcard matches the template and the image is just right. Choose the number of pages to print, confirm the other settings, and click Print at the bottom of the left pane.

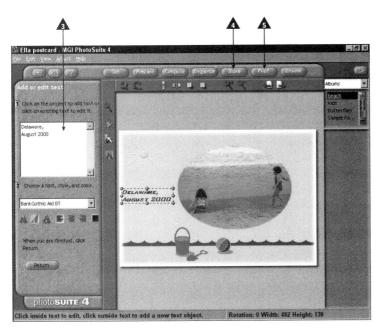

Figure 6-27. Add text to attach something personal or descriptive to the picture.

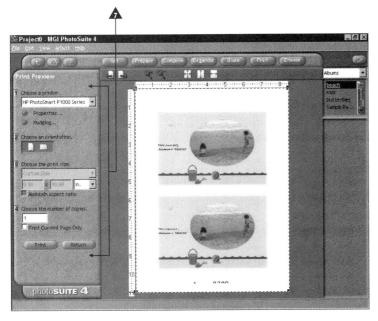

Figure 6-28. This figure shows the placeholders replaced with an image — the postcard. Make sure to select Fill Placeholder in the previous step, which means that your postcard will nicely fit the placeholder, as in this figure.

6

For the Whole Family

Posters

Posters do a lot more than add life to a drab wall. As gifts, they seem special because of their size. They're also a good way of showing off your best (and sharpest) photos. And they can commemorate homecomings, birthdays, and other special events.

Most graphics programs offer poster features. PhotoSuite offers strong designs that print well across several sheets of paper. Just follow these steps:

1 In PhotoSuite, click Compose and then click Photo Layouts⇨Posters in the left pane.

2 From the drop-down list, select a category (the current choices are Funky, Event, or Elegant). Then, double-click a template such as Mt. Rushmore, shown in Figure 6-29. The template appears in the work area.

3 Get rid of unwanted elements (such as the shooting star effect in the Mt. Rushmore template) by using any of PhotoSuite's selection tools.

4 To add photos, text, or clip art, click Compose; click the Add Photos, Add/Edit Text or Add Props button; and then follow the instructions in the left pane. (For more on adding photos, text, and clip art, see the bookmarks activity in Chapter 5.)

5 Many of PhotoSuite's poster templates have an *image placeholder,* a gray area where you can insert your own digital picture. To use a placeholder, click the Add Photos button, retrieve an image, and drag it onto the placeholder.

6 Save your work by clicking Share and then clicking Save in the left pane.

7 To print a poster, Click Print on the navigation bar and then click Print (not Print Multiples). In the Print Preview menu that appears, click Properties and choose the Poster setting on your printer so that the printer can print your single file over several pieces of paper. Click Print at the bottom of the Print Preview menu when you're ready to go.

8 After your pages print, line them up to create your poster, trim any white borders you may have, and then securely tape your pages together.

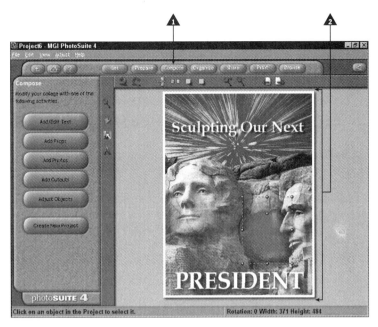

Figure 6-29. This poster template is available in the Funky category. PhotoSuite stands out for the quality of its designs and its avoidance of overly cute themes and styles.

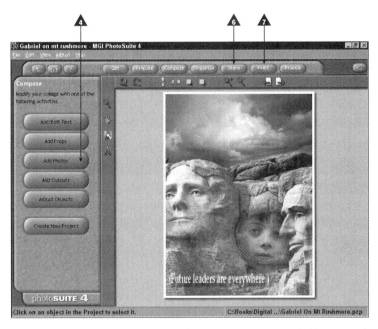

Figure 6-30. In the template, I select and cut out a transparency to hold a stormy sky. A child's photograph replaced the existing transparent placeholder. The text has been moved, changed, and visually deemphasized as well.

Additional PhotoSuite posters are available in Compose mode by clicking Create New Project⇨ Collections⇨AJ Gray Posters. These posters were designed for printing as they are.

Not all printers support poster printing. Consult your printer's manual.

You can use cutout tools to create *transparencies*, which let another picture placed in the background (click Move Back) show through the transparent opening, as in the case of the child and the clouds. To make a transparency, use the Edge Finder or other selection tool to define the area and then click Cut to Transparent. If the selection is imperfect, use the Effects Brush's transparency effect (from drop-down list) to clean up the transparent opening. In this case, the brush made room for the clouds.

6

For the Whole Family

Recipes

Always searching for something to make for dinner? Consider using the computer to both find new recipes and manage your favorite old ones. Rather than use an expensive database program to keep track of your recipes, you can try a lower-cost alternative. Recipe Center Software 2000 is a great recipe database program that you can try for free and then purchase for a nominal charge to continue using it.

The following activity shows how to add a new recipe to Recipe Center Software 2000, which you can download from the Recipe Center Web site (www.recipecenter.com).

1. Go to www.recipecenter.com/software.htm to download and install the Recipe Center software and then start the software by double-clicking the Recipe Center icon that appears on your desktop.

2. From the Recipe Center toolbar, click the Add a New Recipe icon. The New Recipe window opens. Notice the tabs along the top labeled Information, Ingredients, Procedure, Picture, and Nutrition Facts. Clicking any of the tabs opens a set of fields where you can enter information for each recipe.

3. Click the Information tab. Complete the fields for your recipe. Choose keywords for your recipe — important for the software's database function — from the list or type your own keywords in the box to the left of the Add Keyword button. For each keyword you choose or add, click the Add Keyword button.

4. Click the Ingredients tab. Type in the quantity, units, and description of each ingredient in your recipe.

5. Click the Procedure tab. Type the step-by-step instructions for preparing the recipe.

6. If you happen to have a picture of the dish, then use Windows Explorer to first copy the picture into the C:\Program Files\RecipeCenter\Photos folder. Then click the Picture tab and use the Browse button to select your photo file.

7. Click the Nutrition Facts tab if you happen to have this information available.

8. When finished, click the Save & Exit button at the bottom of the dialog box.

9. Your recipe appears on the left in the List of Recipes. Click the recipe to display it on the right side of the screen.

10. Print your recipe by clicking the Print button on the toolbar. To change the way the recipe prints, choose Recipes⇨Options and use the options on the Print tab.

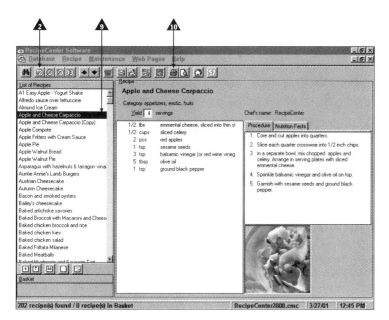

Figure 6-31. After you add your recipe information to the database, it appears in a neat, consistent format and can be used to generate shopping lists. All this data enables you to search for recipes with specific ingredients or characteristics.

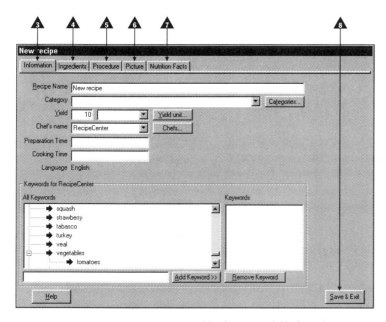

Figure 6-32. A recipe management system like the one available from the Recipe Center helps you organize and illustrate your favorite recipes.

Find It Online

Want recipes? Choose AOL Services⇨Recipe Finder from the toolbar to visit AOL's Food & Recipes center. Look for recipes by course, type of cuisine, special diet, and name of dish. Use My Recipe to contribute to the online collection.

Find It Online

If you are happy with your trusty recipe box and just want a way to make your recipes neat and readable, try the recipe card templates available in the Home and Hobby section of AOL's Print Central. You print the attractive forms and fill them in by hand. This form is ideal for ordinary sharing and less impersonal than a printout.

Tip

If you don't need the raw power of a commercial database such as Access or Filemaker, check out Instabase, which lets you keep your recipes, show pictures of them, and easily search them. Unlike a special-purpose program like Recipe Center, you can use Instabase for other purposes, such as maintaining a property inventory for insurance purposes. The software, part of the AOL GraphicSuite 2.0 CD, can be found at AOL Keyword: **AOL Store**, under Interactive Learning (click AOL Learning).

6

For the Whole Family

Return Address Labels

If you grow tired of scrawling your name and address over and over again on bills and letters, make yourself some stylish return address labels to keep on hand. You can make them plain or fancy, or make different kinds to suit your various mailing needs (for personal letters, clients, and bills, for example).

This activity shows how to use Avery.com's free online service to create a simple return address label with a graphic. Before doing this activity, you will want to have return address labels for your inkjet or laser printer.

1 From the Avery.com home page (`www.avery.com`), click the Print tab and on the next page, click Start Now. You see a list of Avery products that you can create online and then print on your inkjet.

2 When prompted to select a category, click Return Address Labels. From the list that follows, select the kind of label you want (laser or inkjet, and the number of labels). In a moment, you see a choice of label designs. You can choose different text alignment (right, center, left) and whether to include a graphic. Click the design most appropriate for your needs.

3 Type a name in the Name field and choose a font type and font color from the drop-down lists.

4 To include the address for the name provided in Step 3, scroll down a bit. Under Select Another Field To Change, click Address and then type your address in the Address box that appears. If you want to add an image, scroll down a bit again and click the Select an Image radio button. If you're not adding an image, skip to Step 6.

5 If you clicked the Select an Image radio button, the Select an Image screen appears, where you can either select a graphic from Avery's clip art or import your own image from your hard drive.

6 Click Finished when you're all done, which takes you to the final screen.

7 Click Preview and Print. In a moment, you see your mailing labels displayed as an Acrobat PDF file.

8 You can send your labels directly to your printer by clicking the Print icon on the Acrobat Reader toolbar. When printing, be sure to use the Avery label sheets for the kind of label you specified in Step 2.

9 You can save your mailing labels on your computer for future printing from Acrobat Reader by clicking the Save icon on the Acrobat Reader toolbar. You can't edit saved labels offline, however.

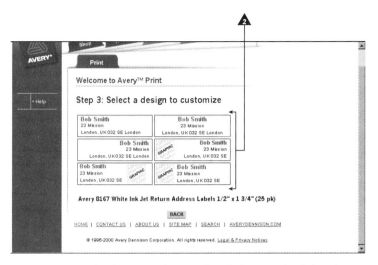

Figure 6-33. Note that the Avery Web projects have built-in wizards, which guide you one step at a time toward creating your own labels. In this figure, Step 3 of the wizard lets you select a *type* of label.

Figure 6-34. Add a graphic to your labels.

Use colorful labels to organize, decorate, or differentiate objects other than letters. You can find a variety of label templates at AOL's Print Central for kitchen storage and other purposes.

For related activities, see the sticker project in Chapter 5 and "CD Labels" in this chapter.

Use only labels that are suited for your printer type. Discard labels that are partially used, bent, folded, or peeling, because they can get stuck in your printer.

6

For the Whole Family

Scrapbook Pages

A *scrapbook* contains many of the same elements as a family tree, but it aims to tell a fuller story of the featured people and situations. Often created as gifts for parents or grandparents, scrapbooks bring together everything about the subject, including newspaper clippings, letters, marriage papers, transcribed interviews and stories, and, of course, lots of photos.

Graphics software and digital pictures can provide key scrapbook elements. In this activity you make photo pages. Other scrapbook pages can contain clippings, letters, and other documents. Before starting this project, make sure to have your pictures available in digital form; when you're ready to print, you may want to use photo paper for inkjets.

1 In PhotoSuite, click Compose. From the Projects menu in the left pane, click Photo Layouts⇨Scrapbooks.

2 A number of scrapbook templates appear in the work area. Double-click the one that corresponds to the number of pictures you want to display on a page and the amount of text you want to include on the page. The Scrapbooks menu appears in the left pane.

3 To add your pictures, first select the placeholder (gray rectangle) to which you want to add a picture. From the menu, click Add Photos to identify the source of the picture to go in the placeholder. Usually your photos are on your computer's hard drive; find and double-click a picture. Repeat for as many pictures as you want to add.

4 Change the size of your pictures as needed by clicking a corner of the image and dragging in or out. To move a picture relative to its opening, click and drag any part of the picture except the dotted border to move it to a new position.

5 Click the Add/Edit Text button on the Compose menu to add captions that identify the people in each picture or provide other information, such as the name, date, or location. For more on adding text, see the bookmarks activity in Chapter 5.

6 Save your scrapbook project by clicking Share and then Save. Be sure to replace the default filename (Project01.pzp) with something more memorable.

7 Print the pages on good inkjet paper by first clicking the Print button on the navigation bar, then Print (not Print Multiples), and then choosing the options you want in the left pane. When you're finally ready to print, click the Print button at the bottom of the left pane.

8 Gather your scrapbook pages in a folder or three-ring binder. Most of the work on this activity is offline.

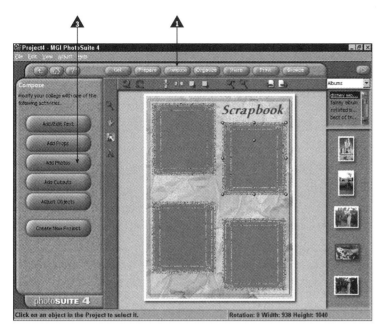

Figure 6-35. After a picture has been placed in a template placeholder, it is simple to resize it and move it around.

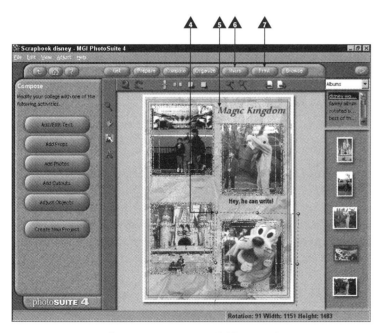

Figure 6-36. Pictures from a trip to Disney World fill the template.

Find It Online

You can explore every aspect of scrapbooking at online destinations like the following: Scrapbooking (AOL Keyword: **Scrapbooking**), the Crafts & Home Decor area of Moms Online (AOL Keyword: **Moms Online**), Graceful Bee (www.gracefulbee.com), and Hot Off the Press (www.craftpizazz.com).

Tip

Use acid-free paper and acid-free adhesive on your scrapbook pages. Pens should be acid free, waterproof, and archival quality (ask at a photography or stationery store).

Note

Several graphics programs are devoted to scrapbooks, for example American Greetings Scrapbooks & More, DogByte's Creative Photo Albums, and Ulead's PhotoExpress: My Scrapbook. All three can be found at Shop@AOL (AOL Keyword: **Shopping**).

6

For the Whole Family

To-Do Lists for Children

Making a to-do list for a child is a great idea and requires little more than a word processor and a few digital pictures. Before starting, collect digital pictures representing various tasks, and you might want a picture of the child for whom the list is being made.

1 In Word, click the New button on the toolbar to start a new document.

2 To place a child's image in your new document, first position your cursor in the document where you want the image to appear and then choose Insert⇨Picture⇨From File from the menu bar. The Insert Picture dialog box appears.

3 Use the Insert Picture dialog box to navigate to the folder containing the graphics file you want. Double-click the file to insert it in your document.

4 Resize your picture by clicking and dragging any of the four corner handles.

5 On the toolbar, choose a large font size (at least 36 points) from the Font Size drop-down menu and a decorative font from the Font menu. Then, type a title for your to-do list.

6 Hold down the Shift key, click the picture and title, and then click the Center button on the Word toolbar to center both these elements neatly at the top of the page. Press Enter a couple of times to insert a few spaces after the title.

7 Choose Table⇨Insert Table from the menu bar, and the Insert Table dialog box appears. For a weekly list, type **9** in the Number of Columns box (seven columns for the days of the week, one column for a heading, and one column for a digital image). Add a row for each task or responsibility plus one extra, for the row of column headings. You can always add and remove rows. Click OK to place the table in your document.

8 Place your cursor in row 1, column 3. Set your font size to 14 or 16, and type **Mon**. Tab to move to the next column and type **Tues**. Continue for all days of the week.

9 Position your cursor in column 1, row 2, and type the first task on the list. Tab to the second column in this row and insert an illustration of the item by choosing Insert⇨Picture⇨From File. Resize the picture by dragging any of the corner handles until it fits nicely in the table. Repeat for each task.

10 Click Save on the toolbar to save the file and give it a name.

11 Click Print on the toolbar to print the file; plain paper is fine but colored paper is more fun. Kids can put a check or sticker in the box as they complete their chores.

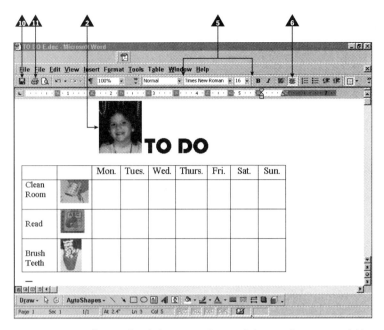

Figure 6-37. An illustrated to-do list is a good way to help even the youngest children start watching out for themselves. This list, created in Word, uses a table and a few digital pictures.

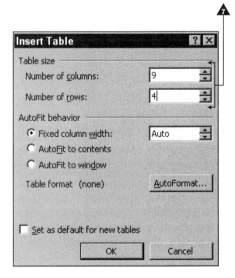

Figure 6-38. Use the table feature in Word to make a neat-looking to-do list. Kids will be proud to take part in making it.

Definition

A *table* is a grid consisting of *columns,* which go up and down, and *rows,* which go right and left. A *cell* is the box where a row intersects a column.

Find It Online

For preprinted to-do lists for adults, which you can fill in by hand, visit AOL Print Central's Home & Hobby section. In the For the Kitchen area, you can find to-do lists.

Tip

PhotoSuite has weekly school schedules and homework charts for middle- and high-school students. Just click Compose and, in the left pane, click Business⇨Stationery. The schedules are in the Education category.

Tip

Kids can use stickers or marker stamps to check off completed activities on their to-do lists.

Wallpapers, Desktop

In the world of computers, *wallpaper* is a picture or image that you display on your *desktop,* the place where you see program icons. The purpose is, well, decorative, just like the wallpaper you put on the walls of your house. You can use one of the wallpaper patterns that comes with Windows or make your own with digital pictures. With PhotoSuite, you can combine several images into one file and use it as your desktop wallpaper. Here's how; you will want to use your own photos and other elements.

1 Click Compose and, in the left pane, click Collages⇨Blank Canvas⇨Landscape.

2 Click the Add Photos button to retrieve an image from your hard drive or other source and repeat for each photo you want to use. Arrange the photos on the work area until it's covered entirely. Change the size of individual photos if necessary.

3 In Figure 6-39, I arranged eight images around the edge of the work area and then placed one slightly larger image in the center. To place this image on top, select it and click the Move Forward button, above the work area.

4 For a special effect, you can select a photo, click the Adjust Objects button on the Compose menu, and use the Edge Fading slider to blend the edges of a photo into neighboring ones. In Figure 6-39, the center photo's setting is 45.

5 Click the Share button and save your project. To set the image as your Windows desktop wallpaper, click the Share button and select Windows Desktop⇨Set Photo as Wallpaper. The Windows Display Properties dialog box opens for you to adjust the display options and click OK. (These instructions are for Windows 98 and higher).

To use a single photo as your wallpaper, simply follow these steps in Windows:

i. From the desktop, choose Start⇨Settings ⇨Control Panel. In the Control Panel window, double-click Display to open the Display Properties dialog box.

ii. Open the Background tab and click Browse. Select a BMP (bitmap), GIF, or JPEG file from your computer and then click Open. You see a small version of your picture in the middle of the box.

iii. Choose one of the three options available in the Display drop-down box. *Center* places the image in the middle of the desktop at its original size. *Tile* repeats your picture across and down your desktop. *Stretch* fills the desktop with your image by scaling it up or down, depending upon its original size. Stretching distorts the image if its proportions aren't the same as the display.

iv. When you are done, click Apply and close the Display Properties dialog box.

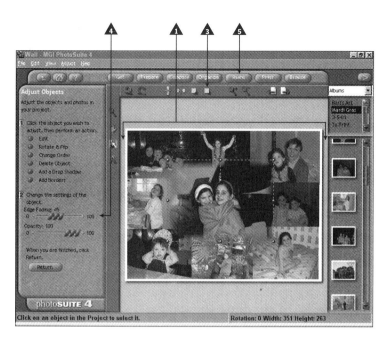

Figure 6-39. To view a selection of your favorite photos all at once on your monitor, create a composite of several pictures. Whenever you use the Windows desktop to open a program or folder, you'll see a selection of your favorite pictures.

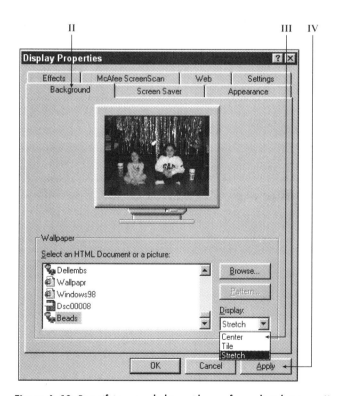

Figure 6-40. Beautifying your desktop with one of your digital pictures. Use the Background tab on the Display Properties dialog box and select an image from your computer.

Note

Wallpaper created using PhotoSuite will be named MGI PhotoSuite Wallpaper. You can find it in the Wallpaper list on the Background tab of the Windows 98 (and higher) Display Properties dialog box. If you create another wallpaper from PhotoSuite, it replaces the previous image. Use the list of wallpapers to select a new one.

Find It Online

For a good selection of Windows wallpaper, (seasonal, decorative, and wacky) visit AOL Keyword: **Desktop Makeover**. For some scenic photographic wallpapers (all available as online jigsaw puzzles), check out www.northernimages.com/gallery.

Tip

If your Windows properties are not set to Active Desktop, your best choice of graphics is a BMP (bitmap) format file. Use the Save As option in most graphics programs to convert a JPG, GIF, or TIF file into a BMP file.

Wrapping Paper

With all the gifts you can start making with your software, pictures, and inkjet printer, you'll need more wrapping paper. Why not make that yourself, too? You need either a high-resolution image (so that a quarter or less of the image would look OK enlarged and printed on its own sheet of paper) *or* a more complex design that can be printed several times and taped together. Either way, you also need quality paper that won't easily tear. Consider premium or bright white for the quality more than the color. But don't take the paper too seriously; wrapping paper is meant to be torn, after all, at least by kids.

1 With PhotoSuite open, choose File⇨New⇨Photo from the menu bar. In the New Photo box, choose Portrait or Landscape; this choice matters more to you (how you like to work with a specific image) than to the recipient, who may be seeing only part of the paper. I've changed the dimensions to 8.5 x 11 inches, the size of a sheet of paper.

2 To add color and brightness to your gift, select a background for your paper. Click the Color radio button in the New Photo dialog box and click a color in the color palette that appears. Back in the New Photo box, click OK to confirm your choices.

3 Click Compose and, in the left pane, click Collages⇨Current Photo to continue using the background created in Step 2. You're back in the familiar editing window where you can add text, clip art, and photos.

4 Click the Add Props button, apply as many images from PhotoSuite's clip art (or *Props*) library as you want. Experiment with the images' sizes and orientations until the design looks just right.

5 Using the Add/Edit Text button, add a message to make the paper both personal and specific, as in Figure 6-42. Such touches set your paper apart from store-bought wrapping paper.

6 Save your file by clicking Share and then Save. Give the file a name.

7 For a larger gift, you probably need to print one design over several sheets of paper. To make that happen, click the Print button on the navigation bar and then click Print in the left pane. In the Print Preview box that appears, click Properties to bring up your printer's Preferences box. My own printer has a tab called Features, which includes Poster Printing — a good option for printing wrapping paper. Poster Printing offers four choices: 2 x 2, 3 x 3, and 4 x 4 pages. The first choice (2 x 2), for example, takes your one-page design and divides it into a grid of two rows and two columns; it then prints each rectangular "cell" of the grid on a separate sheet.

8 After printing, you need to trim the sheets and tape or glue them together.

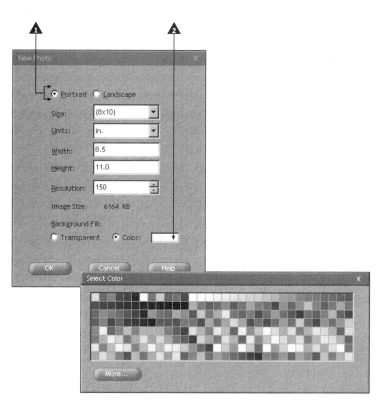

Figure 6-41. In PhotoSuite, you can create a clip-art design on a colored background. Or, to save ink, use no background.

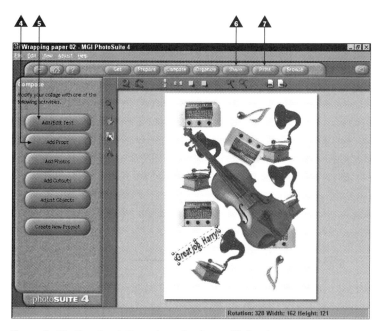

Figure 6-42. PhotoSuite's Music clip art has been added to this paper. In Compose, I rotated these clip-art objects and added text.

Note

Not all printers support poster printing. Consult your printer's manual.

Tip

PhotoSuite simplifies the creation of attractive gift tags. Some of the several dozen templates let you insert digital pictures. To create tags, click Compose and, in the left pane, click Cards & Tags⇨Gift Tags.

Find It Online

Print Central has many gift sets (from the AOL toolbar, choose Print⇨Print Central, and search for *wrap*). These sets include matched wrapping paper, gift tags, bags, and boxes.

Cross-Reference

For more about printing posters, see "Posters" in this chapter.

6

For the Whole Family

IN THIS CHAPTER

▲ Defining your business image with a logo

▲ Marketing yourself with a résumé and business card

▲ Promoting your organization with signs and brochures

▲ Informing customers with visual instructions and presentations

▲ Protecting your property with an inventory

Chapter 7

For the Home Business

For better or worse, work and home are starting to blend into each other in all sorts of ways. Perhaps you work in an office, store, or lab and routinely bring work home. Perhaps you run an accounting, collectibles, carpentry, or candle-making business on the side, and are starting to need more space than the kitchen table can provide. Or, you may have exchanged your cubicle for a corner in the den from which you telecommute. Perhaps your kids conduct a pet-sitting or lawn-cutting business out of your home. The publishing needs of the home-based business can be very broad, but as you'll see in this chapter you can meet many of your needs yourself, using common software, an inkjet printer, AOL, and digital pictures.

Any businessperson knows what it means to look continuously for opportunities to promote and protect a business, expand relations with customers, and work more efficiently. You want to do things easier and, wherever possible, at less cost. You also want potential customers to notice and remember you, and be able to contact you easily.

Ideas for some marketing materials can be found in Chapters 5 and 6, which might seem as un-businesslike as possible. Some business activities in this chapter are really business versions of more generic activities like making signs and club ID cards, covered in Chapter 5. Or, have you considered making magnets or calendars for your customers? These useful things can also be quite attractive and, of course, they keep your image and contact information in front of your audience. Likewise, consider sending customers a bookmark, a holiday greetings card, or a postcard. You can find all these activities in Chapter 6.

Marketing Essentials

The largest grouping of activities in this chapter consists of ideas and activities for promoting your products and services. Consider starting with a logo, a strong image that you can use on all your marketing and other materials. The "Logos" activity starts with the most important part of logo-making: clarifying the image you want to convey and identifying your logo's graphical and textual elements. The creative process of making a logo involves many calculations and a fair helping of inspiration. Your logo will look entirely different from the one roughed out in this chapter, but start here to find out about the brainstorming process and the tools.

Two other tools for promoting your business are brochures and business cards. Print brochures must make a quick, strong impression; be quickly skimmed, then effortlessly retained; and provide, where appropriate, a way for the reader to respond (for example, a mail-in form that is part of the brochure). In the "Brochures" activity, you use Microsoft Publisher to make both a print brochure and a Web-based brochure. All the software used in this book has Web-publishing capabilities, by the way, although this book doesn't have enough space to elaborate on all the possibilities. AOL Hometown has tools that can help you upload your brochures and products to the Web.

Cross-Reference

Chapter 3 has all the procedures for using AOL Hometown.

Business cards, by contrast, are still for the most part tangible things that customers can keep and to which they can refer at any time. PhotoSuite includes some well-designed card templates many let you use your digital pictures. An illustrated card will definitely set your card apart from the many others in your clients' stacks of cards.

Say It with Pictures

Pictures, brochures, and cards all relate to your company's outward appearance. For day-to-day functioning, you can use AOL, an inkjet, some pictures, and a bit of software to create a professional operation. Fax cover sheets emblazoned with your logo are easy to put together and then customize for different purposes. With products like Microsoft Publisher, you can also use graphics to make custom receipts, invoices, and purchase orders (not covered in this book, but quite straightforward using Publisher's step-by-step wizards). Print Shop also offers highly visual business products.

Digital pictures are at the center of "eBay, Preparing Photos for." eBay is the world's largest online auction site, a true online marketplace, and you can reach it directly by going to AOL Keyword: **Ebay**. For this activity you need to upload images to AOL Hometown, as shown in Chapter 3.

Finally, to protect your investment (especially if it's a home-based business) you can use digital pictures to put together a property inventory, showing all your rooms and valuable items.

7

For the Home Business

Brochures

Custom-made brochures used to set you back a good deal of money, especially if you only needed a few copies or made frequent changes. With productivity tools like Microsoft Publisher (part of the Microsoft Office suite), you can create your own spiffy-looking brochures for less. Better yet, you can convert your brochure into a Web publication and publish it using AOL's free Web services.

This activity uses a handy Microsoft Publisher wizard to make a print brochure and matching Web brochure. Just follow these steps:

1 After starting Microsoft Publisher — which automatically opens the Microsoft Publisher Catalog — click Brochures in the Publications by Wizard tab. Double-click to select a template from the available choices.

2 The wizard steps you through a series of choices in which you determine color scheme, paper size, number of panels, whether to include the customer's address, whether to include a response form, and so on. Click Next to proceed from one step to another. When you finish making your choices, click Update and Finish.

3 Your brochure now appears. Notice the wizard items at the left, which allow you to revisit and adjust all the choices made in Step 2.

4 Place your cursor in the main text box and edit the placeholder text with your words, in your own style. Repeat for the other text boxes.

5 To insert a different digital photo from the one in the template, double-click the placeholder photo frame, choose Insert➪Picture➪From File from the menu bar, and navigate to the picture file on your hard drive. Select the file and click the Insert button. To add a different logo, double-click the placeholder and choose Insert➪ Picture➪Clip Art.

6 When finished, click the Save button on the toolbar. In the Save As dialog box, give your brochure a name. Click the Print button to print a copy in order to proof it, examine the layout, and share with others.

7 To convert your brochure into a Web site, select Convert to Web in the Brochure Wizard and then click Create. You can have the wizard make the choices, or do it all yourself. Your new Web brochure now appears on-screen.

8 To complete the process, choose File➪Save as Web Page. Publisher automatically creates a new folder called Publish to hold your saved Web page and places it in the same folder where you originally saved your brochure. You can then upload the Web page to AOL Hometown and anyone can view it.

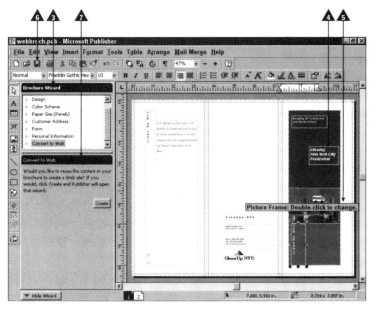

Figure 7-1. Creating a brochure for a fundraiser, business, or community event is a snap with Publisher's Brochure Wizard.

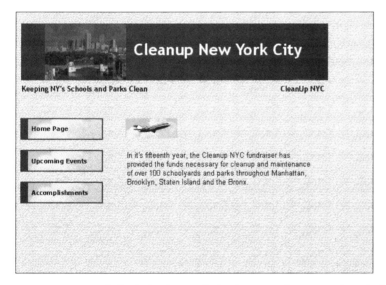

Figure 7-2. Here is the finished Web page of a brochure opened in AOL. On the Web, the plane in the picture is an animated GIF — it appears to move.

Note

Make sure to create a special folder in My FTP Space just for your brochure files. After you're connected to your FTP space, click Create Directory, type a name for your folder, and press Enter; the folder name becomes part of your brochure's URL, so choose it carefully.

Tip

Brochures printed on your laser or inkjet look better on matte or glossy brochure paper. These heavier-weight papers, available at Shop@AOL (AOL Keyword: **Shopping**), are already scored, so they fold properly. Type **inkjet brochure paper** in the Shop@AOL search box to find the latest prices for such papers from different vendors.

7

For the Home Business

Business Cards

If you work for a company, your boss usually gives you a business card; if you're on your own, you need to make cards yourself. Luckily, you now have access to better tools than many bosses do. With digital pictures, a card can show a logo or personal picture. A graphical design can say something about you and your work ("reliable," "fast," or however you want to characterize yourself). And an online card can be available to everyone, impossible to misplace, and never out of date.

Most important, good tools help you do simple things better by allowing you to focus on what counts — who you are, what you do, and how you can be reached. This activity uses PhotoSuite to make a business card.

① In PhotoSuite, click Compose and, in the left pane, click Business⇨Business Cards. From the Miscellaneous category, look for a template with an agreeable arrangement of text and pictures. Double-click the template to select it.

② If you selected a template with a placeholder for a digital picture, click the Add Photos button and then select the source for your picture from the menu in the left pane — Computer or Scanner, for example. Retrieve your image and drag it onto the placeholder.

③ To add your name, company name, address, and other contact information, first select an existing text box. Then, in the left pane, type over the placeholder text with your own. For new text, click Add/Edit Text, click the spot on the card where the text is to go, and type your text in the field on the left. Don't forget to include your e-mail address!

④ To add an additional digital image, click Add Photos again and follow the procedure listed in Step 2. To use PhotoSuite's clip art, click Add Props. (For more on adding photos and clip art, see the bookmarks activity in Chapter 5.)

⑤ In Compose mode, you can add a new border by selecting the entire card, clicking Adjust Objects in the left pane, and then clicking Add Borders. Choose a frame style, select a width, and click Return.

⑥ Click Share and then, in the left pane, click Save to save your work.

⑦ To print several cards at once, click Print on the navigation bar and then click Print Multiples in the left pane. Choose a template with two columns of five cards each, such as 8373 (ten per sheet) in PhotoSuite's Avery Letter category. Select Fill Placeholder, and click Next. Preview your cards and click Print, doing a test copy before using the expensive business card paper.

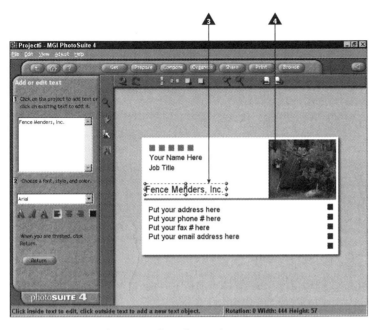

Figure 7-3. A generic business card template in PhotoSuite.

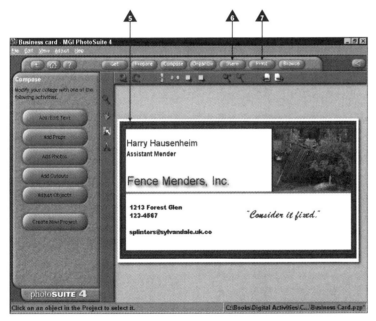

Figure 7-4. The completed card, with picture, text, wooden frame, and effects.

Tip

Use your logo on your card. Don't have one? See "Logos" in this chapter.

Find It Online

Netscape's Business area offers free Netbusiness cards, available to others online. For the details, visit `netbusiness. netscape.com`.

Find It Online

To keep your card from getting lost in someone's stack of tattered cards, print it on a refrigerator magnet. Avery.com's Print area (`www.avery.com`) provides business-card templates that let you print on magnet sheets. (See the magnets activity in Chapter 6.)

7

For the Home Business

Definition

A *table* in Word — and other programs — is a grid-like structure of rows (across) and columns (down), used for clearly displaying information that has some kind of structure, like a bus schedule. In some programs, like Excel, you can use tables to perform operations such as adding the numbers in a column.

Documentation and Instructions

Digital pictures and simple graphics can do much of the work whenever you have to create step-by-step instructions and simple instructional or directional signs. Chances are, well-illustrated procedures can turn a complex process into less work, with less chance of failure. Visual instructions can create a standard for anyone who has to perform a task, and they can minimize the possibilities of misunderstanding among non-English speakers.

Any word processor that has a table feature can create visual documentation that includes digital pictures. For this activity, I use Microsoft Word:

1 With Word open, click the New button on the toolbar to create a new Word document.

2 Create a two-column table, where you can put text in the left-hand column and pictures in the right. To do so, first choose Table⇨Insert Table from the menu bar. In the Insert Table dialog box that appears, type **2** in the Number of Columns box. In the Number of Rows box, type a number corresponding to the number of steps for your instructions. Click OK when you're finished.

3 Type text in the first cell of the left column for your first step. Optionally, you can start by labeling the column heads *Step* and *Illustration*, or something similar.

4 Insert a digital picture into the cell on the right. First, make sure your cursor is in the correct cell. Then, choose Insert⇨Picture⇨From File and use the Insert Picture dialog box to find the picture on your hard drive. Double-click the file to insert it in your table.

5 Edit your text and pictures. Large text (14 points or bigger) is more legible, but the easiest way to make your text easy to read is to simplify the content and focus on the actions required. As for your pictures, chances are that the pictures will be too big for the cell. Reduce a picture's size by grabbing a corner and dragging it toward the picture's center. For more editing options, (such as adding a frame and background), right-click the picture and choose Edit Picture from the pop-up menu.

6 Repeat Steps 3 to 5 to complete your documentation.

7 Click Save to save your document and then click Print to print a copy. Make your documentation available to those who need it, wherever they are. To save your document as a Web page, choose File⇨Save As and select either HTML Document (for Word 97) or Web Page (for Word 2000) from the File of Type drop-down menu. Upload the page to AOL Hometown. (For more on uploading Web pages to AOL Hometown, see Chapter 3.)

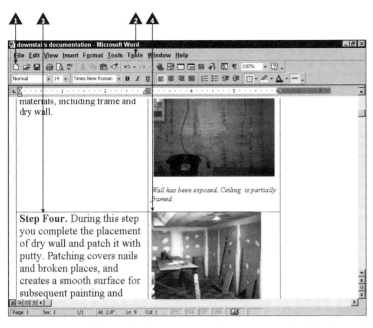

Figure 7-5. A simple layout for documentation, showing a step in the left column and a picture illustrating the step on the right.

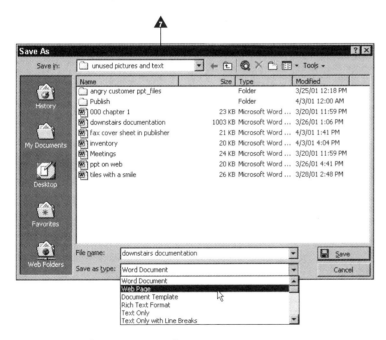

Figure 7-6. Word 2000's Save as Web Page option.

Note

The way you save as a Web page varies in different versions of Word. In Word 97, choose File⇨Save As and choose HTML Document in the Save as File Type box. In Word 2000, choose File⇨Save As, and choose Web page in the Save as File Type box.

Tip

When you create a document in Word and want to share it on the Web, you have two choices. Uploading the DOC file makes it available with its original layout and formatting, where people can read it online. Saving it as a Web Page has several benefits. HTML files tend to be quite small. You can also create links easily, and other pages can link to you. In addition, you can add video and audio. Note that DOC files, because they're big, can take a painfully long period to download and display in a browser.

7

For the Home Business

eBay, Preparing Photos for

If you buy and sell things as a hobby or part of your job, run a collectibles business, or need used office equipment, then you probably already know about eBay, where online auctions take place around the clock and all over the world. If you are selling on eBay, a picture can grab a potential buyer's attention faster and describe items better than words alone. Providing a picture requires that you upload it to a place like AOL Hometown, where it has its own Web address. Then, you provide that address in eBay's Sell Your Item page, along with descriptive information, minimum bid, length of auction, and other data. This activity shows how to provide a picture for something you are selling on eBay.

1 Go to AOL Keyword: **My FTP Space** to view your online storage space. In the My FTP Space window, click See My FTP Space. A dialog box appears, displaying any files you are storing online.

2 In the See My FTP Space window, click Upload. The `members.aol.com` box appears, as shown in Figure 7-7.

3 In the `members.aol.com` box, type the name by which the file is to be known in eBay (`brownbeany.jpg` in this case). Click Continue. The Upload File box appears.

4 Click the Select File button and use the Attach File dialog box to navigate to the folder containing your file. Double-click the file to select it.

5 Click Send.

6 Your digital picture is uploaded and, after a moment, appears in the See My FTP Space window.

Now that your image is safely stored in My FTP Space, all you need to do is let eBay know how to access it. For that, you need to provide the Web address for your picture on eBay's Sell Your Item page. From AOL Keyword: **Ebay**, click Sell, and choose a category to arrive at this page. Fill out the rest of the information and use the Page URL box to enter your picture's Web address:

`http://members.aol.com/screenname/filename.jpg`

For your URL, replace `screenname` with your own screen name and `filename.jpg` with the name of the remote filename you chose in Step 3. When you set up your auction on eBay, be sure to use this address when you're asked to specify the location of your image file.

Cross-Reference

See Chapter 3 for more on My FTP Space.

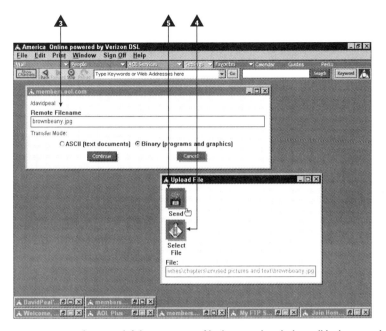

Figure 7-7. In the upper-left box, give your file the name by which it will be known online (usually the same as the name it already has). In the lower-right box, select the file from your hard drive and send it.

Note

According to eBay, digital pictures should have a file size less than 50K, so don't use your digital camera's highest resolution.

Tip

PhotoSuite can help you decrease a picture's file size. For example, in Figure 7-8, I removed the photo's background with the Magic Wand tool and replaced it with a solid light-green color (using the Flood Fill tool and Effect Brush). Increasing the picture's compression can also reduce the size. In PhotoSuite, choose File⇨Save As, click Prompt for Options, and lower the Picture Quality when you are prompted to select one.

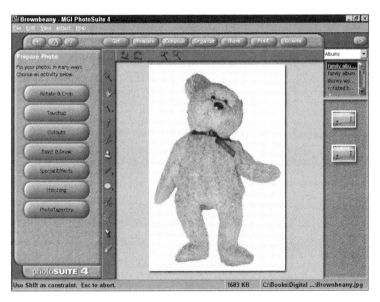

Figure 7-8. A familiar brown plush toy, photographed and uploaded to AOL Hometown for an eBay auction.

Tip

How big is that picture? Offline, you can use Windows Explorer to find the digital picture on your hard drive and view its size using the Size column. Online, you see the size of uploaded files at My FTP Space.

7

For the Home Business

Fax Cover Sheets

Fax cover sheets, like other business forms, can project an image of your company, which really matters if *you* are the company. A cover sheet's main purpose is to provide information about the document itself, along with a way of contacting you if the fax didn't come through legibly or in its entirety. Microsoft Publisher automates the creation of many standard business forms, including cover sheets, but I use Print Shop in this activity because its templates are highly graphical yet easily edited.

1 With Print Shop open, choose Business⇨Fax Covers from the project selector (Print Shop's opening screen).

2 Click Personalize a Quickstart Layout and then click Next. In the Fax Covers screen, select Business and click Next.

3 Choose a template that best matches the image of your business and click Finish. The template now appears in Print Shop.

4 To replace an existing image, first select the image and then double-click to open it in Print Shop's Art Gallery. In the Art Gallery, choose File⇨Open from Disk to find the digital picture, logo, or other image you want to have as your replacement. Select the image and then click Open. The image appears in the cover sheet.

5 Editing text is simple. Double-click any existing text block to select the *text,* and you can then make your changes right in the box.

6 To add another image, click the Insert Graphics button on the toolbar. The Art Gallery window opens again, where you can add a piece of Print Shop clip art or a picture of your own (refer to Step 4).

7 To add new text, click the Text/Headline button on the toolbar.

8 Consider adding a *watermark* — a lightly shaded bit of text — as background for your fax cover sheet. Just click the Panel Effects button on the toolbar and then click the Watermark button to call up the Watermark dialog box. From there, you can type your text and format it as you see fit, changing the font style, font size, color, opacity, and so on. When done making your changes, click OK to insert your watermark. (Don't make the watermark too indistinct — it might not show up when faxed!)

9 Click the Save button on the toolbar to save the file.

10 To use the cover sheet, print several blanks and fill them in by hand. Or prepare sheets with commonly used recipients' addresses and print them. Note that your recipients won't see any colors you use, unless they have color fax machines.

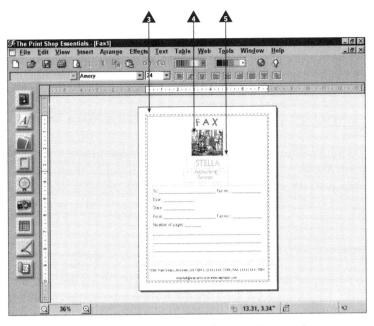

Figure 7-9. You can edit every item on a Print Shop cover-sheet template.

Figure 7-10. To modify the template, I added a new image, edited and moved text, rearranged the contact info section, changed the address at the bottom, and added a watermark. You can modify just about everything with Print Shop.

Tip

In the Art Gallery, choosing File⇨Open from Disk transfers a file directly from your computer into your Print Shop document (one file at a time). If you choose File⇨Import File, the image opens in the Art Gallery, and you can add it to a collection of images. You can then import several files at a time from the gallery into your document. From the Art Gallery itself, you select from several sources, including Print Shop's clip art and an online collection.

Find It Online

AOL's Print Central includes several fax transmittal sheets. Choose Print⇨Print Central from the AOL toolbar, and on the Projects tab, go to Entrepreneur. These sheets are Acrobat (PDF) files that let you enter sender and recipient information.

Tip

Print Shop's zoom tool is located in the lower right (Print Shop 6) or left (Print Shop 11). In Print Shop 11, click the plus and minus signs to zoom in and out. Click the number between the signs (showing the current magnification) to see a menu of zooming options.

7

For the Home Business

Insurance Inventory

For your home and business, an inventory can provide indispensable documentation if your property is ever stolen or damaged in a fire or natural disaster. Digital pictures can show what you own in context and in detail.

Authorities recommend that you photograph both the inside and outside of your house or apartment. Outside, don't overlook patio furniture, the garage or shed, and the contents of your car. Inside, you want to photograph every room, standing in the middle and photographing every wall. For valuable items, you need close-up shots. A professional in your community should appraise older valuables, including paintings, jewelry, coins, plates, and so on. For those newer valuable objects, you should record information such as purchase date and price, as well as serial or model number and any warranty information.

In this activity, you make a property inventory with two parts:

▲ A written inventory listing every type of property in your possession, with purchase price and date information where available. All you need to do is print and complete the inventory form created by the Insurance Information Institute (www.iii.org/individuals/home/inventory.html).

▲ A photographic inventory of all your rooms and valuable objects to substantiate the written inventory. For each photo, you use PhotoSuite to create a label for the back of the photo.

In this activity, each page of the inventory features a picture (top) and description (bottom). You can then print the pages and store them in a metal box, archive them on a disk, or turn them into Web pages, or all three. The following steps use Print Shop because it's easy to use and has excellent text handling capabilities:

❶ With Print Shop open, choose Business⇨Blank Pages from the opening project-selection screen. (Selecting Blank Pages lets you create a sheet without any design elements or specified purpose.) Click Next, select either Tall or Wide format, and click Finish.

❷ To insert a picture, click the Insert Graphics button on the toolbar. From the Art Gallery, choose File⇨Open from Disk. Find your picture and click Open. The picture appears in the Blank Pages template.

❸ Resize the image so that it fills the top half of the screen. To resize the image, click to select it. Sizing handles appear at each corner of the image. Click and drag one of the sizing handles until the image is the size you want.

❹ Now add a text box. Click the Text/Headline button and then click and drag to draw a text box in the lower part of the document.

5 In the box itself, type your descriptive text. I recommend that you use a consistent format for your descriptive text, such as the format shown in Figure 7-11. Whatever format you use, it should be appropriate to the picture and contents you are describing.

6 At the bottom of the screen, type today's date and your name, or other information indicating where and when this inventory page was created. Such dating information is important in evaluating any references to time in the description itself (for example, "2 years ago").

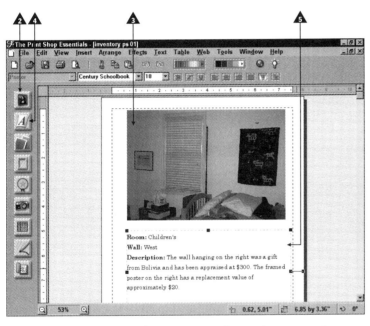

Figure 7-11. This sample page from a systematic photographic inventory shows one wall of one room in a house.

You can save anything you make in Print Shop as a Web page with supporting graphics. With the document displayed, choose Web⮕Publish to Folder. This step automatically converts the document into a Web file, which you can then upload to AOL Hometown as described in Chapter 3.

Kodak provides information about photo inventories; start at www.kodak.com and search for *inventory*. For the property inventory, visit the Insurance Information Institute at www.saftek.com/ insurance/1/ takinive.htm.

Instabase is a handy database that makes it easy to quickly put together an insurance inventory, with digital pictures. You can even save your inventory online at AOL. Just select *Publish to Web* on the Instabase menu bar: for FTP site, type **members.aol.com**; for User, type your e-mail address; for password, type **anonymous**. The software, part of the AOL GraphicSuite 2.0 CD, can be found at AOL Keyword: **AOL Store**, under Interactive Learning (click AOL Learning).

7

For the Home Business

Logos

Logos are everywhere — in kitchen pantries, on computers, in magazines, everywhere. Their purpose is to capture an organization's purpose or image in a graphical and memorable way. Logos must also be flexible enough to be used in different media and situations. Think of McDonald's Golden Arches, which appear everywhere, in every media, and effectively stand for a company and its product.

A logo's elements often consist of some combination of graphics, type, color, and pattern. Sometimes a letter, acronym, or a word does most of the work, sometimes pictures. To brainstorm a logo and its elements for your organization, start with your product or service. Consider the impression you want to project, such as easy, reliable, fast, or friendly. What words, colors, letters, and images convey this impression?

The following activity makes a logo using PhotoSuite and Learning Company's ClickArt, a collection of hundreds of thousands of crisp and usable, but also *copyrighted* images.

1 With PhotoSuite open and with the ClickArt CD in the CD drive, click the Get button and choose the source for the image — in this case, Computer — from the menu in the left pane. Use the Open dialog box to navigate to the CD drive and find the file for the image you want. (You need to use the print catalog to get the image's numeric filename.) Double-click the file to open it in Prepare Photo mode.

2 Depending on the art you are using, you may want to linger in Prepare Photo mode to trim your image, enhance its colors, apply special effects, and so on. Click Return when you're done.

3 Click the Compose button tighten and, in the left pane, click Collages⇨Current Photo⇨Next.

4 Click Add/Edit Text, type the text for your logo in the left pane, and then format the text the way you want. When you're done, click Return at the bottom.

5 In the work area, select and enlarge the text box so that your text is visible and use your mouse to drag the text box where you want it.

6 To add other lines of text, repeat Steps 4 and 5. For Figure 7-13, I used a more personal type-face and rotated the text *(with a smile)* with the selection handle in the middle of the image.

7 Save the file by clicking Share and then Save. If you are using the logo in different media, such as a print brochure and a Web site, you need to save it in a commonly used file format such as JPG. For print-only purposes, use TIFF, a high-quality format that cannot be used online.

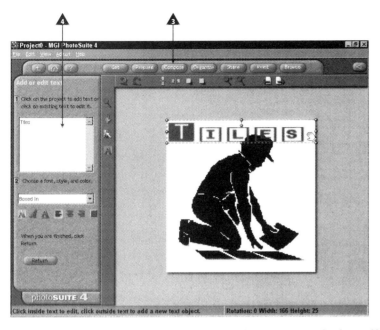

Figure 7-12. This strong image (the silhouette) comes from ClickArt. Text has been added — the word *Tiles*—and positioned above the image.

Figure 7-13. The handwritten-style text adds a personal touch, but because it is a bitmapped (not vector) text, it doesn't display particularly well on an angle or enlarged. Here's where a professional graphic artist can help.

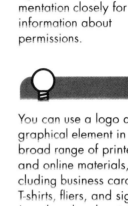

Caution

Clip art is often copyrighted. Read your documentation closely for information about permissions.

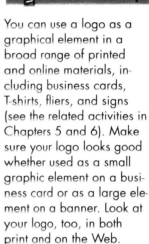

Tip

You can use a logo as a graphical element in a broad range of printed and online materials, including business cards, T-shirts, fliers, and signs (see the related activities in Chapters 5 and 6). Make sure your logo looks good whether used as a small graphic element on a business card or as a large element on a banner. Look at your logo, too, in both print and on the Web.

Find It Online

For a tool to make a text-based logo, try CoolText (www.cooltext.com).

7

For the Home Business

Presentations

Business presentations can be used to explain a new strategy, mobilize a team, or provide an overview of a new skill for training purposes. Like slideshows (see the activity in Chapter 5), you usually show a presentation to your audience, but slideshows can also be set up to run either automatically or at a viewer's pace.

The leading tool for making presentations is Microsoft PowerPoint. The idea is pretty simple. Think of a PowerPoint slideshow as, well, a stack of slides. Although each slide should make an impression, the slide sequence as a whole should keep people's attention and leave the audience a little better informed. In this activity, you make a simple PowerPoint presentation with a digital picture.

1 Open PowerPoint. A dialog box asks you how you want to start making a slideshow. For our purposes, select the Template option and click OK. The New Presentation dialog box appears, displaying the available template options.

2 Click a template to bring it up in the Preview pane, where you can see the overall visual design. When you find a template you like, select it and press Enter.

3 In the New Slide box, click the icon for the Title Slide — the one in the upper-left corner — and then click OK. The Title Slide template appears

4 In the Title Slide template, click in the Click to Add Title box to add a title. Do the same in the Click to Provide Subtitle box to add a subtitle. When you're done, choose Insert⇨New Slide from the menu bar to return to the New Slide box.

5 Choose a layout for the first substantive card. As Figure 7-14 shows, you have a broad range of options, so you can probably find one that fits your needs.

6 Click in the horizontal placeholder at the top of the slide and then type a title summarizing the slide's contents.

7 Click in a text box (if your layout has one) and add your text as a series of automatically formatted bullet points — those short lines of punchy text introduced by a big dot, square, or other graphic.

8 If your design has a placeholder for an image, click the placeholder and choose Insert⇨Picture⇨From File and find the image you want to use. After finding the image, double-click it to add it to your slide.

9 To view your slides, click the Slide Show button, pressing the space bar to advance from slide to slide.

10 When you're done with your content slides, click the Save button to save your presentation as a PowerPoint file (PPT).

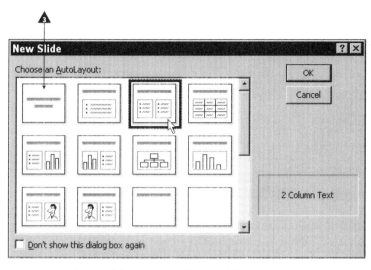

Figure 7-14. The New Slide box lets you choose a slide layout.

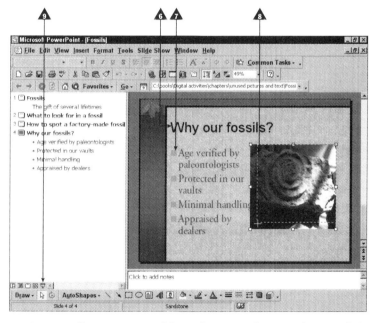

Figure 7-15. Effective PowerPoint slides combine text and pictures. Choose words that make a point quickly and directly and make sure the pictures support the text.

After you start, you can change every design element with the choices on the Format menu: Background, Slide Color Scheme, and Apply Design Template.

Learn to use PowerPoint's multiple views by using the small pictures to the bottom left of the screen. The Normal and Outline views allow you to see your text and your slides at the same time, so that you can enter text in either the outline (on the left) or the slide itself (on the right). The Slide Sorter view lets you see all the slides as a series of tiny squares; use this view to change the order of your slides.

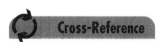

See Doug Lowe's *PowerPoint 2000 For Windows For Dummies* (Hungry Minds, Inc.). A new version of the software is included in the latest version of Microsoft Office (XP).

Résumés

Electronic tools have changed both what employers expect in résumés and what job seekers can do to help themselves. Many employers are perfectly happy to receive e-mail with a plain text résumé as the message (or a word-processed document attached to the message). Job services like Monster (AOL Keyword: **Monster**) provide an online form that you fill out with standard information and make available to all potential employers or use to apply for specific jobs. In both cases, you sacrifice visual impression to convenience (yours and the employer's). Web-based résumés combine the graphical advantages of the traditional paper résumé with the advantages of *anything* online — it's always available and can be quickly updated at little cost. In this activity, you find out how to assemble a Web résumé with AOL's Easy Designer.

1 Go to AOL Keyword: **Easy Designer** and click Create a New Page. After a few moments, the program loads; you see a Click to Get Started button. Do so.

2 In the Easy Designer box, you make a series of three choices. First, choose a template. In this case, make it All About Me (Category) and My Résumé (Topic). When you're done, click Next.

3 Choose a layout for your résumé. All include picture placeholders; some hold more text than others. Generally in résumés, you want to feature as much pertinent information as early as possible. Make a choice and click Next.

4 Choose a color style for your résumé. A simple backdrop won't distract from the impression you want to make with job-related information. When you click Next, your template appears.

5 Adapting template items means modifying each of them in turn. You do this by selecting an item and clicking the Modify button (or just double-clicking).

6 Start with the most important part of your résumé, the text. The template's placeholder text actually gives you advice on what kind of information goes in which text box. Double-click any text box to edit it. Select the text in the box, and type text of your own.

7 To replace the placeholder picture, double-click it to bring up Easy Designer's Picture Gallery. Click Upload Picture. In the Upload Picture box, click Browse to find the picture, and double-click to upload it.

8 Especially important in a résumé is an e-mail link; in Figure 7-17, the link is the underlined Tile Guys text in the text box in the middle of the page.

9 When you are done, click Save, give the page a name, make sure the file extension is HTM or HTML, and press Enter. The Web page appears with your résumé's e-mail address.

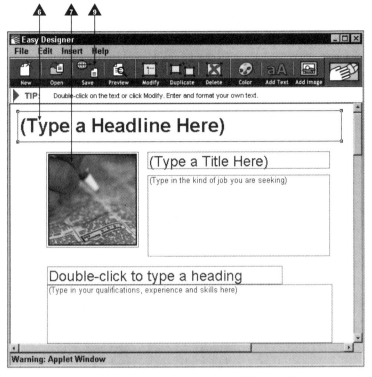

Figure 7-16. In Easy Designer's résumé template, notice how the placeholder text — such as *Type a Headline Here* — gives you hints for laying out your content.

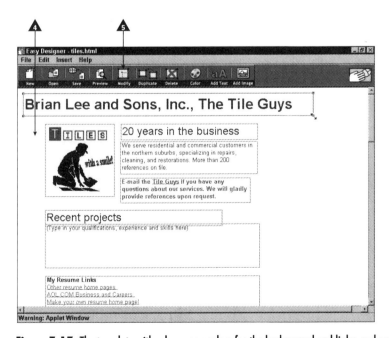

Figure 7-17. The template with a logo, new colors for the background and links, and some of the text common in any résumé.

Tip

In Step 4, consider a non-distracting color style such as Manila Folder, Off White, Parchment, Résumé, or Stationery.

Find It Online

For general advice about writing résumés and cover letters and for assistance in posting an electronic résumé on Monster.com, visit Post Your Résumé (AOL Keyword: **Resume**). Monster is a very large source of nationwide employment listings, with numerous services for both employees and employers.

Cross-Reference

Other activities in this book also use Easy Designer, such as the pets activity in Chapter 5 and the newsletters activity in Chapter 6. Chapter 3 covers all of AOL's free Web services.

7

For the Home Business

Signs with Tear-Offs

Signs provide time-and-place details about local services, events, sales, and other happenings. In this activity, you make a sign that has tear-off strips at the bottom with a name and phone number. The following activity requires Microsoft Publisher:

1 After starting Microsoft Publisher — which automatically opens the Microsoft Publisher Catalog — choose Flyers in the Publications by Wizard tab and then Informational. Double-click to select a template from the available choices.

2 Click Next to start the wizard, which takes you through the process. The first step asks you to choose a color scheme. Colors apply to headline text as well as to decorative lines and boxes. Make a choice and click Next.

3 Now you're asked whether you want to keep the template's image placeholder. In this case, click Yes and then click Next.

4 In the next screen, you're asked if you want to add tear-offs at the bottom of your sign. Scan the list of types of tear-offs (phone tear-offs and coupons), and select one. Click Yes and then click Next.

5 Now you have the option of providing customer information. Doing so adds a second page to your flyer for the customer's name and address, allowing you to mail your flyer. If you are using tear-offs, you likely don't want to mail the flyer, so click No and then Next.

6 If you want, provide personal information for use in this project: your name, business, contact info, and so on. This data will be available to all other Publisher projects. If you click Update, the form appears, where you add this data. Click Finish to view your template.

7 With your flyer displayed, you can modify it. First zoom in to see what you're doing by pressing F9.

8 Editing text takes place right on the flyer. Add a title and other text elements.

9 To change the color scheme, select that item from the wizard menu on the left and choose a new scheme (refer to Step 2).

10 To change the template image, double-click it. In the Insert Clip Art dialog box, click Import Clip to look for a new image. Double-click the image. Back in the Import Clip dialog box, right-click the image and select Import.

11 Click Save to save your sign, and Print to print it out. Snip the tear-offs.

Need a simple sign without tear-offs? In Step 5, click No instead of Yes. Such signs can serve all sorts of everyday purposes. PhotoSuite and Print Shop can churn out these standard signs in minutes, with messages like Keep Out, Beware Dog!, No Smoking, Use Other Door, and directional signs with big arrows.

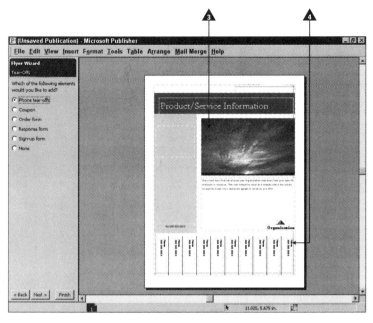

Figure 7-18. Microsoft Publisher sign template with tear-offs. You can change the size and location of text and graphics boxes and add more images as required.

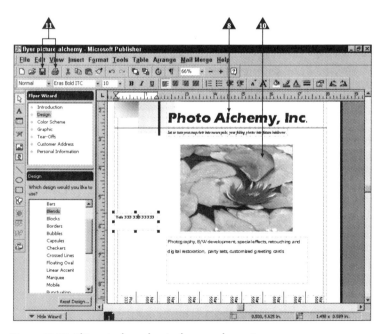

Figure 7-19. This revised template is almost ready to print.

7

For the Home Business

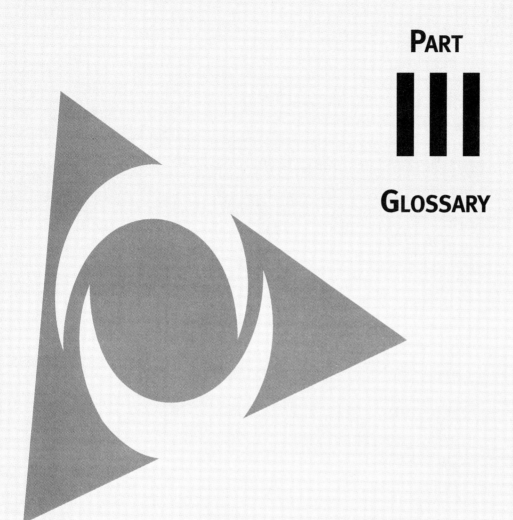

Glossary

A

album

A collection of digital pictures. Albums can be used to organize your digital pictures and share them with others, as in "You've Got Pictures." Many home image-editing programs let you make digital photo albums.

analog

A format that attempts to represent actual sounds, images, and movement with as much accuracy as possible. A film camera is an analog device, for example, because it captures a scene's continuity of colors and tones. See also *digital.*

angle

A camera's perspective on the subject. The camera angle can be altered to affect the composition and the mood of a photograph, as when you shoot the subject from the side, above, or below, rather than straight on.

animated GIF

A series of simple images that is stored in a single GIF file and displayed sequentially to simulate simple animation on a Web page. PhotoSuite has a module for creating animated GIFs.

AOL Hometown

A large community of Web sites where AOL members and non-members alike can create and post their Web pages. Anyone with Internet access and a Web browser can create, add, search, and view Hometown pages. Use AOL Keyword: **Hometown** or go to hometown.aol.com.

AOL Keyword

A word, abbreviation, or phrase that acts as a shortcut to a specific AOL area. Type keywords into the AOL address bar and press Enter to visit an online destination.

AOL Search

AOL's solution to finding information and people online. You can search AOL, a database of millions of choice Web sites, newsgroups, AOL's message boards, the White and Yellow Pages, and more. Click the Search button on the AOL toolbar to visit AOL Search.

aperture

The opening in a camera that lets light pass through to expose the film (or, in a digital camera, to "expose" the CCD). The size of the aperture is called the f-stop. Increasing the aperture lets in more light and creates a broader depth of field (amount of the picture that is in focus). See also *f-stop* and *CCD.*

archive

Files grouped for a purpose: to be compressed, transmitted, stored, or simply made available for others to view. Also, a collection of digital pictures on your hard drive or other storage device.

attachment

A digital picture, word-processing document, or other file sent with an e-mail message. When you use the built-in e-mail program in "You've Got Pictures," digital pictures are sent as attachments.

autofocus (AF) lens

A type of lens that uses a motor to focus the lens automatically. Most digital cameras come with autofocus lenses.

AVI

The standard format for Windows video files. Some digital cameras make video clips in this format, which can be played in AOL's media player and most other popular video players.

B

background

Part of a photographic image against which a subject is set. You can blur or crop a background that distracts viewers from the subject. See also *foreground*.

bandwidth

The amount of data that can travel over a network in a given time. See also *bps (bits per second)*.

bit

Short for *binary unit*, also know as *digit*. The basic unit of computer storage, a digit can be only a 0 or 1.

bit depth

Describes the number of colors (or shades of gray) that any pixel can display and hence the number of bits needed to record colors. If eight bits are used to define a pixel's color, the pixel can display up to 256 colors. If 24 bits are used, more than 16 million colors can be displayed.

bitmap

A type of graphic file that stores information about colors and tones in small dots of colors called pixels. BMP, JPG, and GIF files are made up of bitmaps. See also *vector graphics*.

BMP

A file saved in a standard Windows bitmapped file format for graphics.

bps (bits per second)

A measurement of the speed of data transmission. The higher the bps rate, the quicker your data travels to or from your computer.

broadband

High-speed network access. On AOL, the main types of broadband are delivered over either cable wires or phone lines, and a special modem is required. Broadband access greatly speeds up the rate at which data travels from AOL to your computer, but has less effect on the rate it travels from your computer to AOL. Visit AOL Keyword: **AOL Plus** for more about AOL's broadband content and services.

browser

An application used to view information on the World Wide Web. AOL has a built-in browser and develops a popular browser called Netscape Navigator, which you can use with your AOL account.

byte

A unit of computer-readable data made up of eight binary digits or bits. Typically defines a single character, such as a letter or symbol, but can store other information. A byte is the standard unit of file size, used to measure the capacity of a hard drive or other storage medium. A kilobyte is a little more than 1,000 bytes; a megabyte, more than a million bytes.

C

cable release

A cable that can be attached to some cameras, allowing a photographer to release the shutter (take a picture) at a distance away from the camera.

CCD (charge-coupled device)

The light-sensitive electronic device in digital cameras used to record information about the amount of red, green, and blue at any *pixel*. The more pixels in a CCD, the sharper the *resolution* of the recorded image.

CD-R (compact disc recordable)

Optical digital storage drive that lets you save files on a CD. CD-R disks can be *written to* only once. See also *CD-ROM* and *CD-RW*.

CD-ROM (compact disc read-only memory)

A standard method of storing and distributing software libraries, reference works, games, application software, and multimedia software.

CD-RW (compact disc rewritable)

A type of optical digital storage drive that lets you repeatedly save files on a CD, as you do with floppy disks or tapes. See also *CD-R*.

channel

A major category of AOL content, which also contains a collection of related AOL forums. For example, the House and Home channel is home to Hobbies forums, which include photography-related areas. The Computer Center channel provides reviews, background information, and other information about digital cameras, printers, and scanners.

clip art

A collection of digital images designed for use in Web sites, presentations, and other uses. Easy Designer (see Chapter 3) includes clip art, as do image-editing programs such as PhotoSuite and the Microsoft Office applications.

CMYK

Shorthand for a method used in printing to describe any color as a combination of four different ink colors: cyan, magenta, yellow, and black. See also *RGB*.

color depth

See *bit depth*.

compositing

Technique of combining several images in one document for dramatic or unusual effects.

contrast

Range of brightness between the light and dark areas of a photograph or other graphic image. A high-contrast image has strong blacks and whites, with little gray; a low-contrast image has less black-white range and more gray.

copyright

Legal right to publish and distribute an artistic or intellectual work.

crop

To trim a photograph or other graphic image down to the portion you want to edit, print, or display. Cropping is an excellent way to improve the composition of an image. AOL's Picture Finder provides a quick, easy cropping tool.

cursor

Small movable arrow on your monitor that you control with a mouse. The shape of the cursor changes from context to context, always indicating what is possible at any time while you're using a program. An *insertion* cursor, for example, is a thin vertical bar where you can type text, and the standard selection (arrow-shaped) cursor changes to a pointing finger when you hover it over hyperlinked text or pictures.

D

database

Structured and searchable collection of data in the true sense of data — discrete information items. To organize your digital pictures, you can use database products like Filemaker and Microsoft Access, shareware like Instabase, or the organizational tools built into PhotoSuite.

depth of field

In photography, the portion of the total depth of a photograph that is in focus. Wide-angle lenses offer greater depth of field than lenses of longer focal length. Any lens has a greater depth of field at a smaller aperture setting. Aperture settings are measured in f-stops — the higher the f-stop, the narrower the aperture and the greater the depth of field. A narrow depth of field can be a good way to emphasize a subject.

desktop publishing

The use of a personal computer to set type and add graphics to produce highly formatted publications such as newsletters and brochures, intended primarily for print.

digital

A way of representing complex images, sounds, video, and text (and more) as discrete patterns of binary numbers (1s and 0s). The purpose of digitizing is to make extremely diverse types of information easy for computers to manipulate and transmit. See also *analog*.

digital camera

A camera that captures images digitally rather than on film, using a CCD and computer memory. You can download the digital pictures as files to a computer, where you can edit, share, and use them in many ways.

download

To transfer information from one computer to another, usually from a remote networked computer such as a Web server to a personal computer. You also download when you transfer images from other devices (such as cameras and scanners) to a PC.

dpi (dots per inch)

A way of measuring the resolution (or sharpness) of an image. Changing an on-screen image's dpi determines the picture's size and resolution when you print it.

driver

The software that a computer uses to operate a piece of hardware such as a printer, monitor, scanner, or mouse.

E

e-mail (electronic mail)

A message from one person to another via the Internet. You can attach digital pictures to an e-mail message or insert them within the message. E-mail is available in many forms on AOL, depending on where you access your mail: Click the Read or Write icon on the toolbar for standard mail, go to www.aol.com/aolmail to read your AOL Mail when you don't have access to the AOL software, or use the e-mail integrated into "You've Got Pictures" to share digital pictures with one person or several. AOL also offers AOL Mail on the Web for handheld computers and Palm devices.

emulsion

The light-sensitive chemical coating on film that records the colors and tones momentarily let in through a camera's lens.

exposure compensation

Overriding your camera's light meter reading in response to difficult lighting situations, such as backlighting (where a strong light comes from behind the subject, hiding the subject in shadow). Some cameras, including point-and-shoots, have an exposure compensation control that allows you to overexpose or underexpose in small steps to compensate for such situations. Consult your camera's manual for advice on using this advanced feature.

exposure mode

Exposure is determined by two main factors: how long the shutter opens to let in light (shutter speed) and how wide the aperture is (f-stop). The faster the shutter speed, the better the ability to capture movement and detail. The higher the f-stop, the narrower the aperture and the greater the depth of field.

F

Favorite Places

On the Internet, *bookmark* is the generic term for a saved link to a specific site. In Microsoft Internet Explorer, the term is *Favorites*. On AOL, the term is *Favorite Places*. On AOL, you can save anything as a Favorite Place, including a newsgroup, an e-mail message, an AOL area, and so on.

file compression

Storing a file in a format that reduces the file's size to speed up transmission and reduce storage requirements. (1) On AOL, files are automatically compressed when you attach more than one file to an e-mail message. (2) JPG files, a common graphics format, can be compressed to download more quickly, which makes JPG files the best kind to use on the Web. JPGs can represent complex images. Compressing doesn't reduce the number of colors recorded in a JPG, only the number of pixels; hence, highly compressed pictures lose sharpness.

file extension

The letters that follow the period in a filename and that describe a file's format, for example *JPG*. See also *file format*.

file format

A standard manner in which a file is stored that enables an operating system (for example, Windows) to determine what application is needed to open the file. The format is usually represented by a period and a few letters following the filename, such as BMP, JPG, and GIF (standard bit-mapped graphic formats for use on the Web). The period is usually omitted in this book.

film speed

The measure of a film's sensitivity to light, which is typically a numerical rating such as ISO 100, 400, or 1600. The higher this number, the more sensitive the film and the better it handles dim lighting. A lower ISO number provides better, finer-grained images. Some digital cameras can emulate film speed, so you can take pictures in different lighting situations on the same memory card.

filters

(1) Electronic filters are common in photo manipulation programs like Adobe Photoshop and MGI PhotoSuite to provide image-editing enhancements and special effects. (2) In traditional photography, glass or plastic rings are used to compensate for unusual lighting and to alter color and contrast. Photographers may use clear or *skylight* filters simply to protect the lens.

FireWire

An easy-to-use (plug-and-play), generally fast means of importing files from a peripheral device (such as a digital-video camera) into your computer. Also known as a 1394 serial bus. FireWire is now standard on the Mac and a common option on new PCs.

fixed-focus lens

A lens that doesn't have a variable focal length. Point-and-shoot cameras often have a fixed-focus lens, as do many digital cameras.

flash

Brief, intense burst of artificial light used to illuminate the subject. Can essentially replace or augment sunlight or indoor lighting. A *fill flash* is used for short-distance situations where you need to light up the shadows of your subject.

floppy disk

A relatively small, portable storage medium for computer data. This disk isn't really floppy, and it's usually 3½ x 3½ inches.

font

A complete set of characters (numbers, uppercase and lowercase letters, and common symbols) in the same typeface.

foreground

(1) The area of a photographic image closest to the viewer. In a portrait, your subject is usually in the foreground. (2) When you're working on a graphics project with more than one element, the foreground is the topmost layer, which covers elements that it overlaps. In PhotoSuite's Compose mode, when you are using a template and a digital picture, you usually need to bring the template to the foreground or the picture to the background.

freeware

Software made available to the public free of charge by the program's author, even though the author retains exclusive copyright. See also *shareware*.

f-stop

A measure of the aperture setting; the standard settings are f/2, 4.5, 5.6, 8, 11, 16, and 22. From one f-stop to another, the higher f-stop (for example, f/16 to f/22) involves a halving, not a doubling, of aperture size. The strange numbering system is derived by dividing a lens's focal length by the size of the aperture. See also *aperture*.

FTP (File Transfer Protocol)

A standard method for transmitting files from one computer to another via the Internet. Often used to share large files or upload HTML files from a personal computer to a Web server.

G

GIF (Graphics Interchange Format)

A graphics file format common on the Internet and nearly universally supported by browsers. Most commonly used for solid-colored images, logos, buttons, cartoons, and other simple images. See also *animated GIF*.

gigabyte (GB)

One billion bytes or 1,000 megabytes (MB). The capacity of newer hard drives, high-capacity disks, and CDs is measured in gigabytes. See also *byte*.

grayscale

A black-and-white representation of an image that can include many shades of gray.

H

hard drive

Primary file storage hardware on a PC. Uses magnetic storage media.

hardware

All the devices that can connect directly to a personal computer, including scanners, digital cameras, hard drives, Zip drives, modems, video cards, monitors, and keyboards. See also *software*.

home page

(1) The opening page of a Web site. (2) A personal page. (3) In your Web browser, the Web page to which the browser automatically opens.

Hometown

See *AOL Hometown*.

HTML (HyperText Markup Language)

The script (code) used to format ASCII text files into documents that a Web browser can use. Browsers download HTML files and display them as Web pages.

HTML editor

Software used to create Web pages. HTML editors automatically generate the underlying HTML so you can focus on the content — the words and pictures you want to communicate.

hue

Hue specifies a color's position along the spectrum of all colors. See also *saturation.*

icon

A small graphic image displayed on a computer screen. An icon represents a program (like Word on your Windows taskbar), a function (like Print on the AOL toolbar), or a destination (like "You've Got Pictures" on the AOL Welcome screen). By clicking an icon, you open the application, perform the function, or jump to the destination.

image map

A single Web graphic that provides a set of links to different destinations.

inkjet printer

A type of printer. Inkjets produce good results on a wider variety of media (paper, canvas, sticker paper, stock paper, and so on) and for a more affordable price than laser printers. The name comes from the nozzles that spray very small dots of color. See also *laser printer.*

interactive

(1) Software that lets you express your preferences by giving you the chance to make choices (click buttons), enter text (as in a search engine), and so on. (2) Software that lets you communicate with other people over networks.

Internet

A worldwide system of networked computers. Supports the globally shared standards according to which computers share files and other kinds of information.

ISP (Internet service provider)

A company that provides subscribers with a plain connection to the Internet, usually by modem, without original content or unique interactive opportunities.

JPEG or JPG (Joint Photographic Experts Group)

A graphics file format widely used on the Web. It compresses well, enabling transmission of large, complex graphics such as photographs, with more or less loss of image quality depending on the amount of compression.

K

Kbps (kilobits per second)

Measure used to describe relatively slow data transmission, such as via a modem. See *bit*.

L

landscape

In many applications, you need to decide whether you want to design and print a document in *landscape* or *portrait* orientation. Landscape means wide; portrait means tall.

laser printer

A printer that uses a small laser beam to transfer an image to a photosensitive surface (usually a drum). The surface is then sprayed with toner, which is in turn applied to paper. Usually more expensive and higher in quality than an inkjet printer. See also *inkjet printer.*

LCD (liquid crystal display)

A type of display commonly used on laptop monitors, digital camera viewers, and other types of hardware. On a digital camera, an LCD viewer usually lets you view the following: a scene before it's captured; an image after it's captured; and a menu of choices for controlling cameras, managing pictures, and so on.

lens

Ground glass or plastic that focuses light on film or, in a digital camera, on a CCD surface. See also *CCD.*

library

On AOL, a *library* is a collection of digital pictures for uploading and downloading by any AOL member. Usually the libraries can accept only those files that have a standard graphics format, such as JPG, GIF, and BMP. These letters — known technically as a file's *extension* — come *after* the period in a filename.

light meter

A usually built-in camera component that measures light in order to help you produce properly exposed photographs. See also *exposure mode.*

link

On the Web, a link takes you from one document to another when you click it. On AOL, links take you to related AOL and Web pages. See *visited and unvisited links*.

M

marquee

A marquee is a box, outlined in dots, that indicates where any object will appear. In PhotoSuite, a text box is defined by a marquee.

megabyte (MB)

A measurement of digital storage capacity equal to approximately 1 million bytes. See also *byte*.

megapixel

A way of measuring the maximum resolution of a camera's digital-picture files. A megapixel camera records more than 1 million pixels in an image by recording, for example, 1152 x 872 pixels. The resulting files are often required for good print and project quality, but are usually too big for good Web quality. Some current cameras now top 4 megapixels.

message board

An AOL community feature that lets members read and post messages to a public, online message board devoted to a specific topic. On AOL Search, you search AOL's message boards for discussions about many topics in digital imaging.

modem

A hardware device that takes digital computer signals, converts them to analog waves, and sends them across phone lines to another computer, where they are again digitized. Broadband (high-speed) connections require a special type of modem. Some modems go inside your computer, and others are external. The word *modem* is short for modulator-demodulator.

My FTP Space

Online storage provided for AOL members, based on *FTP.* Used for storing Web files and other documents meant for sharing with other people on the Internet. AOL Keyword: **My FTP Space**.

My Pictures

My Pictures is the part of "You've Got Pictures" where you can view, manage, and share your pictures and albums. It is available at AOL Keyword: **My Pictures**.

O

opacity

In PhotoSuite, opacity refers to the extent to which an effect (such as the Touchup brush) covers up the underlying image. At 100 percent, the image is covered up completely. At less than 100 percent, you can create a softer effect to blunt those jagged edges you often get with cutouts.

optical resolution

Actual physical resolution that a scanner or printer is capable of recording in dots per inch (dpi). See also *dpi (dots per inch).*

overexposure

Application of more light to capture a photographic image than a light meter reads as necessary for a correct exposure. Can be used intentionally to alter the image or compensate for difficult lighting situations that might fool the meter, such as backlighting.

P

page

A page is the unit of the World Wide Web. A page is defined by a single file, usually in the HTML format. Pages can contain text, links, images, and other objects meant for presentation in a Web browser. After uploading a page to an Internet site like AOL Hometown, a page has its own Web address, which other people use to access the page.

panning

Photographic shooting technique in which you move the camera to track a moving object. When you pan, the background blurs, while the subject remains sharp relative to the background. Required for panoramic images. See *panorama*.

panorama

A photographic image with a broad angle of view that captures very wide horizons, large group pictures, and so on; usually created with software by compiling several photographs. Some cameras (like the *APS,* or Advanced Photo System) let you take panorama shots as a standard format.

parallax

A camera's viewing system that provides a view of the subject that approximates but may not be identical to the actual view exposed on film or CCD when the shutter is released.

PC (Personal Computer)

Originally, the brand designation of personal computers from IBM. Now used to describe any personal computer that uses the Microsoft Windows operating system. Sometimes used to refer to any personal computer.

PDF (Portable Document Format)

Created by Adobe, a popular file format used to present highly formatted documents, especially word-processing documents, to publish on the Web. The Adobe Acrobat Reader is freely available at www.adobe.com, but to create Acrobat documents, you must purchase the full Adobe Acrobat software.

peripheral

A hardware device connected to a computer, such as a monitor, scanner, or printer.

pixel (picture element)

The smallest unit of a bitmapped (standard) digital image, a pixel is a small square made up of a specific color; similar to a dot. The number of colors a pixel can display depends on its color depth, which is determined by the number of bits available to define a color for any pixel. See *bitmap*.

plug-in

Software created to work within another application, expanding that application's capabilities. Browser plug-ins enable viewers to view additional Web content, particularly multimedia files (such as RealAudio, Shockwave, and Flash). In image-editing software like Photoshop, plug-ins provide additional special effects and other enhancements that you can apply to a selection or an entire image.

portrait

See *landscape*.

processing

In photography, developing, fixing, and washing exposed film or traditional photographic paper to produce negatives or prints. Unnecessary in digital photography, where image editing takes place with software and a computer.

program

See *software*.

prop

In PhotoSuite, a *prop* is clip art, including photos, drawings, and word balloons. Props are arranged in categories such as Word Balloons, Music, Hats, Hair, and Special Occasions (including pictures of Santa Claus and graduation caps).

R

removable media

Computer storage consisting of a drive (usually the personal computer, with a slot) and removable storage units such as floppies, Zip disks, CD-Rs, and CD-RWs.

resolution

The sharpness or fineness of a digital picture, either printed or on-screen, measured in *pixels* or *dots*. Also describes the sharpness that a monitor can display, a printer can output, or a scanner can capture.

RGB

A way of defining colors as combinations of red, green, and blue light for on-screen use (because screens are lit from behind by moving beams of light). See also *CMYK*.

S

saturation

The amount of color at any point in an image. A saturated color has much color and little gray; an unsaturated image has duller colors and more gray. The greater the saturation, the more intense the color. See also *hue*.

scanner

A piece of hardware that converts a paper-based text or image, such as a photo or document, into a digital file that can be manipulated with image-editing software or used on a Web page or elsewhere online.

screen name

Your way of identifying yourself on AOL and the Internet. Your Internet address is your AOL screen name followed by @aol.com.

screen resolution

Measures the number of pixels that appear on your monitor, usually as a vertical by horizontal measure, such as 640 x 480. Most monitors let you set resolution at various levels; the higher the *resolution,* the smaller but sharper any individual image appears on-screen.

screen saver

A *screen saver* is a type of software that shuts off the monitor after a certain period of inactivity and goes blank, or displays a moving image of some sort. Originally, screen savers prevented screen images from being burned into the monitor. Today, monitor technology makes burn-in unlikely, and screen savers are simply for fun — another way of displaying your digital pictures, for example.

search engine

An online tool that searches for Web sites and other types of content according to keywords you type in a text box. AOL Search is AOL's search engine.

selection tools

Indispensable in image editing, selection tools allow you to identify the part of an image to which you want to apply effects and changes and thus protect the rest of the image in the process. Software varies widely in the number and type of selection tools provided, but common ones include rectangular, elliptical, magic wand, and freehand (also known as lasso).

serial port

A plug at the back of your computer that you use to attach a cable to modems, digital cameras, and other devices. Today, the USB port has superseded the serial port for many uses.

server

A networked computer that many users share.

shareware

Software that you can download and use freely for a trial period. Shareware sometimes comes with restrictions until the user pays a fee to the software maker.

shutter

Mechanically controlled camera opening that enables exposure of film (traditional photography) or digital card (digital camera).

shutter release

In both film and digital cameras, the button you press to open the shutter, capturing the light required to represent the image you want in your photo.

shutter speed

The length of time the aperture is open during exposure (see also *exposure mode*). Shutter speed is usually represented as a fraction of a second (for example, ⅛, ½₅₀, ½₀₀). More and more digital cameras come with an adjustable shutter speed.

slide show

AOL and many software publishers use the term *slide show* to describe the display of a series of pictures, often accompanied by sound. Microsoft PowerPoint is used to create slide shows, and many image-editing programs (including MGI PhotoSuite and ThumbsPlus) create slide shows based on your digital pictures.

SLR (Single Lens Reflex)

Common film camera type in which you compose a photograph through the lens, closely approximating the actual picture. SLRs often use interchangeable lenses (of different zoom capabilities and focal lengths). The advantage of SLRs is their typical support of an adjustable aperture and shutter speed. Only the most expensive digital cameras offer quality and features comparable to good film SLRs.

software

Any program that enables computers to do something such as start up, manage a scanner, organize or edit pictures, browse the Web, send e-mail, and so on. Software is often divided into the *system* software, which your computer uses (for example, Windows), and the *application* software, which you use to do something (work with numbers, words, images, and so on). Application software is created for specific system software.

still

A single frame of a video clip. Like digital pictures, stills capture a moment. Video stills tend to be lower in resolution and lack the compositional controls of a picture made with a still camera.

stock photos

Collections of digital pictures made available for publication or other use, often for a fee. Many such services are available over the Web.

T

telephoto lens

Lens with a longer-than-normal focal length and narrow field of view (for example, 105mm).

template

A fill-in-the-blanks document that you use in AOL's 1-2-3 Publish, Easy Designer, and many graphics programs. When you use a template, a *wizard* often helps you quickly create a highly formatted yet personalized document.

text

The most common way of representing simple English letters, numbers, and characters on computers, also known as ASCII (American Standard Code for Information Interchange) text. In most programs, saving a document as text creates an ASCII file with a TXT file extension (format). Web pages are text files that carry an HTML extension.

text-only

Files that contain only standard, near-universal text characters. Excludes colors, text formatting, and graphics. Text-only files can usually be shared easily among different types of computers.

thumbnail

A small version of a digital image, viewed on-screen. Often used to ease locating and organizing graphics files by allowing multiple images to be viewed on-screen simultaneously.

TIF (Tagged Image File)

A graphics file format used with both Windows and Mac operating systems. This format retains a great deal of image information but produces large files. Sometimes, the name of this format appears as TIFF.

toolbar

A row of icons or buttons in application software that provides ready access to the program's major functions.

TWAIN

Software that lets you import an image from a scanner or digital camera directly into a graphics application. What this means is that you control key hardware functions, such as downloading pictures from a digital scanner or initiating a scan, using graphics software.

U

underexposure

Application of less light to capture a photographic image than a light meter reports is necessary. Can be used intentionally to alter the image or compensate for difficult lighting situations that may result in a faulty reading by the light meter.

unvisited link

See *visited and unvisited links*.

upload

To transfer a file from your personal computer to another (usually larger) computer. On AOL, you use AOL Keyword: **My FTP Space** to upload files for anyone with Internet access to download.

URL (Uniform Resource Locator)

The address of an Internet resource. Begins with a standard prefix that identifies the type of Internet resource, such as `http://`, `ftp://`, or `news:`. Must include the computer's name, which identifies the site (`www.aol.com`), and sometimes a directory path and specific file on that computer. Web site URLs begin with `http://`, but on AOL, you can leave that part off when you type a URL in the box on the AOL navigation bar.

USB (Universal Serial Bus) port

A newer, personal computer plug designed for nearly any peripheral device. USB devices, such as printers and scanners, can be plugged into each other. Most digital cameras can use USB ports, to which the camera is attached via an inexpensive cable.

utility

A broad term for software accessories that improve your computer's ability to carry out a specific function such as compressing files or viewing an unusual image format.

V

value

In PhotoSuite, the amount of gray in an image. You control this amount by using the Fix Colors field (click Prepare, and then click Touchup➪Touchup Filters➪Fix Colors).

vector graphics

Graphic image represented by mathematical formulas rather than a series of pixels as with bitmapped graphics. Vector graphics can be enlarged without loss of resolution. Web pages display bitmapped graphics (JPGs and GIFs). To make vector graphics, you need to use a special graphics program such as Adobe Illustrator, Macromedia Freehand and Flash, or CorelDRAW.

video adapter

Hardware that enables the computer to import camcorder or digital-video files for editing, playing, and sharing on a computer. Also called *video card* and *video board*.

viewfinder

On a traditional or digital camera, the window that you look through when composing your picture. Usually differs slightly from the actual area captured in a photo. Most digital cameras offer an LCD viewfinder in addition to a standard viewfinder.

virus

A program that you can inadvertently download with other software or as an e-mail attachment. A virus is designed to change files on your computer, often with malicious intent.

visited and unvisited links

A *visited* link is a link that someone viewing the page has clicked already; an *unvisited* link has yet to be visited. On the Web, unvisited and visited links are usually displayed in different colors to help your users avoid revisiting pages and quickly identify pages they haven't yet visited.

W

WAV file

Standard Windows sound file format.

wide-angle lens

A lens with a shorter than normal focal length and a wide field of view.

wizard

Walks you through the process of personalizing each step of a publication in a program such as PhotoSuite, Print Shop, or Publisher.

WYSIWYG (What You See Is What You Get)

Pronounced *whizzy-wig*. Used to describe a graphical software user interface in which the editing view closely approximates the final printed or on-screen appearance.

Z

Zip

(1) A generic term (verb) for file compression. (2) Extension of a set of zipped files. (3) A type of storage medium that holds more data than a floppy — 100MB or 250MB, instead of 1.44MB.

zoom

(1) In photography, you zoom in with a telephoto lens to make a subject appear closer. (2) In image-editing software, you zoom in to a picture to do fine edits and zoom out to view the overall image.

zoom lens

A lens with a variable focal length, which lets you capture more or less of the main subject.

Index

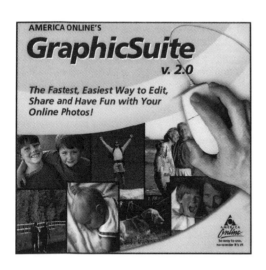

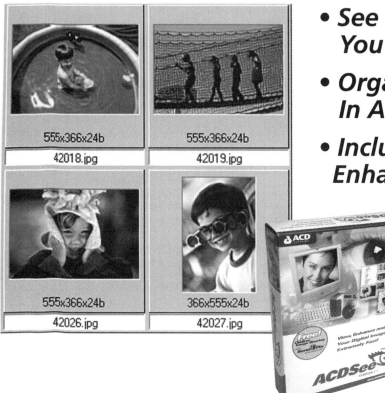

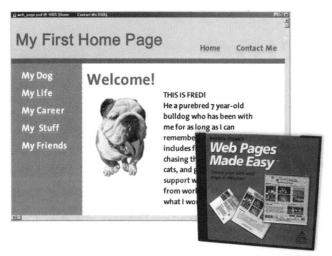